THE GANG THEY COULDN'T CATCH

DEBRA WEYERMANN

THE STORY OF AMERICA'S GREATEST
MODERN-DAY BANK ROBBERS—AND HOW
THEY GOT AWAY WITH IT

●

SIMON & SCHUSTER

NEW YORK LONDON TORONTO SYDNEY TOKYO SINGAPORE

SIMON & SCHUSTER
Simon & Schuster Building
Rockefeller Center
1230 Avenue of the Americas
New York, New York 10020

SIMON & SCHUSTER and colophon are registered trademarks
of Simon & Schuster Inc.

Designed by Pei Loi Koay
Manufactured in the United States of America

1   3   5   7   9   10   8   6   4   2

Library of Congress Cataloging in Publication Data
Weyermann, Debra
The Gang They Couldn't Catch: the story of America's greatest modern-
day bank robbers—and how they got away with it / Debra Weyermann
        p.   cm.
Includes index.
1. Bank robberies—United States. 2. Brigands and robbers—United
States. 3. Thieves—United States.
I. Title.
HV6658.W49   1993
364.1'552'0973—dc20   93-4341
                                               CIP
ISBN   0-671-73131-9

All photos courtesy of the Grandstaff family.

For my father, Andrew Weyermann,

who named me Faith and then taught me how to feel it.

And for my mother, Wilma Weyermann,

who would say that she saw it coming.

ACKNOWLEDGMENTS

●

With gratitude to:

Bob Hirsh and Jeffrey Minker, who provided hundreds of hours of court tapes and thousands of pages of collaborating documents when the authorities refused to cooperate.

Friends Chris Fotheringham, who did a preliminary edit; Ben Mc-Nitt, for his ear; Paul Hutchinson of the *Denver Post* and Dan Sorenson of the *Tucson Citizen,* for helping track down elusive newspaper clips.

George Weir, Terry Lee Conner, John Oliver, Mike See, Clyde and Lori Brown, Sharon Grandstaff and family, and a host of others who cooperated.

Terri and Kenny Kauzlarich and their sons, Kenny Jr. and Mark, for their hospitality and their insights.

Michael Nordstrom for putting up with my snits and kicking my butt when I got discouraged.

And in New York:

Jim Silberman, for seeing the value in all this to begin with. Dominick Anfuso and Casandra Jones at Simon & Schuster, and Suzanne

Gluck and Susan Jensen at International Creative Management, for pulling me through what turned out to be quite the labyrinth.

A word about how this thing was put together:

This story spans several decades. More than 100 people were interviewed, some for longer periods of time than others. I reviewed court documents, police reports, library files, and newspaper clippings. Some people requested anonymity and I honored their requests. They were minor characters and their names were changed.

Some characters, notably Bruce Fennimore, declined to be interviewed or there were limited subjects they would discuss.

It should be noted that the FBI, the Federal Bureau of Prisons, and the U.S. District Attorney's office declined participation for various reasons on several occasions. Prosecutor Dan Knauss said he could not stand to think about the outcome of the case and did not wish to jeopardize any future proceedings, should there be any. The activities of these agencies are documented with thousands of pages of their own reports, an equal amount of court motions, and hundreds of hours of taped court testimony.

CONTENTS

PROLOGUE

•

David Grandstaff never intended to become a notorious bank robber. He entertained the same dreams all kids do when they think life is unspoiled. His family was very poor, but he dreamed he could become a dentist and heal people whose teeth hurt as badly as his did when there was no money to fix them. He would do it for free when people couldn't pay.

Early, he realized he was going to have to play the hand he'd been dealt. Poverty and drink. Sheets over the grimy windows so people could not see into your shame. A life cleaning revolting septic tanks or working in the stink of the slaughterhouses.

David didn't like the cards, so he changed them.

He brought along some others who felt they'd been dealt from the wrong deck. A host of The Boys were all from Iowa, or thereabouts. A modern James Younger Dalton gang who operated in tandem no matter what part of the country they were in. Midwestern boys who said "please" and "thank you" and "yes, ma'am"—when it was appropriate. They had all wanted to join the party, but were never allowed.

Tired of the jokes about their clothes and their backgrounds, they robbed at gunpoint for a living. In twenty years, in various combinations of men, they never hurt anyone but made off with perhaps $12 million. They are not sure. The authorities don't know either. There was very little evidence.

What is certain is that, on April 22, 1981, the largest robbery of a standing bank in American history was accomplished. Millions of dollars were lost. The FBI was angry. The Boys were amused. They had vowed never to be laughed at again.

They weren't.

PART I

THE CROWN JEWEL

1

The day would soon be an eye-shattering blue, but now, at sunrise, the mountains around Tucson glowed orange and red under the emerging fireball of the desert sun.

It wasn't exactly hot. Yet. Yellow and purple wildflowers that had sprung up after the winter rains were abundant and there was still a green tinge to the Catalina Mountain foothills. But the promise was there. The promise of the strange, ethereal heat that would come in a month. The flowers would shrivel; those animals that could would head for the high country and the rest would pant a lot. David wanted to be out of there before then. He and The Boys enjoyed the Arizona desert only in winter and spring.

As usual, he'd been up since 3 A.M. He'd hauled Doug's and Bruce's asses out of bed at the same time, although they constantly grumbled about his obsession with breaking down their weapons, cleaning them, and reloading every single time they were going to make another try on the bank depository.

"Do we have to wipe the goddamn cars down again, too?" Bruce grumbled.

They'd purchased three vehicles—including a van now painted to look like a telephone truck—for this job. David required anyone driving them to wear Krazy Glue on their fingertips and to wipe them down after each use to erase any chance of fingerprints. They were parked in different locations every night to avoid detection.

"It's good therapy," David informed him quietly. "And it's professional. It prevents mistakes."

They'd been watching the bank for about three months. Actually, it wasn't a bank. It was one of those mythical places the bank robber community had never been sure existed. A kind of warehouse for money. Stacks and stacks of it in an unmarked building with very little security.

They'd tumbled to it because the bank David had initially selected— Valley National on the corner of Broadway and Country Club— looked too complicated. Although he estimated the huge structure might have as much as $10 million on the premises at any given time, there were too many employees around the vaults, and vaults were the only areas David was interested in. He had no desire to risk his life or anyone else's for the petty cash the tellers guarded.

Posing as a janitor, David had walked through the cavernous basement where the vaults were and ascertained that bank management had staggered employee duties so that at least a half dozen people were in the area at all times. David had to admire it. He also admired the fact that the employees all arrived at work at the same time—another practice he knew was not an accident. It would be almost impossible to control twenty-five people.

"Too risky," he'd finally told Bruce and Doug, though he was reluctant about it. Bruce and Doug groaned that they'd already invested a month in surveillance. The money looked good, but someone would certainly get shot, David said. In twenty years in the business, he'd never shot anyone and he didn't intend to start now. He wasn't greedy enough.

However, he'd noticed a ton of armored cars going to and from the great white whale—as he called the bank. There were many more than normal. Tailing them led the trio to the depository at Broadway and Swan.

Sometimes David would sit at the bus stop across the street eating an ice cream. Sometimes in the coffee shop down the way eating breakfast. But in a month or so, he knew every procedure the depository followed. He found it incredibly stupid that they followed the same routine every day, but he chalked that up to Bud Grainger (nicknamed Bald-Headed Bud by David and his partners). From his observations, David felt Grainger was a man who couldn't stand change and was very controlling. Ordinarily, such a personality might present a problem—try some heroics. But David didn't think so in this case. Grainger seemed more at ease with bullying his subordinates.

The morning of April 22 would be their ninth run at the job. Bruce, who was the driver and the only one who could see out of the front of the van they were using, had always found some reason to call it off. An old woman at the bus stop. A one-armed man handing out religious pamphlets. A kid crossing the street. David was sick of it. He thought Bruce was just scared.

"This time, we go," David told him firmly as they loaded the van. Bruce put on his sullen expression. "I don't care if the Pope is having a parade. We've got to get out of here."

That much was true. The FBI had been scouring the country for David Grandstaff, Bruce Fennimore, and Doug Brown for nine months, ever since the men jumped bond on a $1.5 million jewelry heist.

Not that David had ever been charged with the robbery. The FBI had trouble finding any evidence on him. But they knew he'd done it. And he was considered the most dangerous of a group of a dozen or so armed robbers—most of whom had grown up together in the poor area of Des Moines, Iowa. They were thought—between them and in various combinations—to have stolen right around $10 million in the course of their exploits, and they were getting a kind of Robin Hood image the FBI found extremely upsetting. More galling, even a few of the local police and federal prosecutors liked them. Grandstaff was dangerous because he was considered the most controlled and brainy of the group. He was the planner and they wanted him bad.

They had no idea where he was, though. Charlie Virgil was about to find out.

●

Like most people who lived in the desert year-round, Charlie Virgil didn't spend valuable time worrying about the upcoming heat. He had long since accepted the desert, being one of a tiny minority of black men who made Arizona home. Charlie had worked for the same janitorial firm for almost ten years, although he sometimes moonlighted with other companies to get ahead. And that's what he was worried about today. He had worked all night at his second job. Now, at 6:45, he had to roll right into his second one, which was cleaning the First National Bank cash depository. He was dog-tired. He had brought his house slippers because he hoped he might be able to get a small rest before the bank manager arrived to let him in. It wouldn't be a long rest. Maybe fifteen minutes. But that was enough to prompt Charlie to bring the slippers.

Charlie had keys to most of the offices he cleaned. Usually, there was no one around when he cleaned because he mostly worked nights. But this job was different. He had to wait for Bud Grainger, the depository manager, or David Harris, the assistant manager. The two managers alternated opening the small building for reasons Charlie didn't know but was vaguely suspicious about. Although he had no reason to believe it, Charlie felt that Grainger was always looking to "put one over" on him. He didn't know what that would be and he didn't know how varying who opened the depository could accomplish it, but there you had it. It was just a feeling. He remembered uneasily that a week earlier, he had emerged from his night job to find all the tires on his truck had been flattened. It had been so puzzling. But the worst part about it was that it threatened to make him late to the bank, where he imagined Grainger waiting triumphantly with his clipboard detailing the transgression. Charlie could only thank his lucky stars that he'd finished a little early at the office building. At the same time, he was angry that his fifteen minutes of solace had been spoiled by a bunch of rotten kids, because those were the only people he could imagine pulling such a stunt. He would find out only years later that Bruce had deflated his tires in an effort to have fewer people at the bank when they went in.

Naturally, the depository's function contributed to Charlie's unease. The building was identifiable only by a small sign in front announcing that it was a First National branch office. There *was* a small branch office there, but Charlie knew what the real purpose of the building was. In a way, he wished he didn't. The location of the cash receptacle for all of the branch offices in southern Arizona was a closely guarded secret, at least as far as the bank was concerned. Charlie didn't know how many millions were in his reach as he moved a soggy, gray mop over the concrete floors, but he knew there were millions. Grainger kept a very sharp eye on Charlie and the thirty-odd women who worked there. It was part of his job to detail their activity, even when they had to leave the room for hygienic reasons.

Charlie didn't know how anybody in the neighborhood could overlook the fact that dozens of armored cars pulled up to the metal garage doors daily, loading up millions in cash to be distributed to any branch office in the southern part of the state. It seemed pretty obvious that this was not the tiny branch office it appeared to be. But a U.S. depository had never been robbed, so Charlie guessed the bankers knew what they were doing when they refused to give him even the phone number to the place. Arizona was a state dominated by white men, and pretty conservative white men at that. He'd just as soon have someone watching him work in case the count came up short.

Traffic at the intersection of Broadway and Swan was still light at 6:45 A.M. In another hour, all four lanes would be jammed. It wasn't exactly uncrowded now, but Charlie knew he would not have to summon his fatigued faculties yet to fight maniacal traffic. Arizonans, Charlie reflected glumly, drove as crazily as Californians. Only they did it without the benefit of freeways. Tucson traffic frequently moved at around 55 mph on city streets marked "Speed Limit 30," with drivers pretty much loath to mess up their time by slowing for yellow lights, even when they'd been yellow for ten seconds. Nobody watched or looked for anything. It was so common that you had to be driving in a stupor or hit something valuable to be ticketed. At peak hours, the situation required full attention.

Charlie watched the traffic, knowing he would not see Bud Grainger's car until 7 A.M. or later. Grainger didn't get to the bank earlier than that. Charlie didn't know why this was true, but it made him feel less paranoid about putting on his house slippers in case this might be one of the infractions Charlie imagined Grainger scouting for.

The depository sat on the Broadway/Swan corner, a small, nondescript brick building with an even smaller parking lot, maybe half the size of a tennis court. From the front of the building to the busy intersection was no more than fifty feet, a fact that made it hard to rest as the trucks and impatient motorists screamed through yellow lights on their way to another workday. But, from where Charlie had parked, it would give him an opportunity to see Grainger pull in and time to get the slippers off. He didn't notice the telephone van thirty feet away from him parked to his left and rear.

By 7:05, it was clear Grainger was going to be late. Far from feeling satisfied at this no-no (as Grainger called breaches of rules), Charlie became slightly worried. Was this a test? Should he call someone? He was deciding what to do when the driver's door flew open and hands grappled all over him. Something cold and hard hit his temple. At first, he thought he must have fallen asleep and hit the steering wheel or something. He couldn't imagine what else could be happening.

"Behave yourself now, and don't make a murder out of this," someone close to him said, but Charlie didn't assimilate it right away. He was fixated on the face. There was something terribly wrong with it. Something so grotesque that Charlie screamed like a banshee over that alone. He continued screaming at the top of his lungs, even though he now knew the thing that had hit his head was a gun.

"Son of a bitch," a second voice said, almost amused. "He's screamin' like a goddamn girl." The second voice was grabbing his arms and Charlie started to kick. He connected with something. A chest maybe. He wasn't sure. He didn't know how many there were.

"Just get him the fuck out of there before he causes a fuckin' riot," the first voice answered tersely, but very businesslike. The man sounded like he was carrying out a transaction at the grocery store.

The traffic screamed by them only fifty feet away, but Charlie now saw that the view from the street was blocked by a white telephone van he would have had to smash into, even if he had seen it pull up behind him in time to move his truck. Based on the viselike grips on his body, Charlie thought there might be two men attacking him. But Charlie was a slight man, weighing about 130 pounds at five feet six inches. Everyone said he was kind of dignified looking, and small boned, like a junior high math teacher or a librarian. These men were larger. Much larger. Whatever his kick had found was as hard as a football player's padding and it hadn't daunted the recipient in the slightest. Charlie was already spent, but the men with him seemed to be just getting started. He felt helpless.

And then he was being pulled. He was sliding and scooting over the vinyl seats, his arms and legs clenched in so tightly he could barely struggle. The truck's open door looked like a yawning abyss that, if he passed through it, would swallow him into eternity. If he went through that door, he would never come back. It would be like falling off the face of the earth. He realized he was still screaming.

"Son of a bitch, motherfucker," the first man swore in calm annoyance. "Shut the fuck up." Charlie felt he'd become some kind of technical problem.

Why couldn't anyone hear them? Charlie wondered as he was pulled toward the bright, white light outside the cab's door. He knew he was leaving the truck.

At that moment, falling into eternity didn't seem to matter as much as the fact that one of his house slippers had fallen off. That slipper was new. He hadn't even had time to wear it down properly. His wife would kill him. He realized the thing that was wrong with the faces was that they weren't faces at all. They were Halloween masks. Plastic of some kind. Ugly.

And suddenly it was over. He was quiet, on the floor of the van feeling his saliva accumulate over the gun barrel that had been shoved in his mouth, hitting the back of his throat. There was no taste to the barrel. It had been cleaned and recleaned, he knew, because he owned his own guns. Perversely, he wondered when he'd last cleaned his own guns that well.

"Charlie," the first voice said, "don't move or I'll blow your fucking brains out." The man banged the gun against the back of Charlie's throat for emphasis and Charlie believed the man completely. The mask was over him as if framed in a goofy camera angle from a bad horror movie. Except Charlie was the camera and what was happening was not a movie, a thought that almost made him faint. He stopped moving, in part because he was awed that the mask knew his name.

Slowly, very slowly, the gun receded from his mouth. "Let's quit this fuckin' screamin', too, Charlie," the mask said, almost wearily. "It's damned undignified."

Charlie nodded, feeling the gun barrel leave his lips with a small pop. There was a metallic taste now, but no trace of powder. He reminded himself that the gun had not been fired recently. For some reason, that was reassuring. Charlie felt able to look around.

There was a tarpaulin covering what looked like an arsenal of very serious weapons. He recognized a shotgun under the lump because the barrel was protruding. Charlie saw that the front part of the van— the driver's part—was partitioned off. He could not tell how many people were inside the van. For no logical reason, he assumed there were two men in front he couldn't see because of the partition. Then the two here in back. They were binding his hands. It felt like tape.

He was trying to see more when, to his amazement, the first mask pulled him into a sitting position and sat down right next to him, as if they were school chums about to share a lunch. The man sighed. Charlie nodded numbly. The man was patting him down. He removed a pager Charlie carried so that the janitorial service could reach him. Charlie winced as the man took it. It would be something he would have to pay for. Just like the slipper.

"Now, Charlie," the mask said, assuming a calm tone, "this is just a routine bank robbery. It's got nothin' to do with you. Do you understand?"

"Fuck this shit!" a voice screamed from the front of the van. "Make him tell us what the fuck is going on or we'll cut his goddamn fingers off. Where the fuck is old Bald-Headed Bud Grainger, Charlie?" the voice yelled. "Tell us or I'll be back there directly with my knife to cut your balls off, too!"

A hot, greasy sweat erupted on Charlie's forehead as he thought for the first time that he would die. There hadn't been enough time to think about it before, but now it seemed perfectly logical that he would die today and he could not even react to the fact that the men knew not only his name, but Grainger's and Grainger's schedule. The voice in front terrified him. It did not have the same composure as the man next to him, who said nothing in response to the outburst.

"Maybe Bud and Rose stayed up screwing too late," the second mask said languidly. There was a flat sarcasm in the voice that Charlie found unnerving. He didn't even dare look at the second man, who was sitting with his knees up opposite Charlie. For some reason, he turned to the man next to him for reassurance. The robber patted Charlie's shoulder paternally.

"Just calm down, Charlie," he said. "We don't want to hurt you. We feel for you and this fucking job you've got."

"Fuck it. Let's just cut his fingers off," the man in front yelled again. Charlie cringed, but the man next to him seemed to ignore the remark.

Charlie felt like ice, though the temperature inside the closed van had to have been at least twenty degrees warmer than it was outside. The man beside him patted his shoulder again.

"What about that, Charlie?" the man next to him prodded.

Charlie struggled to remember the question. Grainger and Rose. Staying up late screwing. . . . But Grainger's wife's name wasn't Rose. It was . . . Betty. Yes. Betty. And come to think of it, it had been her birthday yesterday. Grainger had talked about the party he was going to throw. Yes, Grainger had thrown a birthday party for his wife. It was probably why he was late.

"Yeah," the second man broke into Charlie's struggling thoughts. Charlie could feel him watching, perfectly at ease in the van, and enjoying. "Because Rose is a pretty good lookin' woman. Don't you think, Charlie?"

"Betty," Charlie said numbly. "You mean Betty. And he's probably just late because of her birthday party last night." Charlie didn't see the men exchange quick glances as he said it.

"Right," the man next to him reassured. "Betty."

It was then that Charlie realized the telephone van's engine was running. It must have been running all along, although it did not seem they were moving. That didn't mean anything. They could be driving along one of a thousand remote desert roads that could have been reached in the eternity he'd already spent in the van. He thought about the stories that dotted the Tucson newspapers, of people found months after their deaths, bleached and whitened by the desert sun, and police saying they were still trying to make an identification. . . .

"Okay, now, Charlie," the man beside him said. It seemed important now to please that man. "We know about the double lock on the door. Is there a trip alarm inside? Don't lie to us now, Charlie. Because we'll know if you lie."

Charlie shook his head that he would not lie. He felt sure they were telling the truth.

"Now, here's the thing, Charlie," the man said, checking the tape. "Is this too tight? If it is, I'll loosen it. I'm sorry about having to do this, but you can understand what it's about, can't you?"

Charlie nodded.

"I just want to talk to you a minute, Charlie. Are you okay enough to listen to me?"

Charlie looked at the hideous mask but felt calmer. He nodded again.

"You may not realize it, but you and us are really no different. You got more to do with us than them bankers whose toilets you've been cleanin' for years. You're gonna go in there and clean them toilets again today, Charlie. For three bucks an hour after workin' all night. And they probably don't know your name. I'll bet they don't know as much about you as we do."

Charlie listened, now completely still. They knew. They seemed to know everything. But there was something to what the man said. There really was. Charlie always felt like someone in the bank was trying to trick him into doing something wrong. The mask nodded, appreciative of the reaction. Charlie felt he was on the right track.

"Listen to me, Charlie. We've been kicked in our asses all our lives, just like you. We ain't never had nothin' either. We ain't out to hurt nobody. We're just out to even things up a little bit. You understand? These bankers wouldn't never give you nothin' but a boot in the ass anyway. Why should you risk your life for them? Do you understand?"

Charlie nodded slowly, because he did.

●

Bud Grainger—his real name was John, but everybody called him Bud—was a little late to the cash depository that morning exactly because he'd been celebrating his wife's birthday. He consoled himself with the knowledge that he wasn't so late as to be caught. He was there in plenty of time to beat David Harris, who never arrived more than thirty seconds before or after 7:30 A.M.

Not that Harris would say anything. But there were procedures and, as it was, Grainger was in violation of two of them. One, he was late. Two, he possessed both keys to open the building when he should only have one. Harris should have the other. It was part of the First National Bank's security policy. Nobody could enter the inner sanctum without another trusted employee. Bud felt sheepish that he'd taken both keys last night as a matter of convenience, but he wasn't nervous about it. He didn't see the telephone van across the depository's parking lot as he pulled in. He was hurrying.

He wheeled his vintage white 1966 Mustang into his normal space, noticing Charlie Virgil's white pickup parked in its usual place, two parking spaces down from the innocuous door to the depository. Charlie did not seem to be in the cab. That was irritating, this glitch on top of his other concerns. He needed Charlie to get right with him so he could get inside the bank and put this security breach behind him. Charlie was probably asleep in the cab, Bud decided. The scuttlebutt was that Charlie had been working two shifts lately. Bud had not had a chance to check on that yet.

Bud walked to Charlie's truck and slammed his shoe into the front bumper of the pickup. The truck rocked a bit, but there was no response. He didn't bother to look in the truck because he felt the kick had been hard enough to roust the sleeping janitor. He walked to the front of the building—the small branch office that Charlie also cleaned when he was finished with the depository. It was possible that Charlie had become confused and tried to enter this part of the building first.

Peering through the windows, Bud saw that Charlie wasn't inside and wasn't waiting outside. Frustrated, Bud walked back to the rear of the building and began opening the depository doors. One key in at the top and it clicked. One other key at the bottom and as it clicked, the door would open. There was a screeching noise that Bud identified as tires burning rubber, but he didn't turn around because the traffic at the intersection had become intense and he had become accustomed to accidents. It was not until the wind from the halting vehicle hit his face that he realized it was directly behind him. He turned quickly and was confronted by a sight that couldn't be true. There was a telephone company van with the cargo doors thrown wide open. Two men with deformed faces knelt in the bay area, pointing guns at him with remarkably steady arms.

"Now, Bud," one of the men said quietly, "don't do anything dumb. Just be calm. This is just a routine bank robbery. And if you want Betty to have another birthday like she did last night, you'll do what I say. Now get in the van."

"He's got both keys," the second man said, surprised. "He's got both the damned keys."

Bud was highly irritated. A joke was a joke, but for the comptroller's office to pull this kind of a stunt simply because he had one lapse in twenty years was unforgivable. After all, it was only a key. And that van had come dangerously close to hitting his car. Bud was willing to take responsibility for the time and the key problem, but they had really carried it too far. The Halloween masks were particularly perverse.

The gun that hit Bud behind the ear in the next three seconds was not plastic and he felt his skin inflaming. It was a revolver, he knew from his army experience. He also thought the cylinders were empty, but he decided against mentioning it because he now knew this was no comptroller's joke. He was too stunned to move. He could only concentrate on the fact that one of the masks had a small tear in it. What shoddy workmanship, he thought ridiculously.

He didn't have long to ponder the inanity of his thought processes. One of the men yanked him forward with power that almost took him off his feet. His terror was starting to jell as he fumbled with the second lock. He remembered that they'd known his name. They had known his wife's name. He almost panicked at the thought that something was happening to her, too. There was at least one man behind him and a second one in his face, pointing another gun at his forehead. He was vaguely aware that Charlie was standing there with his hands behind his back. He was in house slippers, except he wore only one.

"You can stay in the van, Charlie," the man in front of Bud said. "You're done here."

"No!" Charlie shrieked. "I wanna come with you!" The thought of becoming separated from the calm man terrified Charlie. Bud watched in wonder as Charlie scrambled clumsily from the van and stood beside the man as if he were a guardian angel.

"Let him come," Charlie's benefactor told the man holding the gun to the back of Bud's head. "He don't want to stay with the asshole and you can't blame him."

Bruce waited till Charlie, Bud, and his guys were inside before throwing the van into reverse. He careened around the rear of the building, backing into the garage they'd observed the armored cars using when they made pickups and deliveries. When David heard the van inside that area, he made Charlie push a button to close the door, so the van would not be visible from the street. Bruce climbed through the trap door used to move the money bags into the garage.

Over and over Bud could remember hearing the three men warn him not to set off any alarms. Bud had been in the army. He was a baseball coach at the University of Arizona. He was involved in civic activities. Over and over he thought he should do something. The men told him they had guns trained on his wife who at this moment he knew would be walking around the house with the curtains wide open, making coffee. Betty always let the morning desert sun in while she made coffee.

●

David Harris arrived at the depository exactly on time. Seven-thirty A.M.—no sooner, no later. He buzzed the intercom that would allow Grainger to let him enter a locked "mantrap" that served as a security area before anyone could be admitted into the main building. Grainger would see him on a video camera and admit him to the mantrap, and then look at him through a glass window to make doubly sure before letting him in. Everything happened normally, except that Grainger looked a little peaked peering through the window once Harris was inside. But that was to be expected given the party that had gone on the night before. Grainger buzzed him inside.

Harris started to sign in, but felt himself flying through the doorway to the inner sanctum. It happened so fast, he didn't register how his face had ended up on the concrete floor or why his shoulder ached like it was on fire. The janitor was standing there, tied up. Bud Grainger was standing with some men who had hideous faces. Grainger looked bad, too.

"All right, David," he heard someone tell him, "get on up off of there and don't do anything stupid. This is a routine holdup. Nobody has to get hurt."

It made perfect sense, Harris thought dazedly. Just a routine holdup. Just do what you're told and everything will be routine. No hitches in the routine. It was a good plan, he decided. He heard Charlie reinforcing Grainger's persistent assurances that he was not going to set off any alarms.

"That right, Charlie?" the men would ask every time Grainger denied that his movements would cause an alarm.

"That's right," Charlie would answer confidently. He didn't seem nearly as freaked-out as Grainger. Harris certainly hoped Grainger wasn't going to do anything out of the routine they'd embarked on. Grainger had a tendency to dislike insubordination. Harris kept his face on the cement floor. He had every intention of cooperating. He was not going to risk his life over a job.

"We have to sign in," Harris heard Grainger croak. It was policy for everyone to sign in, in the morning.

"Jesus Christ, Bud," came a flat, sarcastic voice Harris didn't like one bit. "Why don't we just forget about your fucking little sign-in sheet. Live a little. This morning, we're gonna break the rules."

Harris was hoisted to his feet and shuffled to the vault with Grainger. He and Grainger held dual combinations to the main vaults, although Grainger could open the inner vaults by himself. Once the main doors swung open, Harris was led back to Charlie, and both men were laid on the floor and bound with duct tape. Harris saw a third man, obviously their guard, fiddling with a police scanner that had been laid on the filing cabinets. There was a lot of chatter about an accident on 22nd Street. There was nothing about an armed robbery in progress.

"Be cool, David," the janitor whispered. "Just stay cool." Until that moment, Harris had been unaware that the man lying next to him knew his name.

●

Inside the vault, Doug and David watched Bud Grainger go to work on the money drawers. Both watched with increasing irritation. Grainger was fumbling and bumbling with the combinations, pretending he didn't know them. I ought'a go over there and kick him in the ass, David thought, just to knock some wisdom into him.

In all his years in the robbery business, David had never been able to comprehend people who were willing to risk their lives to save someone else's money. Their own money, yes. He could understand. He had never robbed small businesses for this reason, though it didn't have so much to do with his fear of resistance as his feeling that it was somehow not right.

But a bank's money? Next to insurance companies, banks were the worst possible institutions in the country. They were responsible for half the wars going on around the world and they wouldn't give two nickels for a dime for Bud Grainger's life if he had begged for it. Yet here he was fumbling around, first pretending he couldn't open the vault at all and then saying he couldn't open the shining steel cash drawers.

"Bud," David snarled, "I'm not gonna tell you again. We'll nail your wife this minute if I don't see some cooperation." David motioned to Doug to stay where he was. Doug's fuse was quite a bit shorter than David's and he was displaying inclinations to get physical.

Now Grainger, defying instructions again, was opening the drawers that held the singles and five-dollar bills, which David had no intention of taking. They were too heavy.

Why was Grainger doing this? If he was so worried about his wife, why was he playing with her life like this? Of course, there was no one at his house, but Grainger didn't know that. And if he didn't care about his own life or hers, what about the other two idiots out there? Cops, he could understand. Cops were trained to shoot at robbers. It was their raison d'être. And even if they didn't particularly *want* to get into a shoot-out, they'd never be personally able to live it down if they didn't. For this reason, David had always been particularly wary of off-duty cops who might have wandered into the target area to simply cash a check or say hi to someone.

But why wasn't Bud Grainger happy with his nice house and nice car and nice family? Why did he, too, have to pretend that this was some matter of principle and not what it was—just a simple crime of economics. David did not consider himself a violent man, but he was not opposed to violence. It was sometimes necessary. Now he thought about giving Grainger a simple kick to the rear to get his attention. A knock to the head might disorient him, or even knock him out.

David, Doug, and Bruce were all a long, long way from home and it had been a trying time. None of them had contacted friends or relatives (or so David believed at the time) because of suspected FBI wiretaps and surveillance. All that bickering between his partners over video games had worn him out. Those damned games were ruining the youth of America, he'd said many times. Nobody went out and kicked a football around anymore. They all sat in the house like zombies.

And he was sick of the hotels. Hotel after hotel in every city in the country, most of them low-rent because he did not want to call attention to himself by staying at the finer places. Once, they'd even bought $1,600 worth of camping equipment, thinking that would be better than places like the Pink Flamingo, where they were staying in Tucson. But Doug and Bruce had gotten into one of their squabbles and the brand-new equipment was tossed out the window going 65 mph on Interstate 25 outside Denver.

This job could put an end to all that. This job could put something back together, perhaps. It could quite possibly be the last one and he might buy a house someplace green. Someplace that at least reminded him of home, even if he could never go back there.

Now this idiot banker was screwing around, messing up the plans. It was 7:40 A.M. They absolutely had to be out of the bank well before 8:00 A.M. when the first armored car came for a pickup. They had a lot of packing to do between now and then. David nodded at Doug.

●

"Bud, I want you to stop fucking with us!" Grainger heard one of the men snarl. It was not the man Charlie seemed to like. "Open those goddamn drawers on top and stop fucking around or I'm gonna blow your fucking brains out."

Grainger felt, rather than saw, the man move up behind him. The man moved closer, so that Grainger could feel his menace at his back.

David rolled his eyes under the sweaty mask as Grainger continued his pretense. And then, Grainger did what David considered to be his stupidest move so far. He started clutching at his chest and gagging.

"Motherfucker! The asshole is pretending to have a heart attack," Doug said, also astonished at the folly of it. Both men had seen it before.

In fact, Grainger was pretending. He would later testify that he'd seen the move on numerous television programs. It always worked there.

"It might be for real," David suggested noncommittedly. "Have a quick look." Doug took another look.

"It's not a heart attack," he said definitively and was on Grainger's throat with a knife in a second. "Goddammit, I'll show you," he hissed.

Doug yanked Grainger by his collar, pressed the blade into the skin of his neck, banged his head into the steel drawers, and told him: "You are no good to us dead, you cocksucker. So if you're gonna die, why don't I just finish you right now?"

Grainger was inches from the man's face but would later remember nothing about him, not even the color of his eyes. Grainger's terror was overwhelming. He returned his breathing to normal and the knife receded.

"Open those goddamn drawers, Bud," David said. "Before you really get hurt."

Grainger saw that this man—the one who seemed to be in charge—was also losing his patience. This time, he really did miss the lock, he was so frightened. He shook and tried not to panic, thinking how ashamed and humiliated he was that he could not stop this. It was just unthinkable that these hoodlums could walk in here and take all that away from him. How could he face people if he did not resist them? He had been trusted. He was in charge. But he could not afford to trip the alarm. He had others to consider. He did not know that if his fear had prevented him from opening the lock on the second try, he would have been shot.

●

Grainger was returned to the room containing Charlie and David Harris, where he persistently tried to look up at the man guarding them. Unlike Harris, he did not believe the police scanners were real and did not heed instructions to keep his face down. This prompted his second encounter with a knife to his throat. To Grainger, this man seemed less sure of himself—perhaps more likely to overreact—and Grainger decided to give it up, though a part of his dignity died forever with the decision.

"Be cool," Charlie soothed. "Just be cool. I don't think they want to hurt nobody."

This struck Grainger and Harris as ludicrous. Both of them were thinking the same thing: "They are going to come back in here and put bullets in our heads. We are helpless. They are going to kill us and we'll never see it coming." Both men thought of their families.

Now there was the sound of duffel bags being opened and knives slashing through containers. The men on the floor had no idea how long it went on. At some point they heard a couple of the robbers yell at their partner, calling him a moron and telling him not to mess with the small bills. Grainger knew the "small bills" were three duffel bags containing about $300,000 that had not been counted or deposited the day before. He already knew what they thought about the small bills in the vault.

"Charlie, I want you to help us out," Grainger heard a calm voice behind him. Charlie nodded and was helped to his feet.

"Everything is okay and you guys are fine," the man said. "Don't move for ten minutes or we'll be back." Grainger assumed Charlie went with him. He thought they might be taking him hostage. He did not know that Charlie had been enlisted to close the garage door at the armored car entrance. The telephone van had been pulled into one of the garages and the gate shut while the money was loaded. Now that it was time to go, the door had to shut again so that the first armored car that arrived would not think anything was wrong. Before David left, he tossed Charlie his pager and the slipper lost in the parking lot. David had retrieved it before entering the bank.

●

It was 7:50 A.M. and Grainger croaked at Harris to cut him loose. One measure of pride Grainger had been able to salvage was that he had turned the "tripper" on when he opened the depository. It was not an alarm, but a beeper that indicated a vehicle had left the garage. If Charlie was with them, there was not much he could do about it now except escape.

Grainger had believed that if he kept his hands spread during his binding—like he'd seen in the movies—he would be able to just wriggle out of them. Instead, Harris was free and he was still writhing around.

"I think there's a scissor in the desk," Grainger said desperately. Harris got it, cut his hands loose, but for some reason didn't think about his feet. For that matter, neither did Grainger. He hopped around with his arms free without thinking to untie his feet. Making it to the phone, he knew he should call the police but simply had to call his wife first.

"Betty!" he yelled when she answered.

"Goodness, Bud. What's wrong?"

"Are you all right? We've been robbed!"

"The branch office has been robbed?" Betty asked, thinking her husband meant the minor branch office at the front of the depository.

"No! No! They got to us! Get down on the floor! Don't go to any windows!"

Betty was in tears when he hung up to call the police. U.S. currency littered the floor as if there had been a green snowstorm. The robbers had left $750,000 in small bills scattered all over the place.

Their take would turn out to be $3.3 million—the largest robbery of a standing bank in U.S. history.

2

Dan Sorenson, a journalist for the *Tucson Citizen*, was sitting in the pressroom in the basement of the police station when the first call on an armed robbery crackled over the scanner at 7:57 A.M. A veteran reporter, he was accomplished at hearing the police scanner without actually listening to it. He would be instinctively alerted by changes in the dispatcher's tone or by unusual calls. Bank robberies and drug busts are common in Tucson, and reporters—especially reporters unlucky enough to draw the hated early morning police shift—do not pay particular attention to either of them unless somebody has been shot or taken hostage. Hostages are unusual, but shootings happen with some regularity. Both the *Arizona Daily Star* and the *Tucson Citizen* feel a duty to report them, even though they are boring occurrences and a general pain in the neck for the reporters. Sighing, Sorenson kept one ear cocked to the radio while he continued perusing his competition, the *Star,* to see what might have been missed yesterday by his own colleagues.

The calls about the robbery continued, not unusual in itself. But Sorenson's innate radar was beginning to penetrate his concentration on the morning paper. He turned his full attention on the scanner without knowing exactly why. It came to him soon enough.

The cops were using a scrambler on their transmissions, which prevents eavesdropping. The cops do it only in extreme situations because it can backfire on them if one of their own can't hear a crucial transmission. Sorenson felt sure they would not be using it unless there was a terrible hostage situation or the biggest bank robbery in the history of the United States.

When he realized that nearly every available officer in the city was heading toward the bank, he picked up the phone to call his city desk. The phone was ringing as a heavily armed cop ran by the pressroom door, flanked by a bunch of guys in suits. The FBI. Now Sorenson was sure. Not a hostage situation. The biggest bank robbery. Technically, the FBI has jurisdiction in all bank robberies, but they pick and choose their cases very carefully. Often they don't get involved unless the locals run out of steam and even those are rare cases. In fifteen years of reporting, Sorenson had never seen them rush to the scene so shortly after the event.

The rewrite man, Keith Carew, finally got on the phone, but he did not share Sorenson's conviction about the robbery's significance. It was close to deadline and he didn't want to have to restructure his pages. After fifteen minutes of exasperating arguments, Sorenson slammed down the receiver and prepared to write a three-inch brief on the robbery. He would be tormented for weeks by his competitors with snipes about how he had missed the story of the biggest bank robbery in the history of the United States—a story that would capture imaginations from coast to coast and lead to one of the most extensive FBI investigations ever.

●

At 7:57, Officer E. Smith heard the first radio call at the same time it was monitored by Dan Sorenson. It was also monitored in two cleanly registered cars—a Buick and an Olds—doing the speed limit on Interstate 10 to San Diego.

The Buick contained Doug and Bruce, plus a load of pistols and three AR-15s, which had not been needed to blow out the engines of police cars that might have gotten to the bank in time to give chase. Safely ensconced in westbound interstate traffic, the Olds contained David, $3.3 million, and a pump shotgun, which had not been needed to blow away a police officer who had innocently pulled up behind David at a stoplight as he was leaving the city.

When he heard the radio transmission, David smiled. Officer Smith did not.

An armed-robbery-in-progress call does nothing for a cop's sense of security. Especially if you happen to be cruising the area a block away—as Smith was. He was alone and would have to respond to a life-threatening situation. He had no idea when backup might arrive.

In fact, David had always assumed he had at least two minutes to leave a robbery scene—even after an alarm was sounded and even though a cop might be having coffee next door. He believed the police would rather track robbers than engage them in a firefight. He'd had some experience with it in his younger days.

Smith approached the depository carefully from the east, then sat quietly, watching the parking lot. When he saw no movement, he went in.

As he entered the bank with his weapon drawn and his emotions in a severe state of flux, Smith found Charlie Virgil walking around in the front of the depository. Virgil was, to Smith's way of thinking, calm. He had seen people in shock before, but this didn't seem to be the case with Virgil.

After assuring Smith that the robbers had left, Virgil told him that there had been four men, ranging from about five feet eight inches to six feet tall, wearing different colored windbreakers and holding a variety of guns, including a .32-caliber pistol and a 12-gauge pump-action shotgun. A couple of the men wore tennis shoes; the other two wore Hush Puppies. All wore masks and brown gloves, Virgil said. They wore different colored pants. Smith began radioing the information to the two dozen officers wailing toward the scene with blue and red lights flashing. The cars eventually fell into line on Broadway as if they were late for an important funeral.

●

By the time Sergeant Schreiber got his call, he knew how serious the situation was. He reacted by dividing the city into quadrants for a fifteen-block area surrounding the bank. At least a half dozen cops screaming toward First National were diverted to the quadrants to begin a street-by-street search for the telephone van.

But the depository's parking lot was still a carnival light show of police strobes when Sergeant Arndt arrived. It was eerie and Arndt reflected that there were an awful lot of cars for a crime scene where no one had died. Arndt was not sure who was there when he entered the building.

Inside, the place was a mess, but the kind of mess that could only happen in a daydream. Bundles of cash, still in the bank wrappings, littered the floor like rag dolls cast away by bored children. Loose bills carpeted what areas were not taken up by the bundles. Police officers stood looking around in awe. Several men wondered what necessities could be bought if they simply took what was plastered to the bottoms of their shoes. Others wondered how much was gone, if this had been too small to take.

Arndt saw Smith taking victims' statements. The bonds of adhesive tape were still dripping off Bud Grainger and David Harris, a fact the two bankers seemed unaware of as they wandered around the depository, bumping into cops. One officer noticed that Grainger could not seem to stay off the phone long enough to talk to anyone in charge. He appeared to be checking on his family and friends, apparently not realizing that the police had already dispatched men to the victims' homes. Given the threats that had been made, it seemed a wise thing to do.

Eventually, Grainger said there had been three robbers, all wearing maroon windbreakers, brown Hush Puppies, and jeans. They had ranged in height from five nine to six three and all weighed about 180 pounds. Harris said there were three robbers, one wearing blue slacks and the other wearing black silk slacks. He didn't see the third one, only sensed him. Harris repeated that he'd taken his instructions seriously and not lifted his face to look at the men, but he thought they were all about six feet tall.

At 8:44, Officer J. Starr found the telephone van at the El Con shopping mall, about two miles from the bank. He radioed his discovery excitedly and the cruisers searching the city quadrants screeched toward the shopping mall as the Buick and Olds neared Picacho Peak, about forty miles northwest of the city limits. Out of radio range now, the men inside no longer amused themselves with the police chatter. They cruised leisurely like all the other businessmen making their way to Phoenix this bright April morning. Instead of worrying about the papers in their briefcases, however, these men passed their time dismantling a serious arsenal of guns, which were to be buried 800 miles away.

At the mall, Starr circled the van warily, noting that it was not a telephone van after all. It had only been painted to suggest one. Some psychologists, these guys, he thought. On closer inspection, the paint job wasn't all that good either. The bottom looked like it had been roller brushed and there appeared to be bits of sand ingrained, as if it had been done in the desert.

Inside, Starr could see a mask under the front seat. He assumed it was a robber's mask, but he did not touch it. He was there only to secure the scene and wait for the detectives. But he did note that the van was completely empty except for the mask and completely clean, as if it had just been washed and hosed down.

When the other cops arrived, they split up, looking for witnesses. Any kind of witness. It would not be easy, because the mall did not even open until 10 A.M. and the lot was empty. But they did find a few. One woman on her way to work felt sure that several men had been staring at her from an intersection. Another thought a couple of men in a big American car seemed to be awfully busy with something in the backseat when she arrived, but she'd noticed only because she had to move her car around them to park. A couple of Mexican nationals, who had been at the lot all morning under the mistaken impression that a small bank branch office there opened early, said they saw nothing. Nothing at all. Their green immigration work permits seemed to be in order, though. Another mall worker said he'd noticed the van because he'd realized it wasn't an actual telephone van. He was the only one who had.

When Sergeant Arndt heard Starr's radio message, he prepared to leave the bank. Coming in was Lieutenant Jerry Reeves and his special problems unit along with several grim-looking FBI agents. Well, well, thought Arndt. We won't have this case for long. It looks like it's too big for us. He did not speak to the FBI men as he left the building.

●

Police chief Peter Ronstadt, the brother of singer Linda Ronstadt, was at a fund-raising breakfast the morning of April 22. Ronstadt had lived his entire life in Tucson and he did not dread these necessary chicken and pea appearances anymore. At population 500,000, Tucson was just big enough to afford privacy and just small enough to require camaraderie, even if you happened to be in the midst of a political bloodbath with the guy sitting next to you. Ronstadt's father was German, his mother Mexican. Unlike in cities in the north of the state, the combination was normal, accepted, and sometimes even necessary to get ahead. Tucson was a very integrated city. Maybe it was the city's proximity to a poverty-stricken and uncontrollable border. Maybe it was the fact that the city was rough with drug importers whose business in part benefited the economy, even if bodies did turn up regularly in the desert. Maybe it was the summer heat. But Tucsonans tended to wink at situations others might stamp their feet over. They were used to the abnormal and they had a sense of humor about it.

Ronstadt had known everyone at the April 22 breakfast for a long time. There was no need for a staff strategy plan to handle the press. The press sat next to him, working the same causes. Ronstadt was politely waiting for the speaker, who was talking about law and order, to finish when the first police officer approached the head table and whispered in his ear. Ronstadt cocked forward, listened, nodded, smiled, and turned to a respected columnist for the *Tucson Citizen* seated to his left.

"Well, well," Ronstadt said quietly. "I guess Tucson has finally reached the big time. Somebody got a bank depository an hour ago. Must have gotten millions."

●

The FBI agents at the bank were not amused. Glumly, they watched Frank Torres, a comptroller from the bank's headquarters, inventory the money littering the floor, comparing it to what was supposed to be in the bank. The robbers had gotten clean away with about $3.3 million in less than twenty minutes. They had left more than a half million on the floor—presumably because the bills were too small to bother with, or too heavy to carry given the burden they already had.

The agents called their boss, Larry Bagley, to report the bad news. Then they sent a priority bulletin to more than fifteen cities across the country. They did not expect to find the men who committed this robbery lounging around a bar in Tucson bragging to their friends. The agents doubted if they had any friends in town except, of course, the one who helped them pull this job. It was definitely, the agents had decided, an inside job. The robbers knew too much. Before the priority warning had gone out, Charlie Virgil found himself downtown in an interrogation room being threatened with twenty years in prison if he didn't cooperate.

●

By the time the telex went out, the cruising Olds had passed through Phoenix and into open desert on its way to California. The clothing of a half hour ago was long gone, the money was stowed out of sight, and it was a beautiful day for an open country drive. The Boys intended to enjoy it.

"I still say we should have dropped a $30,000 bundle in ole Charlie's truck," Bruce had said when they were burying the clothes under a highway bridge. "He was so helpful. And he was a pretty nice guy. Real polite. You can see he ain't got a pot to piss in. It don't seem fair."

"Naw," David had said. "I told you. They're gonna search his truck and then they would have nailed him for sure. As it is, he's gonna have a shit storm on his hands because he's a black man. They'll go right for him. They won't be able to believe we didn't have help."

"Guess you're right. As usual."

3

U.S. attorney Roxanne Conlin got up the way she always did—in a bad humor. Conlin was only the second woman in U.S. history to become a district attorney, after President Jimmy Carter appointed her. She was not a morning person, however. Though she always arrived promptly at 9 A.M., her staff knew to give her some time with her teapot and newspapers before showering her with the day's disasters, and April 23 was no exception.

The *Des Moines Register* spread before her, she sipped gingerly at her steaming herb tea. None of the major headlines on the front page interested her and she was about to flip it when a small item near the bottom of the page caught her eye.

> Tucson—A record $3.3 million was stolen from a Tucson bank depository yesterday in what authorities are calling the largest bank robbery in the history of the country.
> An undetermined number of armed robbers wearing Halloween

masks took several bank employees hostage during the robbery at the First National Bank cash depository. Police said the robbers called the victims by their first names and seemed to have an intimate knowledge of the layout of the bank. . . .

Conlin's phone was ringing, but this time she would not hit the intercom button and complain to her staff.

"Hello, Ed," she told Ed Mall of the Des Moines FBI.

"Do you think The Boys were in Tucson this week?" Mall asked.

"You've seen the paper, have you?" Conlin was still reading, looking for more details.

"What do you think?" Mall asked.

"I think you'd better give them a call out there."

"Right," Mall said.

"Send some mug shots, too."

"Right."

After a moment, Conlin said, "Dave Oxler is sure gonna be unhappy about this one."

"Maybe not," Mall said thoughtfully. "At least now we have an idea of where they *were*.

●

In a Travelodge motel room in Motel Circle outside San Diego, The Boys prepared to go their separate ways. A stack of wrapped bills had filled the room the night before. Before it was divided, it was four feet high, three feet wide, and five feet long— approximately the size of a very heavy, very cumbersome Spanish chest of drawers—and weighed around 350 pounds. The Boys would walk by it, taking turns picking up packets, and even though they moved swiftly, it still took three hours to cull the green wall into separate piles.

These were packaged in shoe boxes and wrapped in brown paper for shipment by rail, bus, and airline. Each man would take care of his own share privately, with the destinations kept secret. Of course, there was always a risk that a postal worker or a bus depot employee would discover the contents of the innocent-looking packages, or that they'd be lost. These possibilities did not concern The Boys. They had been prepared to die in Tucson rather than fail. After that decision had been made, all other risks seemed too small to consider.

●

The next priority FBI telex went out April 23 and it also went to more than fifteen cities between New York and Portland, Oregon; Louisville and Los Angeles. The code word now printed for the Tucson robbery was "TUCROB," and it listed four suspects provided by a hunch from the FBI in Des Moines, who had been tracking The Boys for years. Although the Tucson authorities had suspects from California pegged for the job, the Des Moines authorities felt such a heist could only have been successfully pulled off by their local crew.

David Lee Grandstaff
Douglas Wayne Brown
Douglas Bruce Fennimore
John Anthony Oliver

George Weir was in prison, or Conlin would have listed him. Michael See was known to be in Des Moines, or she would have listed him. She had just finished a successful prosecution of Michael Gabriel for the $1.5 million Phoenix robbery she'd hoped to try the others on. So he was not with them. She thought about placing the names on the Ten Most Wanted List.

What she, and the FBI, and a half dozen other law enforcement agencies thought was this: They would never be able to indict, much less convict, The Boys for the nearly $10 million in money and jewels they were believed to have stolen over the years. The Boys, Conlin knew, were very good at their work. There was rarely any evidence.

Smaller robberies The Boys were suspected of included countless grocery store robberies following armored car cash deliveries. In one, thirty people were forced to lie on top of one another for several hours while the robbers waited for the armored car to arrive. The take was some $50,000 and, as usual, there was no evidence. Some of the robberies she also felt sure they'd committed included:

- The October 31, 1977, robbery of a Lewis System armored car in front of the Central National Bank in Des Moines, in which an undisclosed amount of cash was taken.
- The December 1, 1978, robbery of an armored car outside the Coca-Cola plant in Des Moines. The take was $500,000 in cash.
- The February 28, 1980, robbery of the Davidson and Licht Jewelers in Walnut Creek, California. The take was $500,000 in jewels.
- The May 22, 1980, robbery of G. Darrel Olsen's jewelry store in Phoenix, Arizona. The robbers escaped with $1.5 million in jewels.
- The February 19, 1981, robbery of the Mid-States' Bank in Denver, Colorado, in which nearly $100,000 was stolen.

And now, $3.3 million from the First National Bank in Tucson.

Grandstaff, Fennimore, and Brown had been fugitives for eight months. It was most likely that they were traveling together. They would not have risked contact with John Oliver, Grandstaff's ex-brother-in-law, who was thought to be operating in the Missouri area anyway. Conlin guessed The Boys would head away from there. Maybe California. Maybe it wouldn't take long this time.

Officers of the First National Bank certainly hoped so. Successful bank robberies, especially record ones, do not make bankers look exceptionally competent and they encourage follow-up attempts. The depository at Broadway and Swan was razed and rebuilt shortly after the robbery to prevent information about its interior from being passed around the criminal community. There was also the matter of insurance. If the bank was found to be negligent in any way, the insurance company would not cover the loss. First National was already having enough business problems without the public thinking a bunch of hoodlums could walk a janitor into a bank and get away with money it couldn't replace. As it was, they had launched an expensive advertising campaign to get new customers. They'd tried to soften the image of a cold, haughty institution by using an average-looking actor who played the role of "Hank," a bank manager who claimed he was just like everybody else. "Come bank at Hank's bank," the ads proclaimed.

The American Bankers Association hurriedly called a meeting and decided to offer a $25,000 reward to *anyone* who could provide the slightest clue about the robbers. The amount was unusually high. In fact, the association usually did not issue rewards at all. But then, its banks usually weren't robbed of $3.3 million in twenty minutes.

●

On April 25, photographs of Grandstaff, Brown, Fennimore, and Oliver appeared in papers from coast to coast. They were front-page news in Tucson and Des Moines. The media's appetite for the robbery—and the robbers—was voracious. Diagrams, police composites, and any shred of rumor reporters could uncover were immediately plastered on the front page. One reporter went so far as to check recent luxury home rentals, concluding in a lengthy article that the robbers had arrived in Tucson a month earlier, lived quietly and well on the west side of town, and moved out the day after the robbery. Neighbors who had merely said hello to the mystery men were quoted extensively. They were effusive, thinking they might have known millionaire bank robbers. A University of Arizona student printed up a mess of T-shirts that proclaimed "I Yanked Hank's Bank." The T-shirts could be seen in shopping malls, movie theaters, and restaurants.

The romance of the deed became so overwhelming that Paul Turner, an *Arizona Daily Star* columnist, felt compelled to quash it. Under the headline "$3.3 Million Daydream Looks Good Until . . . ," Turner wrote: "If you've ever checked out the inhospitable insides of a maximum security prison you're probably not among those who see bank robberies as some sort of made-for-real-life movie."

Still, the daydreaming and speculation went on, and it wasn't confined to Arizona. On April 25, Kenny Kauzlarich was getting ready to go to his job at the post office in Des Moines. Although he subscribed to the *Des Moines Register,* he hadn't looked at it that day. His wife was pregnant, sick, and cranky and he was also trying to get his boat ready for the upcoming water skiing season on Lake Rathbun. Kenny worked nights at the post office, where he maintained the machinery. The U.S. government had sent him to school in Oklahoma to learn about it, a fact he was a little proud of, but rarely discussed for fear of being thought of as a braggart.

Still, it gave him satisfaction that he had learned well and could fix just about anything that went wrong at his branch. Of course, he knew The Boys thought well of him, too, even though he'd taken a different fork in the road after a brief interlude. The Boys had never looked down on the fact that he had wanted something different. In some ways, he thought they might envy it.

He hadn't talked to them in months—not since they'd left. So they weren't on his mind when he walked into work and found the other postal workers whooping it up, holding the newspapers over their heads and shouting "Right on!" and "All right!" Some of them were muttering that "they should all be locked up forever," but for the most part, the mood was exuberant.

"Fuck that bank," one yelled. "They've got it coming."

The mail carriers were congratulating the hometown boys and speculating seriously about what they might do with the money from a record bank robbery. Many lottery tickets were sold in Des Moines that afternoon as news spread through the bars and grocery stores and restaurants. Kenny wished he'd read the newspaper earlier, so that he could have called a half dozen families on the south side who he knew had picked up their papers and smiled. Somebody would be able to make their house payment. Somebody would get the transportation they had to have to qualify for their job. Somebody would get a new dress and somebody would be able to beat off a bank officer who wanted to repossess a car. Courtesy of the First National Bank. As proud as he was, Kenny felt a bit of sadness. This was not one they would let go. Something bad would happen eventually.

In the U.S. penitentiaries at Leavenworth, Milan, Atlanta, and Lompoc, and in state prisons in Iowa, newspapers were passed quietly over chow tables and between cells. Cheering was not recommended, but there was an occasional guffaw or a low whistle. They had beaten those bastards again. Those guys had given the dirty sons of bitches a wallop they wouldn't soon forget. Especially in Leavenworth, there was a decent feeling in the air that day, even if they all believed it would be short-lived. They all had experience with "dollar justice," and there would be no cutting corners, no lack of resources, for the chase.

George Weir happened to be sitting in Leavenworth at the time. A childhood friend of David's and a partner on many scores, he shook his head at the photographs.

"Man," he thought to himself, "I hope you get far away, my friend. There will be no mercy this time."

4

As Roxanne Conlin was reading her paper in Des Moines on the morning of April 23, Doug Brown, David Grandstaff, and Bruce Fennimore were in San Diego, gearing up for a busy day .

Emotionally and physically exhausted from the rigors of the robbery, they'd spent a quiet night in the Travelodge packing their haul into shoe boxes. As usual, David and Bruce stayed together and Doug took a separate room because Bruce and Doug were on the verge of killing each other again. The night before, Bruce had called Doug "Dougo" one too many times, prompting Doug to reinform David that the younger man should never have been allowed in the group.

"All right, all right," David had responded wearily. The complaints had worn him down. "It's over now, anyway. You never have to see him again if you don't want to." Doug had just snorted and quit the room for the evening.

That morning, Doug elected to stay in the room, which now held the contents of the First National Bank depository, while David and Bruce made the obligatory trip into the mountains east of the city. Unlike his associates, Doug did not like long drives. He preferred flying and had more than once taken security risks to avoid drives like the one he'd made the day before. He was eager to fly out today and get back with Linda. He had no desire to make another drive into the hills, unload about fourteen guns that hadn't been thrown out yesterday, take them apart, and cast them to the four winds. The remaining clothing would also have to be buried and Doug was not interested in digging, either. A national bookie and a gambler by profession, Doug liked good wine, gourmet food, and expensive clothes. He'd taken up robbery only because of that FBI sting in Omaha that had landed him in Leavenworth. He would not, and could not afford to, turn over on his very serious Las Vegas counterparts, so he had done the time, but it had made him far too conspicuous to move in that circle again, and he had reluctantly abandoned it.

●

Now Doug watched David and Bruce rub a thin coating of Krazy Glue on their hands as they prepared to leave. Gloves did not provide the dexterity to break down guns and David wanted no prints on the parts. David was not interested in taking chances, even though the chances of anyone putting those weapons together was as remote as a summer snowstorm in Arabia. Bruce sneered constantly about how paranoid it all was. What a punk, Doug thought. Accusing them of being "paranoid." What a punk. The moron had never seen the inside of a county jail, much less Leavenworth. Doug still could not understand how David put up with it.

"Back in short order," David said briskly, and Doug nodded, trying not to sour his stomach by looking at Bruce.

Doug's lanky build made his five-foot-eight frame appear taller than it was. His hair, once coal black, had turned prematurely silver over his thirty-six years and it set off his startlingly blue eyes in a way that would come back to haunt him. He'd met Linda months earlier. Although he liked women, Doug had never been as bewitched by them as, say, George Weir. But Linda was different. The moment he'd seen her eating dinner with a friend in a San Diego restaurant, he'd wanted to talk to her, and that he did. He'd walked over and introduced himself as Jeff Nottingham and they'd been together ever since. The raven-haired consultant from a middle-class background had been surprised when Doug had recently told her his real name and occupation. But she hadn't balked or run. She hadn't been shocked, nor had she condemned him for his subterfuge. She had become the first woman he'd ever trusted. He lay back on the bed, waiting for his time to go to her.

●

It took several hours to get rid of the weapons, although Bruce insisted on keeping one—a sweet Beretta he and David had purchased in Cheyenne. David had given up arguing with Bruce about such matters. It had become his opinion that Bruce was intent on getting everyone arrested with his ignorance and naïveté. The sooner they got away from each other, the better, because certainly Bruce would be arrested. Although none of The Boys had respect for the FBI, Bruce seemed to believe they were first-class idiots, which David knew from experience was not true. It was typical of Bruce to believe he was the only person with a brain cell in his head. David sighed, allowed Bruce to keep the gun, and got in the car. He was too tired to argue.

On the way back to the hotel, David spotted a used-car lot with a nice-looking Ford out front. They would need another car, since there were three of them and three directions. He told Bruce to stop and check the car out. Although many of The Boys disliked Bruce, they all admitted that he was a first-class car man. He had been around cars his whole life, cheating and shaving and wheedling. One hundred years ago, he would have been the best horse trader west of the Mississippi. He was impossible to cheat. It was impossible to hide defects from him. And anything that ever went wrong with a car, Bruce could fix, no matter whether he was in a Detroit auto factory or on the Utah salt flats. He was also an excellent driver and David knew there could be tense moments when Bruce's abilities might help them avoid a shooting spree. Plus, Bruce had protected Marty Brightman when he was sixteen and lied before a grand jury for George Weir when he was thirty-one. It had saved George from a bank robbery indictment, so it was not as if Bruce did not have a stand-up record. David knew why his friends didn't like him, but sometimes he wished they'd all just shut up and remember why Bruce was around. Nobody was perfect.

David sat in the Olds watching Bruce dicker with the car salesman, pointing out this deficiency and that, getting the price down. There was no need for David to supervise the transaction. If Bruce said the car was sound, it was. And Bruce would get the best price possible. No matter what kind of money he was sitting on, David would not be cheated.

"Okay," Bruce said, getting back in the car. "It's cool. You wanna get it now?"

"Let him sit on it for a while," David said, putting the car in gear. "He'll come down another hundred dollars."

●

Back at the hotel, Doug heard Bruce's raucous laughter first. When was that motherfucker ever going to learn to keep quiet and not attract attention? By the time the door opened, Doug had his grip ready to go.

"Well," Bruce said awkwardly, watching the other two men packing up with professional speed. He did not like to be ignored. For that matter, he did not like the idea of being alone. He never had. "I guess we'll all meet up in Kansas City then, eh?" he prodded.

Doug brushed past him without speaking. The money, which had taken hours to divvy up, had been moved to the Olds and Buick in suitcases purchased for the occasion. The Boys were just some businessmen checking out.

"Get going," David told Bruce. "And don't forget to hose that fucking car down. I don't want no fingerprints on that car in case they ever do put it together." Bruce watched the two men move briskly through the parking lot, then started getting his own things together.

Doug drove David to the car lot, where they picked up the Ford Bruce had finally purchased for $3,800 cash under the name of George Bradley, which was really David's alias. The two men followed each other on I-405 up to Los Angeles, found a car wash, and hosed the Buick down, inside and out. The soaked carpeting alone probably added fifty pounds to the car's weight. Then they took rags and wiped it to make sure.

David said good-bye to Doug at LAX. Doug was flying out; David would be driving. The TUCROB Buick was left in a private, long-term parking lot, from where it would eventually be towed and sold at auction. There was no way to trace an owner. That was the way it always worked, anyway.

David was driving northeast on the California interstates around the time Conlin was sending the mug shots to Tucson. He was feeling very good, very happy, as the teeming, chrome cities of southern California began giving way to the open desert, and then to the more rolling hills heralding the approach of the greener states he preferred. He had grown tired of the desert during the extensive planning of the job in Tucson. He knew it had been a record score. It was like a crown jewel in a career. It was exactly like starting in the mail room and working your way up to the executive suites. David did not believe there was any difference. Ralph Nader was about the only man in America he felt was above suspicion. He believed the men in the executive suites committed more robbery than he did.

"The only difference is," he often told Doug, "is that they do it with paper and pens and they keep it. We, at least, put it back into the economy. We buy things."

But, of course, he was well aware of the other difference. He would go to prison for the rest of his life if he were arrested and convicted of this robbery. He thought again uneasily of Bruce. David had made it crystal clear that Bruce was not to return to Des Moines under any circumstances. David felt sure Bruce was smart enough to understand why, but . . . He put the thought away.

The plan he'd been ruminating on for months now was a move to Hartford, Connecticut, where he would buy a three-bedroom-or-so home in a nondescript, middle-class neighborhood and lay down. He'd owned homes in Des Moines that he had renovated, adding new carpet here, some wallpaper there, and in one, a wonderful spiral staircase to the second floor. But he had something more in mind for this one. Not too large. Not too noticeable. This would be home for quite a while.

He'd decided on Hartford because he had never been known to travel east. Most men on the run go to the Sunbelt, especially Los Angeles. The Los Angeles Police Department has had great luck with sting operations in which letters are sent to suspected fugitives informing them of great riches they've won. When the men come to collect, the cuffs go on. David had often marveled at the stupidity of it, but he had to admit that he'd been no exception as far as his choices were concerned. He had spent most of his time west of Iowa. Hartford, he'd decided, was a place nobody would think to look for him.

There were other reasons for Hartford. He knew absolutely no one there. This was a bit lonely—and he was tired of loneliness. But it eliminated the possibility of being recognized or having someone turn him in for money, which was always a concern in the netherworld. It was an activity that could exact terrible retaliatory sums from those who practiced it. Even so, there always seemed to be some rat—a friend, a relative, or someone trying to work off their own legal problems—who was willing to take that chance. Snitches. They were the lowest life form David could think of. He had debated with himself for a while about who was worse: the actual snitches or the authorities who ran them, giving them money, letting them lie, letting them steal, as long as they continued talking to The Man. It seemed to him that the authorities, who said they were interested in upholding the law, had a higher duty. But on second thought, people who sold out their friends and relatives for money or to save their own hides had no claim to being human. At least the cop could blame it on his job. As rotten and hypocritical as that was, it didn't involve putting personal friends in cages. Not that he didn't think they wouldn't, if they hadn't had the money to attend college and get jobs that made them all "Special Agents." Personally, he'd never thought any of them were special.

Experiences with this had given David grave misgivings about the worthiness of the human race on either side of the law. These days, he basically trusted only those people prepared to risk their lives with him. By that, he meant that they had to be ready to get their brains blown onto the wall. No surrender. No negotiation.

Mercy was a different matter. Every precaution was taken to avoid a no-win situation. Plenty of jobs had been aborted because innocents had stumbled onto the scene. It had never been his intention to kill, or to get anyone else killed with poor planning. But anyway, he had to know that his colleagues were capable of it. He had to see it in their eyes. There had been too many times in Leavenworth when he had allowed grace on that issue and regretted it. Now, he was pretty sure of his judgment where character was concerned. He did not worry about The Boys, not even Bruce.

Experience had also taught him to keep his own counsel. David's eyes were often flat mirrors of hard brown. Mike See wore his sunglasses day and night, but David's eyes did not require glasses to disguise emotion. They did not melt during happiness or tear during sadness or light up during mirth. Only movement in his facial muscles gave clues to his mood.

At five feet eight, David was not a tall man, but he was athletically built and fanatically careful about his weight and health. He experimented with diets. He worked out hard every other day. He was meticulous about his dress and his appearance. Blue jeans had to be creased just so. Shirts were tucked and folded before being placed in the jeans. He had more than a dozen pairs of Nunn Bush shoes, all of them looking brand new and lined up in his closet with supports in them. His brown hair turned blond quickly in the sun and he kept it cut short, unless it had been grown out as a disguise. Likewise, the mustache was trimmed with gold scissors daily unless it had been shaved for the same reason. When he was young, his face had a wistful, yearning look, not unlike that of James Dean. There was always a set to it though, and as he aged the set became harder and more frequent until now, the yearning look appeared only sporadically.

He was borderline superstitious. He believed men who smoked pipes were untrustworthy, poking the smoking apparatus into their mouths to buy time to think up their next lie. He disapproved of women who did not wear bright colors. He wouldn't touch meat that was more than three days old. He wouldn't tolerate untidiness of any kind. He liked children but never demonstrated it, although they seemed to sense his affection. They were drawn to him whenever he entered a room.

Unlike some of his colleagues, who had an emotional reaction to "the system," David was a student of politics. He had received college law and government credits in Leavenworth, as well as credits in history. He watched at least two hours of CNN a day. He had taught himself Spanish so that he could communicate with the sizable Latino populations behind bars. His unalterable conclusion was that there were two kinds of people—those with money and those without. Those with it will form alliances to protect it, even if it means sending young men like his brother Danny to war. The greatest symbols of this evil were banks, politicians, and insurance companies. He never felt guilty about anything he did to them.

That night, on his trek toward Wyoming, David finally relaxed. He hadn't looked in the rearview mirror for an hour or so, letting his taped music take over his brain. He'd run over details a dozen times. There was no eyewitness identification from the bank. The cars, purchased with false IDs, were untraceable. The guns were gone. They had changed hotels so often, he was sure there was no problem there. He had misgivings about one of his partner's behavior at a steak house they'd frequented. Bruce had been very loud. But he did not think it would matter much. So it was a shock when he pulled into a Cheyenne gas station on the morning of the twenty-fifth and picked up the newspaper.

His picture stared out at him along with Doug's, Bruce's, and John Oliver's. David dropped his head quickly, cursing and wondering what had gone wrong. The typed lines began to blur and he struggled to fight off a reeling dizziness. He forced himself back into control; forced himself to read the article slowly as he began his breathing exercises.

There had been no arrests, according to the article, so it could not be that someone had done the unthinkable and talked. No one knew they had been in Tucson. There had been a pact not to contact anyone without permission from the others—on penalty of death. It had been a serious pact. Although he trusted all of them, David had a queasy feeling. There had to have been a slipup he just wasn't seeing. And if he couldn't pinpoint it, he couldn't fix it.

His queasiness was heightened by a growing alarm from another quarter. Cheyenne was a small town and his appearance was not that changed from the photograph. As calmly as he could, he walked to the trunk, popped it, and began rummaging through his suitcase like any other tourist who had misplaced a map or his glasses. The galling glasses he hated he would now have to wear. They made him feel old and he was fearful of aging, but they were the only things he had offhand that could alter his appearance even a little. They would have to do until he could get his hair dyed and permed and his mustache shaved. The needed rest he'd anticipated had been turned to sudden flight.

He found a pay phone and gave the regular code to the man who answered in Walnut Creek, California. Ten minutes later, the pay phone he was using rang back. Jimmy Smith was calling from another pay phone for the information.

There was a car, David informed him. A yellow Ford Smith could find abandoned at the long-term parking lot at Stapleton International Airport in Denver, where David intended to drive it. It was to be picked up, driven away, taken apart, and tossed piece by piece in various junkyards. It was not to be sold for scrap. Smith would find $5,000 in the trunk for his trouble. Jimmy Smith understood. He'd seen the papers, too. He would get right on it.

David did not really think any of the cars could be traced to him, but he was taking no chances. He had learned long ago to anticipate the most outlandish events, because those were the ones that got you. He had no way of knowing that the most outlandish, bad luck coincidence of his career had already occurred on April 8, two weeks before the robbery.

●

In the days that followed the robbery, the Tucson Police Department and the Tucson branch of the FBI got a serious workout. Uniformed officers and detectives alike were dispatched to virtually every hotel and motel in the city, armed with Conlin's mug shots. They pored over registration cards, interviewed hotel employees, and searched, in vain, for some clue as to where the Tucson bank robbers might have stayed.

By now, everyone had figured out that TUCROB was of more concern than normal to the FBI and the robbers were more than an annoyance. "I Yanked Hank's Bank" T-shirts began appearing on tourists wandering the malls and on high school students in math class. The newspapers clamored daily for more details. The *Tucson Citizen* scored a coup when reporter John Rawlinson got an exclusive interview with Charlie Virgil. It was splashed over the front page as if Virgil were actually a president of some small country. Reporters from coast to coast began calling him, begging for similar interviews. Supermarket tabloids teased their readers with visions of the missing millions. Even *Time* magazine got into the act, running a breathless article that was mostly inaccurate.

Not to be outdone, *Des Moines Register* reporters camped out at the homes of the alleged robbers' relatives. Sharon Grandstaff, David's sister, returned to her neat three-bedroom south side home with an armful of groceries and was shocked to find a gaggle of reporters in front of her house. She was nearly in tears after pushing through them to the comparative safety of her living room. Kelly Grandstaff, one of David's brothers and a union painter, was working when his phone began ringing off the hook with newspaper people wanting to know if he had received any of the TUCROB loot in the mail. Enraged, he called the *Register,* demanding that no such nonsense be printed. He had four children and he did not want every crook in the country to think he was sitting on a million dollars. The information that the loot was with "relatives" was printed anyway. The paper subsequently apologized, but Kelly, an avid hunter, spent many sleepless nights sitting up with his shotgun, listening for noises in the dark.

The reporters were followed by visitors from the FBI, including Agent David Oxler, who was hated by the Grandstaff and Brown clans for his dogged pursuit not only of David and Doug but of their families.

"He's in over his head now, Sharon," Oxler told David's sister on one of his visits to her home. "He's involved with people now who are different. The only way you can help him is to tell us where he is."

Sharon had just returned from her job as hostess at the Fort Des Moines Hotel and she was tired and confused. The only thing she could think Oxler was talking about was that David was involved with the Mafia somehow. Or that the Mafia would be angry that he had gotten so much money. But it was ridiculous. None of The Boys had ever associated with the Mafia. Most of them were suspicious of any organized group, criminal or noncriminal. She tried to put thoughts of the Mafia out of her mind. It was just another FBI trick. But she couldn't do it completely.

In Tucson, the intense publicity generated an avalanche of calls from the public—all concerned citizens claiming to know something about TUCROB. Many of them had heard about the $25,000 reward. A worker in the Greyhound bus station said a rude man had come in and pulled out a fistful of money. A woman filling her car at a gas station miles from the bank said she saw men looking at her suspiciously and she just knew they were the ones. A bag lady rooting through a Dumpster found some clothing she felt was too good to have been thrown away. After an exhaustive search, the clothing was traced to a man who lived in the nearby apartments. He was bewildered that the police returned his trash.

5

In defiance of all orders, Bruce, who had holed up in Miami for a few days, went to Des Moines. That will show the paranoid son of a bitch, he thought.

And while Bruce was ruminating about David, David was in Hot Springs, Arkansas, enjoying the water. All of the pain, all of the suffering, was over, he thought, sinking his shoulders under the bubbling springs. It was true, he could not go home for many years. Possibly never. But he could help his family. He could help his mother and sister Sharon get on their feet. His brother Danny, he supposed, was doing all right.

He did not know if he wanted a woman tonight. He'd soured on them lately. Even Lori—beautiful Lori—had grated on his nerves with her constant complaining and whining. Women, he thought, simply did not know what life was about. Since Virginia Fry, David had not felt the need for a long-term relationship, although, to be honest, he thought prison might have a lot to do with it, too. He wasn't really prepared to think about that, though. He didn't believe in dwelling on things.

He made a mental note to call Jimmy Smith in Walnut Creek. He needed a car transferred. He would tell Jimmy where. Jimmy could be trusted to keep a secret.

●

David left Arkansas and meandered around the country. The money had been safely stowed in The Network. Now all he had to do was be careful.

He'd once thought of lying down in Miami for the rest of his days, then rejected the idea because the town was so lousy with cops and drug dealers. Still, it was his favorite city. He loved the way the canals and waterways threaded through the buildings, reflecting the clean chrome skyline in shimmering ponds. He enjoyed just taking long walks, sometimes going for hours through areas that reeked of money or poverty. He enjoyed the wealthy areas more, but the poor sections didn't bother him. They reminded him of where he'd come from and he liked the Latin culture. He didn't even mind getting lost. He would make finding his way out a game. It was a kind of mental exercise to remember landmarks and little details, like Hänsel and Gretel finding their way home.

Of course, even the hope of Miami had evaporated when he'd driven there and found Bruce hanging around. That fool just could not stick to a plan. More and more, it was beginning to look like Fennimore was going to bring heat down on himself, and David didn't want to be anywhere near him when it happened.

●

In San Francisco, David took a hotel apartment, bought a used ten-speed for ninety-five dollars, and biked daily across the Golden Gate Bridge to Sausalito. There, he ate lunch in any of the several outdoor restaurants on the pier. One day, a sea gull stole a hamburger off another diner's plate. Under the weight of its score, the bird had trouble getting airborne, but it kept running doggedly across the restaurant floor, flapping its wings and looking backward, waiting for the recriminations it knew from experience would come. The man who had lost his meal raced after it screaming, "Hey! Hey! Come back here!" as if the sea gull would give itself up for arrest under the pressure. David laughed so hard his eyes teared, a rare phenomenon. He laughed during the whole bike ride back.

In Santa Barbara, David met a young woman from Phoenix. Since he knew a little about Phoenix, they had something to talk about. He stayed with her for about ten days. He liked the girl, but ten days was more than enough. Unlike the rest of The Boys, David had no intention of marrying, despite the pleas of a dozen or so women, two of whom had elected to carry their pregnancies to full term despite his assurances that he would not become personally involved. There had been too much damage for that to happen.

He enjoyed Santa Barbara. Enjoyed the quiet and the beaches and the sunsets. He took long walks. He liked shopping in the little places along State Street. He knew they were all tourist traps, but he didn't care. He bought a workout suit with a sunset on the chest. Under the sunset it said "Santa Barbara." He bought jackets and shoes. For some reason he was always buying jackets and shoes. He bought baggy shorts in bright colors that came down to his knees. He hated fitted clothing despite the fact that it flattered him. He especially hated drab colors. After all that khaki in Leavenworth.

He met Doug and Linda and they did a lot of sightseeing in northern California for a while. They went shopping. David thought Doug was too extravagant with his gifts of clothing and jewelry for Linda, but he didn't say anything. They attended a few shows. Then they swung up to Oregon. They went to see the sea lions at a national park and drove on into Washington State to take in the sights in Seattle. The Space Needle. Things like that. It was a pleasant time.

Before leaving Miami, David had given Bruce explicit instructions to meet him in Kansas City. The boy had to be straightened out. He said good-bye to Doug and Linda in California and headed east.

Now in Kansas City, David entered the coffee shop in the Holiday Inn closest to the airport. It was understood that any rendezvous, no matter which city in the country, would occur in the coffee shop of the Holiday Inn closest to the airport. It was June 4, the day David was to meet Bruce.

David was hungry and tired. He bought a newspaper, tossing it on his table so that the bottom half of the front page faced him upside down. At first the picture there looked only familiar and he yawned, looking at it more closely. Disbelief and numbness set in as he turned the paper around and read the headline. Bruce had been arrested the day before.

He controlled his panic as he rose from the table, heading for the pay phones. There were a lot of people to notify. Jimmy Smith in Walnut Creek, for one. Smith would have to come and get the car David was now driving and chop it up as he had the other. Bruce would have an inkling he'd be driving it. He also needed another change of appearance. And another ID. George D. Bradley, who in reality had died in infancy thirty-eight years before, vanished from the earth for the last time as David destroyed the birth certificate and driver's license.

He reached Doug, as always, with Linda in Los Angeles. It was agreed that David would fly to Sacramento. Linda and Doug would drive there and pick him up. Posing as tourists, they spent time in Sacramento, then went to Oregon before heading back toward Los Angeles.

"That fuckhead is going to talk," Doug growled incessantly.

"No," David answered firmly. "He's stand-up. He's good people. He's proven it before. He won't say nothin'."

David really believed it. The brotherhood was too strong. There were too many ties in Des Moines, forged over twenty years. Bruce was part of that now. He couldn't go against it.

But as the trio drove south toward Santa Monica, Bruce had already proved him wrong.

PART II

THE SCHOOLYARD

DAVID

If you ask where the Des Moines city limits begin, Iowans will raise an eyebrow and tell you it's obvious. It's the Big City. It's the place where the cornfields and hog farms end. There are traffic lights.

From the air, Des Moines looks as if it were in danger of being sucked under a lush, green ocean of agricultural prosperity. The city butts its way stubbornly—even defiantly—out of a world of fat livestock and healthy vegetables. The farmland seems to roll right into the downtown area, where an army of young female office workers marches through the streets at lunchtime, dreaming that their jobs with the one hundred–odd insurance companies, which largely support the city, will deliver them from the tiny, single-church towns they fled.

Even downtown Des Moines has startling open areas. The glass office buildings are tall enough to overlook football fields of open space around the Des Moines and Raccoon rivers. It is still a source of civic pride that Lewis and Clark once traveled there by canoe and met their famous Indian guide, Sacajawea, who was said to have been very beautiful. There is a log cabin in a field near the capitol marked for her. People explain its history without being asked, usually throwing in a few off-color jokes about Sacajawea's interest in the explorers.

Des Moines residents consider themselves citified, even to the point of ridiculing their countryside neighbors who sometimes come to town for a meal. In Des Moines, being called "corny" is a humiliating insult more likely to send the recipient slinking off than into a rage.

But fancy is not something the city is comfortable with. Cafeterias are popular eating places. A minimal effort to hang plants or art will earn a restaurant an "upscale" reputation and even the most upscale of these are just as prone to serve grilled cheese sandwiches as lobster. The "better" homes look like carriage houses compared to the ornate architectural flourishes found in midwestern cities like St. Louis and Chicago.

There is a schizophrenia, though. As much as Des Moines tries to imitate the chichi California life-style, its residents are fiercely proud of their state's status as the leading hog and corn producer in the nation. The same remark about "bib overalls" they may have made minutes earlier will be met with great antagonism if repeated by a stranger. Des Moines cannot escape the fact that it is surrounded by some of the richest farmland in the country and that farming is, after all, more than 90 percent of the state's economy.

Perhaps because farming is an intensely individual effort, Iowans have a history of distrust and scorn for authority, particularly moneyed authority. Certain types of banks were not even allowed in the state until 1858. In 1932, 1,400 farmers converged on the county seat to stop New York Life Insurance Company from repossessing a farm. They slapped the sheriff (and anyone else who tried to interfere with them) senseless. This method of averting foreclosures continues to this day. In the 1970s, when farms were failing all over the Midwest, it was not uncommon for ruddy Iowa farmers, known for their conservative morals, to drive their pickups through the front windows of banks holding notes to their farms.

In any Des Moines tavern today, it isn't unusual to hear customers discussing politics as a sinister process in which elected officials are no more than puppets for moneyed interests. It's not a unique thought, but in Iowa its roots run deep. It saturates the social fabric. As long as no one gets hurt, Iowans and plenty of other Americans don't mind seeing a fat cat taken down. The Boys never hurt anybody—at least not physically—and to many, they were regarded as no more of a menace than the Clay County farmers regarded Frank and Jesse James in the 1800s. In fact, The Boys enjoyed a kind of hero status, especially in the Southeast Bottoms, where most of them grew up together.

●

The Southeast Bottoms lies in the lowland south of the Des Moines and Raccoon River fork and has always been prone to fog and a kind of southern swampiness. Smells and by-products from the dumps, slaughterhouses, and other businesses the rest of the city would rather not see often mix with the damp air, giving the whole area a heavy, unclean texture.

The Bottoms has always existed in Des Moines—some say before the city itself. Even in the 1800s, travelers passing through the area described it as "teeming," overpopulated to the point of being a health hazard. The area had been settled mostly by migrant families, who fell prey to the native Iowans' well-documented dislike for newcomers—especially newcomers who were not of Nordic descent. Iowan farmers who had once been immigrants themselves were renowned for their belief that every man should get his own. They'd gotten theirs, and they wanted the newcomers to move on.

When that didn't always happen, native Iowans confined new arrivals to a kind of ghetto some of them never got out of—the Bottoms. Earning power was limited to the menial jobs no one else wanted to perform. When The Boys were born in the early forties, the jobs included hauling shit from septic tanks and boiling down cattle carcasses at the National By-Product plant, a stinking conglomerate that the board of supervisors has only recently seen fit to regulate, mostly because the sickening fumes escape the Bottoms on windy days.

The movies depict westward migration as bright-eyed folks marching off to a new life, eventually establishing the Ponderosa or High Chaparral through guts and hard work. In reality, large families straggled off of broken-down farms in foreclosure, often losing track of one another on some vague trek west. Graves went unmarked. Husbands went off to other states for work and never returned, some marrying two or three times, producing dozens of children of varying parentage. In Iowa, the American-born migrants usually straggled in from Kentucky or Tennessee and landed in the Bottoms. All of The Boys had the soft, lilting drawl common to those states. Although some had tried, many couldn't trace a family tree beyond their grandparents, a fact that bothered some of them.

It wasn't easy to get out of the Bottoms.

Men might beat their wives, drink themselves into a stupor every night, and ignore their children, but if they went to work every day, they were considered successful, even if they never earned enough money for an indoor toilet.

Education—except perhaps to achieve basic literacy—was not valued, as it had no bearing on the job market. Sons usually went to work at the same places as their fathers. High school graduation was acceptable, but not necessary. Many Bottoms Dwellers considered themselves "educated" if they graduated from high school, but nobody got a watch or a car or even a cake for achieving it. In some cases school was considsered a nuisance, since it prevented youngsters from holding down full-time jobs. College educations were not even discussed. College was something spoiled, rich people did before going out to fuck up the world with their stupid ideas, just as they always had.

Entertainment was limited. Las Vegas and Disneyland were considered dream vacations, though few would ever get beyond Des Moines. Cars took on the status of prize art. Young men could spend eight hours at a time just driving around, if they had the gas money. Fist fighting, even among women, was an expected activity and allowed much conversational diversion as one group after another described the altercation in great detail, sometimes for weeks. Eyewitnesses to the fights were prized visitors. Being jailed was, of course, a natural consequence and no one thought much of it. Girls got pregnant early and often—frequently by two or three different men—in and out of wedlock. They would live with other generations of their families in cheaply constructed wood houses whose ill-laid foundations regularly tilted into the damp river dirt. Porches caved in. Windows sagged and poverty doomed the houses to further disrepair. Combined with the fog, the crooked homes gave some streets a carnival fun house mood that induced equilibrium problems.

What sidewalks existed were cracked, tilted, and useless for what they were intended. The cement was sporadic, as if a drunken city worker had just dumped the concrete here and there in an effort to get down the street and back to the bar. There were a few poorly maintained parks and no fences around hazardous industrial areas. Drainage ponds, which accumulated unchecked, presented a constant threat of drowning to the children who played near them.

To this day, three or four Bottoms children drown yearly. In the year 1948, when Truman achieved his surprise presidential victory, David Grandstaff's cousin was one such casualty. David was five years old at the time.

●

Ronald Agee was ten when he drowned. Ronald was the first of the older boys to allow David to tag along on their adventures, mainly because David was an excellent ice cream thief and ice cream was like gold in the Bottoms. His small size, which embarrassed David, was considered a virtue by the older boys, a group that included quite a few of David's numerous cousins. It was a boon for the other children that David could slip under the local grocery store counter unnoticed. He would stuff his clothing with the precious treat, then run to a vacant lot a hundred yards from the store where the older boys had dug "foxholes" covered with corrugated tin scavenged from the surrounding junkyards. There, the children would gorge themselves until they were sick.

But David was too young to risk taking near the water, which was strictly off-limits for all the children. Because the adults could not swim, they could not teach their youngsters how to survive in the water. The solution to the problem was to promise a serious beating if they ever went near it. This made the prospect more enticing, but no one was willing to take two beatings—one for going and another for corrupting the younger children.

On a misty morning in March, Ronald, his brother Larry, and a neighbor boy set off for City Water Works, the city's reservoir located close to the Bottoms. David watched dejectedly from the porch. The boys discovered a dilapidated rowboat in the weeds around the reservoir, which was not fenced. Gleefully, the three boys hauled it out and piled in, splashing awkwardly out toward the middle of the lake. Their shouts and laughter stopped abruptly when a city worker began shouting threats at them from the bank.

For the boys in the boat, the demands to come to shore conjured up images of the juvenile home. In the late forties, the *Miranda* decision was almost twenty years away. Adults had few legal rights. Children had none. Everybody knew somebody who had been taken to the home and held for days—even weeks—at a time. Most had seen policemen take fathers and brothers away in handcuffs. They had stood behind the sheeted bedroom doors listening as mothers were interrogated about someone's whereabouts until they cried. "The Law" is what Bottoms adults called all authority and especially the police. They said it not with rancor, but with the dull, flat tone of surrender The Boys would come to despise.

The city reservoir worker was now threatening dire consequences if the boys did not get the boat to shore and submit to their punishment. At the very least, that would be a beating from him and then from their parents. Larry Agee began panicking. The law would soon be there. Undoubtedly, the city worker had called them before coming out to yell. Larry looked around wildly for the escape routes Bottoms children learned to calculate early and with great accuracy. He could not swim. None of them could.

While Larry panicked, Ronald went into a terrified frenzy. He jumped from the boat without warning. The thrashing and screaming froze Larry and the other boy in stark horror. Ronald's struggling drove him away from the boat and any possibility of Larry's getting him by the shirt collar and pulling him inside the boat. Larry watched his brother in a state of transfixed paralysis, the screams penetrating his brain like sharp spikes. If he jumped in after Ronald, he would be doing the same thing.

Frantically, the two boys tried to paddle the boat after Ronald, but their thrashing was uncoordinated enough to simply start rocking the boat to the point of capsizing. In the interim, Ronald's impotent bat-

tle disintegrated into gulping water between guttural, gurgling noises. When he sank, he did not come up again.

●

What David would remember about Ronald's death was his grandfather's reaction. Clyde Agee was David's mother's father and he had
been raising Ronald as his own. The situation was not unusual in the
Bottoms, where children were plentiful and were often interchanged
among relatives depending on the varying economic or marital status
of the natural parents. Clyde Agee, as far as David could tell, handled
Ronald the way most Bottoms men handled children, which is to say,
very little. Child rearing fell to women.

So David was amazed when he opened his family's door to a pallid
and weak Clyde some weeks after Ronald's funeral. The man looked
as if he'd lost thirty pounds.

"Benny," Clyde said, ignoring David but nodding at David's father.

"Clyde," Benny acknowledged and the two men sat down with the
stiff formality reserved for occasions when it was clear nobody had
arrived to socialize.

"Benny, I come for a favor." Clyde gripped his knees. Benny waited to hear the favor. There could be no doubt it would be granted. Favors were not requested lightly.

"I can't live in that house no more, Benny. I see that boy everywhere
in that house. I can't live there no more. It's tearin' me up inside."
Clyde gripped his knees harder. It was the only time David had seen
him display anything like emotion. It was almost frightening.

Benny considered. Love was a serious and dangerous admission. It
was hardly ever verbalized, at least not by men, and when it happened, it could have serious consequences for the reputation. Benny
knew Clyde was not weak, but if this got out . . . It wouldn't, of
course. It was in the family.

"What do you need, Clyde?" he asked, after a moment.

"I want you to switch houses with me, Benny. You go live in that
house and I'll come here. It's the only way I can think of."

Benny nodded slowly. It was a big request, but if it was the only way
the old man could find peace, he'd do it.

Years later, David was still haunted by Clyde Agee's grief, but he'd certainly thought of other things his father might have done besides switch houses. What about the man who owned the boat? Why didn't they find him and make him pay? What about the city that ran the reservoir? It was bad enough that they allowed water to accumulate all over the place without taking care of their own property. And what about the man on the bank? Why hadn't he jumped in to save Ronald?

And then it came to him. All the raging, yelling arguments about the tragedy that his father would make at dinner were impotent. For all of their swaggering, the men would do nothing to avenge this outrage. Despite all their boasting, they were intimidated by the Gold Dome.

●

The Gold Dome of the state capitol building sits on the highest point of ground in Des Moines and can be seen from almost any spot in the city. It is an eye-catcher.

On bright days, it gleams like a fantastic mirror flashing messages across the countryside. On rainy nights, it looms like some kind of shifting, ghostly castle guarding powerful secrets.

The Gold Dome is clearly visible from the Bottoms, shimmering in the distance like the entrance to an unobtainable Oz. Physically, the Dome is not far from the Bottoms, perhaps only a distance of about two miles as the crow flies. But no streets from the Bottoms go directly to the capitol, and a labyrinth of railroad tracks, salvage lots, junkyards, and fences make walking there impossible.

Once they reached adulthood, most Bottoms people took the Dome for granted and didn't think about the decisions being made in its hallways. The process was not much understood anyway. Bottoms people rarely voted. But the children looked at the Dome simply because it was hard not to. Television was just emerging at the turn of the decade and, although Bottoms children had little access to it, they were exposed to this new source of information. The Dome, they knew, represented the shiny black, big-finned Cadillacs their parents coveted. It meant brand-new clothes bought at real department stores where the air was sweet from glittering bottles of perfume. And steak dinners in restaurants where the waiters called you "sir." And plenty of ice cream.

Years after Ronald's death, when bicycles had been either stolen or scraped together somehow, David and his sister Sharon rode to the capitol building. Sharon Grandstaff was David's elder by two years, but they were the closest siblings in the family. They would conspire in the night under hushed giggles and sneak out windows to run around free in the dark, spying on the activities of the older teenagers, which were not exactly wholesome. Once, imitating some of the better-known Bottoms hoodlums, the pair got hold of some india ink and gave each other crude tattoos that left Ava Grandstaff faint, although Benny didn't seem to notice.

Parking their bikes outside the building, David and Sharon entered and headed straight for the imposing spiral staircase that shot to the top of the Dome. The staircase had long been an entertainment item for Bottoms children, who dared each other to ascend to dizzying heights. Those with the heart to reach the top might write their names in the plaster, a source of endless irritation for maintenance crews. David had more than writing in mind today.

"We shouldn't be doin' this, David," Sharon told her brother with a nervous laugh. They had been to the capitol before, but this time David was slinking up the stairs with a stealth that meant nothing but trouble. The ice cream thefts had progressed through several stages. First to *Turoc, Son of Stone* comic books, which David savored in the crowded room he shared with his siblings. Then to bicycles and minor acts of vandalism. Naturally, Benny found out about some of it. Sharon would cringe in their bedroom as David received the punishing beatings from their father. The beatings never deterred her brother in the slightest.

"David . . ." she began another objection, knowing it was pointless.

"Shut up," David told her. "Go back if you want to."

Miserably, Sharon followed. At the top, when David was sure there was no one else around, he removed a chisel from his jacket.

"David!" Sharon hissed.

"I'm gonna put my name in this thing so deep, it will be here for a hundred years," David told her.

He had already taught himself to swim.

7

When David started school at age four, he realized that many of his classmates had indoor toilets and did not eat potato and onion sandwiches for lunch. Their sandwiches had meat on them and there were cupcakes for dessert.

It did not come as a total revelation. He knew such things existed. He just hadn't realized how much they existed. And he could not abide the sidelong looks and sniggers over his worn clothing and scruffy shoes. Teachers ignored him to the point of rudeness and school became an ordeal. As the years passed, he saw it only as a way to have social contact with others like him. His attendance was abysmal, his grades about the same. He began mental and physical exercises to improve his size and physique. If nothing else, he was a good athlete.

His teachers remembered him only because of what he did later.

"A very well mannered boy," said Richard Scanlan, who would not feel that way about several of the other Boys. "I remember his sisters well. Very pretty girls. Him, I do not remember causing any trouble. He was always exceptionally polite. Perhaps because he wasn't here that often." There was a faint smile on his lips.

Ava and Benny Grandstaff never said much about the schooling, but there was one institution he could not escape. Ava Grandstaff insisted that her children attend church. She herself did not, because her husband didn't. But the kids were picked up each Sunday morning by a bus that transported them to the First Pilgrim Church in Des Moines, a nondenominational church that was borderline Pentecostal.

The Bottoms Dwellers who came closest to religious organization were those who considered themselves Baptists in the southern tradition of fire and brimstone. Bottoms Dwellers did not count themselves as Methodists, Lutherans, Episcopalians, and certainly not Catholics. These denominations, with their grand churches and enormous resources, were too overwhelming to consider attending. In fact, many Bottoms Dwellers weren't sure they were churches. David did not even know there were such things as religious denominations until his teenage years. In the Bottomss, there were just two categories. Christians and non-Christians. David and the rest of The Boys would come to despise all organized religion, based on what was called Christianity in the Bottoms.

To David, Christianity meant loosely organized services where members "witnessed" to one another and called each other "sister" and "brother." Bible-shaking from the pulpit punctuated every point, which usually revolved around the strictest interpretation of God's Law. No drinking. No dancing. No premarital sex (a laughable concept, since half the members had been born out of wedlock). Sometimes, services weren't held in churches at all, but in homes. But church parking lots were jammed from Saturday evening through Sunday.

David thought it very odd that nobody seemed to notice that the same held true of the tavern parking lots. Or that adulterous gossip abounded right after services. Or that out-of-wedlock pregnancies were common and accepted. When he was born, his own grandmother tried to poison the community against his mother by suggesting that David was not his father's son.

David and Sharon hated the First Pilgrim Church, but at least it wasn't as bad as the church their grandmother attended. Ava Grandstaff's mother, Cora, rarely left the house except to attend church, a tiny, run-down wood structure that was once a house. It was clear that offerings were not used for capital improvements. There was no minister. "Spiritual leaders" stood behind the pulpit to "witness." A "leader" was anybody with a hankering to talk.

The first time David saw his grandmother writhing around on the floor screaming about God, he was terrified. After watching this a few times, David's fear gave way to disgust, which was finally replaced by anger. His grandmother was a fool.

Aware of her son's feelings, Ava chose the First Pilgrim Church even though her mother wanted the children to keep attending with her. David endured his Bible classes. He was even open to believing, despite his experiences with his grandmother.

But the preacher's sermons about eternal burning in hell gave him terrible dreams. Behind his eyelids, he could see the flames licking and licking and feel the terrible, unending pain. The instructor had shown them pictures of burned people with their flesh charred like the burned flesh of cattle carcasses at the rendering plants. It was just every now and then that the thought crossed his mind: If Jesus was so great and forgiving, how come he'd allow something like that?

The death blow for religion came during a Bible class in which the instructor, who doted on a girl from a relatively wealthy family, asked her what sin was. Included in her list was "doing it."

David felt disgusted. He had known what "it" was since he was four years old. He and a kindergarten classmate had gone to the classmate's house after school in search of a treat. David knew there were none at his own home.

When they entered the house, they heard grunting and groaning from the back bedroom, which was separated from the living area only by a blanket. The two boys watched the couple make love, at first trying to figure out if they were hurting each other. Eventually, they reached the conclusion that they were not. The older boys later explained the whole thing to David, advising that he should try it sometime because it felt good. It seemed like a reasonable explanation and David could not imagine that feeling good could be sinful.

As for the stealing the girl also listed, well, he did not believe that any great being would send him to eternal damnation for the stealing he had done. He'd taken some ice cream, which he had shared with every kid in the neighborhood and felt they all deserved anyway. He'd taken some *Turoc, Son of Stone* comic books because he was interested in dinosaurs. He'd also had a spree—before the grocers caught on—of stealing milk and fresh bread and eggs from the delivery stoops. Sometimes there were bakery goods. The trucks used to just drop the items off and the grocers hauled them in when they opened shop. Until David discovered the routine. Those items were always delivered to his mother, who would look at him questioningly, but would quickly put the things away. It had given him great satisfaction to see his brothers and sisters able to slurp all the milk they wanted at dinner. His father never noticed because he was absent more and more these days. But David didn't think there would have been an objection if he had.

Several months later, the First Pilgrim Church sponsored a Bible retreat for its young members. Ava forced David to attend.

He boarded the bus in misery. He had no real friends at the church. His clothing and grammar excluded him. Once boarded, he started toward the rear where he planned to sit in silence, but was surprised to see all the rear seats taken. He was forced to take a seat in the front of the bus, directly behind the instructor.

Buildings melted into green countryside and rolling roads. David did not know how long they'd been driving when he became aware of soft giggling and urgent whispers in the rear of the bus. The instructor was asleep, mouth open, his head bumping against the window. The driver wasn't paying attention to anything.

David made his way slowly to the back, grabbing seats for balance. He saw that the other kids—almost all boys—were out of their seats in a ring around one seat. They were far too engrossed to notice his intrusion. He pushed through and saw the "good girl" who thought "it" was a sin sprawled on the seat half dressed as she allowed the boys to take turns feeling every part of her.

"Oh, you nasty, bad things," she giggled.

When he returned from the retreat, David informed his mother that he was never returning to church again. Knowing that argument was pointless, Ava did not inform her husband. It would only bring on another beating. They were so frequent these days.

●

David collected stray dogs, attempting to train them to attack people who threatened himself or his family. Benny Grandstaff did not approve and often ordered his son to get rid of the animals, despite the tears and the pleading. Sometimes, Benny said nothing about the animals and David strove to keep these out of his father's way. One got sick though, and David pleaded for veterinary attention the same way his mother had pleaded to bring him to a dentist.

Benny found the idea well beyond ludicrous. Going to the dentist because the boy's teeth hurt was stupid enough. Just give him some clove oil painkiller and be done with it. He'd relented on that one and it had cost a whopping eleven dollars. Benny figured that the ranting he'd put up over the next few days would have cured the family of any other silly requests. Now, David actually wanted to spend money on an *animal*. Benny Grandstaff slammed the sick dog in the head with a hammer and that was that.

●

Benny Grandstaff came home from his trucking job one night in 1955 demanding the same thing he always demanded when he came home—absolute quiet. The six children now in the family were allowed to speak in their room, but only if Benny couldn't hear them. It was a difficult order.

It was summer and the sky was light until well after 7 P.M. Laughter from other children playing outside rang through the open windows, but Benny, for reasons he never explained, expected his children to be in the house by 5:30 P.M. David's mother had put in a full day working as a maid—a job David hated her to have—and was now cooking. David watched hatefully as his father took the only fan in the house and turned it on himself.

Ava watched anxiously as the children filed sullenly into their room. She worried about David particularly. He was polite. He was clean. But he did not seem to be affected by anything except his animals and Sharon. He spent more and more time away from home. Ava knew that he was not just delivering vegetables as he claimed, though she'd never confronted him with that.

When David was home alone with her, he moved around the kitchen snagging this or that from her dinner preparations and talking animatedly. He was silent when Benny came home.

Except for his disciplinary measures over David's stealing, Benny Grandstaff did not beat his children. He was, however, a man with a temper, a loud voice, and a penchant for expressing whatever thought came to mind no matter how ill conceived or insensitive. His de-

meanor alone was enough to make the children frightened of him. All
except David, Ava thought. Ava, her brother Harold, and his wife, Mabel, spent plenty of energy placating Benny's temper. She did not
know what would happen if David did not.

Accordingly, she'd suggested that Benny spend more time with
David, especially because the boy seemed to be getting deeper and
deeper into trouble. In some ways, Ava was not all that worried about
the stealing. It was really just something all the kids in the Bottoms
went through. When David got a job at one of the plants and married,
he would grow out of it.

Benny, who listened to his wife more than he admitted, took David
on a few afternoon fishing excursions. David hated them. In the first
place, he suspected that he was along only to be watched. This was
particularly true because Benny always brought his friends along.
David sat on the bank of the Des Moines River, slapping bugs, sweat-
ing, watching the boring line bob in the water, and holding his tongue.
He hated listening to the men's impotent spleen-venting about "the
system" that kept them down, which would dissolve in another moment into the national anthem. His family still had an outdoor toilet;
his mother still worked as a maid; the laundry was still hung from
ropes across a living room that had no curtains, so that anybody walking by could see in. Nobody talked about Ronald anymore.

●

Mabel Agee, Ava Grandstaff's sister-in-law, watched with limited concern as her nephew practically moved in with them. It was not all that
unusual in the Bottomss, but David Grandstaff was so *single-minded*.
It was a little unnerving. Mabel knew that Benny Grandstaff's mother had tried to poison Ava's reputation by claiming that David was not
Benny's son. But to Mabel, he seemed very much like Benny. He was
determined to have his own way.

Though they were not blood related, Ava Grandstaff and Mabel
Agee could have been sisters. They were both smallish, almost bird-
like, and had reddish brown hair. (It was thought that certain areas
of Germany produced this particular color, though neither woman
had the slightest idea of where their ancestors had originated.) Now

past the bloom of youth in which both women had been considered pretty, their looks had faded like a winter sunset, the way most poor women's do. Ava's hair, particularly, was starting to fray and thin from too many cheap perms. Makeup, when they bothered with it, was applied carelessly, as though their youthful stabs at self-esteem had been a misguided effort. The women had taken on a tired, white look that came from endless work and childbearing.

Abuse was not something anyone made a big deal out of in the Bottoms. People just got smacked once in a while, and many in the Bottoms viewed it as a character-building experience. But Mabel had to admit that her husband, Harold, was a real sweetheart compared to some of his contemporaries. He never hit her and only spanked the children under dire circumstances, like that time when he'd explicitly told their son Ken not to ride his bike by the river and ten minutes later, on his way to work, Harold caught him doing just that.

But Harold always brought his paychecks home. There were always Christmas presents for the kids under the tree and if somebody needed a new pair of shoes, they got them—no questions asked. This was (she took it) not at all the way Benny Grandstaff ran his house. Good-looking, strapping Benny paid little, if any, attention to his children, and their things were always secondhand—probably bought by Ava with what she could scrimp together from her slave wages. Mabel had seen David on more than one occasion studying Ken's things—not with envy but with a kind of surprise.

"Ava," Mabel said to David's mother over the phone one day. The two were good friends and the couples often socialized. Mabel resented the fact that everyone always had to do what Benny wanted, even if he was the only one who wanted to do it. "He had the car," she would sigh two decades later. "And that was that."

"Ava, David has been here for a week. He's okay and all that, but . . ."

"Well, I know, honey," Ava replied. "He comes by every day to visit."

"Well, he and Ken are best friends. . . ." Mabel was doubtful, unsure of where she was going with this. She was happy to have David at the house. It didn't matter, but she felt there was something wrong.

"Well," Ava said with resignation, "him and his dad ain't gettin' along too good and you know how it is."

Mabel did know. About the enforced silences. About the yelling. About Benny's alleged infidelities. And about David's thievery. She was really hoping that he wasn't getting Ken involved in that, but she knew she'd be powerless to stop it if it were happening. The boys were disappearing at night. They said to go play pool, which was bad enough. But if that wasn't where they were . . .

Not that she had a moment's nervousness about David. The boy was exceptionally respectful and almost fanatically neat. Mabel never had qualms about leaving the grocery money out or her purse unattended. It was inconceivable that David would steal from family or anyone else they knew. In her heart, she knew Ken had been involved with David in some fashion, but, like Ava, she considered it a phase.

Vaguely troubled about Ava's depressed tone, Mabel hung up and walked into the outer room of her Bottomss home to find David and Ken in a discussion.

"What are you doing with my shoe polish?" she heard David ask Ken calmly. "You didn't ask if you could use it."

Mabel herself had three children and had cared for many more. Cousins, out-of-wedlock babies whose mamas still wanted to play, nieces, nephews, the works. She'd never seen a kid as fastidious as David. His clothes had to be just so. Unless he was playing in the mud or bicycling, he insisted on pressed shirts, which he was perfectly happy to do himself. Even his jeans had to be pressed. Her own Ken was happy with whatever she got out for him, as long as it wasn't embarrassing. He was an easy-going kid, content. David was the only child she knew who would spend his money—wherever he got it from—on shoe polish. So that his shoes could be clean.

"That's my shoe polish," David told Ken.

"I know," Ken said in his offhanded way. Mabel knew her son didn't even see the problem coming. "I'm just borrowing some of it. What's the big deal?"

"You can't borrow shoe polish," David said evenly. "You use it and it's gone. You can't return it because it's already on your shoes."

Ken glared. David's statement was hurtful and insulting. It implied freeloading—a crime far worse than theft. Mabel thought about intervening. She had seen the boys go at it over toys or girls or even plans for the afternoon. Although David was still smaller, he was well developed and athletic, as was her son. Both boys possessed a fierce refusal to give up, even when blood was flying. When they were younger, it had simply been cute. Two little tykes pulling at each other on the floor. It had been simple to lift the little bodies apart. But it had reached the point where they might be able to hurt each other— and anyone else who interfered. No matter how much David and Ken cared about each other, they would hurt each other rather than give up.

Still, she hesitated. The boys had to work it out for themselves. They would have to as grown men in the pool halls they were so fascinated with now. Mabel sighed. It was almost time to let them go.

"It's just shoe polish," Ken said sullenly. Mabel knew it was an apology. She wondered if David would accept it or simply strike out with his fists, angry that his possession had been so classified.

"It's *my* shoe polish," David told him again, but Mabel could hear the edge gone from his voice.

"All right," Ken said. Ken extended the shoe polish to David, although he'd completed only one of his shoes. David surveyed the outstretched hand.

"This time is okay," David muttered. "Next time, you have to pay me first."

David quit the room. Ken looked at his mother, shrugged, and continued polishing his shoes. "The poor little shit," Mabel thought, watching David leave the house. "He's never owned anything of his own. He doesn't know how to share."

●

David Grandstaff was saddened to hear about James Dean's death. Leather jackets and young toughs from the East were getting some attention. Dean seemed to symbolize it and David related to Dean. He didn't have great grammar and he didn't take any shit over it. He was like David. The teachers hated him. But he had respect.

David didn't know that Vietnam would later affect his family in a big way. Dean's death was the only world development he knew about except that the price of Coca-Cola had risen from five to ten cents a bottle. This had prompted his stint in Myron Juvenile Hall. That was for stealing the empty Coke bottles people left on their back porches and in their garages for pickup and refund. At the time, David worked a part-time job delivering fresh vegetables door to door. He'd always noticed the bottles and had never done anything about them. There was no need. He stole all the ice cream and candy he needed and his job paid for the Cokes—until they went up in price and the bottles became too tempting to ignore. Then he decided there might be more bottles *inside* the houses. He recruited a friend. They checked it out. What they found astonished him. People in those houses had all kinds of *things*. Radios. Televisions. New curtains when his own mother was still stringing sheets across the kitchen windows to keep people from knowing that she hung the laundry in there. They didn't steal the stuff. They wrecked it. For no reason at all except to do it. Blasted out television screens. Smashed radios. Slashed upholstery. He didn't know why it felt good. He didn't know why they did it. They were caught.

He spent six weeks in juvenile hall. He was not told how long he would be there or what the charges were. He endured the physical and verbal abuse, whimpering in his dormitory, wondering where his mother was. Surely she would have come by now if his father had not prevented her. When his father finally came to get him, there was little said in the car. David stalked into the house, trying to keep his shoulders back.

"Boy!" bellowed an enraged Benny Grandstaff, slamming the front door. "Goddamn you, David! You get your ass over here!" Panting and heaving with rage, Benny thundered around the house looking for his son.

"David! Get your sorry ass over here!" Benny had his belt off and was slapping the buckle against walls.

Ava sat trembling in the kitchen. Sharon threw herself on her bunk, burying her head in the pillow to muffle her rising sobs. The smaller children fled the house. David sat stoically in a darkened corner of the living room. The beatings had ceased to frighten him. He had not had the church fire dream in months.

"There you are, you little bastard," Benny snarled, finally seeing him.

"Here I am."

"Git over here and take your medicine."

Having decided it was pointless to make things easy for someone who intended harm, David stayed where he was.

"You little idiot," Benny snarled as he brought the belt down. David heard it hit simultaneously with the staggering pain in his head. He summoned all the control he had to keep from crying out but was dimly aware that others in the house had. The belt came down again, then once more, and he heard guttural sounds from his father as he struggled with the effort. Somewhere, Ava Grandstaff was screaming. Another blow, he had lost count of them, caught him square on the nose. Blood squirted everywhere. It didn't seem possible that there could be that much blood in a person's nose. David marveled at how it sprayed when he sneezed, and he tried to wipe it away so he could breathe. Then he saw his father. He had backed away, standing with the belt limp at his thigh. He was pale with an expression of thin, ragged shame.

Benny Grandstaff stood there for a moment, looking at his son as if he'd never seen him before. He looked around the room hazily. Then he turned and walked into the kitchen in silence.

The silence in the entire house was deafening. David mopped at his nose, entering the bedroom.

"Oh, my God, David," Sharon cried. "Oh, my God." She threw her arms around him. She was sobbing.

"I ain't never gonna stay in the Bottoms," David told her. "I'm getting outta here. I'll do whatever it takes."

In the kitchen, Benny surveyed his wife. His words could be heard through the sheeted door over her quiet weeping.

"I will never beat that boy again, Ava," Benny said softly. "I've done all I can. It's clear he's gonna go his own way and I can't stop him. No matter what happens, I'll never lay a hand on him again. So help me God. I'm through."

●

So, David thought, now he was really free. Free of the belief that he would ever get to dental school. Free of the hope that life would somehow be normal and calm. But still sure of the fact that he would leave this place by any means available to him.

It would be only a few more years before the FBI heard his name for the first time. And twenty-five years later, they would be combing through Tucson, still trying to stop the rampage.

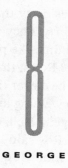

GEORGE

George Weir had encountered his father, again. His eyes now ached and his ribs hurt. George hoped his eyes wouldn't blacken. If they did, he'd have to make up a story about a street fight. He could not admit that his father had administered another unchallenged beating.

George had seen his father's face as soon as he'd entered the house. It was Roy's face after he'd been drinking whiskey instead of beer. It only took an instant to recognize the difference. George didn't mind it when Roy drank beer. For some reason, it made Roy affable and even happy. It didn't affect his face. But the whiskey did. The whiskey made Roy's face red and puffy and put a mean glint in his eyes. His father sitting in his chair in the ramshackle and disheveled Bottoms living room. No drink in sight, but there never was. His father staring at him as he came in the door. The mean glint. George tiptoed around, trying to make his way across the dismal living room to the kitchen. It was a tiny house. It was only a matter of a few yards to the blessed back door, which led to the freedom of the fields. And then on winged feet he would jump over the neighbors' fences, fleeing like a shadow from their outraged shouts as he trampled their plants or lawns, giggling like a madman at the success of it all until he reached David Grandstaff's house and the two of them could go and hunt new, young pigeons from the nests under the river bridges for their covert, prize-bird-raising operation. Nobody knew about that. Nobody knew that George and David were raising prize pigeons in a secret place using only the fowls most people considered a nuisance.

"Boy!" George heard his father shout. "George! I'm talkin' to you!"

And George knew it was over. The principal had called. Or the teachers. Maybe it was the parents of that kid who had yelled and taunted and called his clothes dirty that morning. In fact, George thought angrily, they weren't dirty. They were just old. Old, faded, and frayed. George knew it. He didn't like putting them on in the morning. But whose fault was that? Roy's, that's who. Roy, who had made a mess of the one enterprise he'd ever thought up to get them out of poverty. Then turned back to welding and was content to drink beer or whiskey instead of trying again. Hell, George didn't even know who had ended up with that farm. Roy said it was an uncle or something.

But George had never met him. He'd never met any of them. He'd never met any of the uncles and cousins he supposedly had. The only thing he knew for sure about his family was that some of them had come from Holland. He only knew that because his mother's mother didn't speak much English. She'd come to live with them when she got sick and they'd said she was Dutch. Both she and his mother were fair skinned and light haired, so George figured he must take after his father's side of the family, whoever they were. He had always had a lustrous mop of curly, black hair, although he'd inherited the sparkling, crystal-blue eyes from northern Europe. He had always been tall and well built. Years later, people would remark on how his face never seemed to age—how he always looked young. At age eleven, this was definitely not an asset. He couldn't pull off the rebel image, even in his James Dean leather jacket. He still looked like the kind of kid you wanted to squeeze instead of fear.

His father was about to whip him for what had happened at school that day, he supposed. It was true that Roy did just enough work to feed George, his sister, and his two brothers. But it wasn't good food and that was all he did. They still had to piss in an outside toilet and his mother looked about a hundred years old. She never even talked anymore. Roy sat there drunk from whiskey and now he wanted an argument—and then a beating—out of George's actions. Which were all a kid *could* do at that age, as opposed to what an adult could have done: whipped the hell out of the kid who had made fun of his son's clothes. Roy never asked why he fought, George thought angrily. And he was the reason why it was necessary. Well, screw it. He sure wasn't going to explain it to him. And so, he told himself he would not cry. He took the beating. He went out to see David later, after his father had passed out.

George had met David Grandstaff about a year earlier in the school yard of Nathan Weeks Junior High School. George was new in town. His family had moved around Iowa somewhat after the Albia farm failure. Just one in a series of failures.

His first day at school in Des Moines, George encountered Billy Striker in the hallway. Billy was a big kid for his age, George thought.

"Hey, you!" the big kid yelled. "You sleep in them clothes or does your mama pull 'em outta the garbage?"

The big kid laughed and a gaggle of little girls behind him giggled. George was very fond of girls. He always would be. He felt the heat of humiliation on his cheeks.

But George was patient. Living with older brothers who thumped him regularly had made him that. He approached the Striker boy calmly.

"Why don't you and I meet down in the school yard afterwards and talk about it?" he asked mildly. He kept the burning in his gut out of his mind.

Somewhat surprised but not about to lose face before his audience, Billy Striker agreed. A time was set.

Down the hall, David Grandstaff watched the incident with interest. He had been subjected to similar remarks but had long since silenced his critics and was now established in the school as no one to insult. David did not intervene in the spat. It was not his battle. But the new boy's attitude so impressed him that he felt compelled to strike up a conversation. He ambled over.

"How ya doin'?" he asked George. George looked at him.

"Okay."

"I seen what happened there. That Striker is a puke."

"Yeah . . . well . . ."

"Listen. I'll go with you later."

"I don't need no help."

"I ain't sayin' for help. I'm jus' sayin' I'll go along, if you don't mind."

George shrugged. "Suit yourself."

"My name's David Grandstaff."

"George Weir."

"Glad to know ya, George."

There was an awkward, childish handshake.

●

In the school yard later, George broke several of Billy Striker's ribs, nearly castrated him with well-placed kicks, and left him heaving and moaning on the ground. He did not feel bad about it, as he wouldn't time and time again. The prick had asked for it. He had practically begged to be beaten. When George was finished, he simply dusted off the clothes that had started the whole thing, nodded at David Grandstaff, collected his belongings, and started for home.

George was thrown out of school the same day he enrolled. Was readmitted eventually, but the fights continued. George, David thought, had an awesome kind of temper. He was as calm and mild as a milk cow unless he was provoked. He had an easy-going, country kind of humor. You could definitely tell he'd spent some time in the Iowa countryside. His opponents, to their rue, often mistook this and his childish looks for stupidity.

George was respectful, even in awe, of girls. He defended the least attractive and most ridiculed girls in the school, often taking them out on dates to build their self-esteem. Later in life, George would make projects of several prostitutes, trying to reform them. David was mightily amused by George's penchant for underdogs.

But when George was angered, there was no retreat. He'd wade in oblivious to any kind of pain he might receive. He had one objective. He didn't care what he had to do to achieve it.

The next boy who discovered this was a boy who pushed George in the back. George was watching a group of girls argue in the school yard, along with a smattering of other boys who were enjoying the show. George was thrown forward from the impact, cracking his neck. Ever willing to give the benefit of the doubt, George turned to look at the other boy, thinking the boy himself might have been pushed from behind and merely stumbled forward. But when he looked him in the face, there was just a smirk.

Most of the kids in those days gathered at Frankie's Drugstore after school and that's where George found his quarry.

"I choose you," he said, using the accepted challenge of the day. The other boy had to come forward.

The results of this fight were similar to those of the bashing he'd given Billy Striker, except in this case a teacher came running down the hill from the school yard. He was not in time to catch George, but he did call the police. The boy lying in the dirt seemed injured. He was.

The police arrived at George's home with the injured boy to make an identification. After it was made, George was expelled from school again, and severely beaten by his father. But that would not end it.

●

Sitting in their pigeon roost, George and David looked over their stock. The little shack was camouflaged, out in a dell on private property near the Des Moines River. It was their private place where they nursed one of their dreams: raising prize show pigeons. They had thought of several enterprises by which they could become rich and get out of the Bottoms. The pigeons seemed accessible, since there were millions of them in the city. There was no overhead, because neither boy was afraid to climb to the places they roosted and steal the chicks. There had been the problem of where to keep them, but that was solved on a scouting trip when they found the corner of the dell, indented just enough to conceal them from the house on the property. The boys tried to be quiet when they tended the birds, though. Discovery by the landowner meant instant eviction, if not buckshot to their bottoms.

David examined a plump female. "This 'un's pretty good," he said brightly. "No show bird, but you might could eat her."

George wrinkled his nose. The wild pigeons they took as chicks from under the bridges were obviously stringy. Nobody in their right mind thought about eating them, and inbreeding them had not turned a single one into a show bird.

Frankly, George was getting discouraged by the enterprise. He always got discouraged first.

"I don't know, David," he said dubiously. "Them birds don't look no different to me than the ones shittin' on the Dome."

"They don't shit *on* the Dome, George," David said, exasperated by his friend's lack of vision. "They shit *under* the Dome where the nests are. And the *point* is that this bird is lookin' good on account of what we're feedin' 'em. That's the only difference between them wild birds and the ones Old Man Smith has. His birds don't have to eat all that shit out there. And now ours don't either."

"That ain't the *only* difference, David. Old Man Smith's birds are from totally different stock. They ain't been touched by wild birds for centuries." George was not sure about this fact, but he plunged on with his point. "It's a whole different thing, David. Our birds would kill his birds if . . ."

George was starting to feel helpless. He knew from experience that winning arguments with David was the same as trying to beat him in a race across the Des Moines River. Impossible. David could swim and he couldn't. Unless David got pensive. Which at this moment, he was.

"All right," David said, apparently reaching a decision with himself. "We'll just go get a few of those other birds. That's all there is to it."

''That's all there is to it'' was one of David's phrases that made George nervous. It meant there would be no discussion and certainly no evaluation of consequences. Not that George feared consequences. He just found it annoying that they were never mentioned. Old Man Smith's pigeon hut was his pride and joy. It sat close to his house. There would be difficulties getting in and out without being detected, particularly because pigeons tended to make noise when their area was invaded. Old Man Smith was attuned to those noises. But then, planning was the part David liked best.

"I'll see you on the course tomorrow," David told him, rising. "Five-thirty?"

"Yeah," George said, relieved that they did not have to steal the birds right then. "Five-thirty."

Maybe David would forget about the birds. But George didn't think so.

9

David and George met at the Wakonda Country Club golf house at 5:30 A.M. for two reasons. One, they wanted to be the first of the caddies to arrive to assure they would work. Jobs were assigned based on arrival times. And two, they wanted an opportunity to practice the game. Though it was against regulations, head caddy Al Brock often brought his own clubs to the course. Between 5 and 8 A.M., the caddies chipped and putted, with money on the outcome of every stroke.

Because club members often relied on caddies for advice, and because a caddy's pay was based on how well the members liked his performance, the boys studied the game with a zeal they'd never brought with them to school. Bob Mills, who was two years older than David, could not read or write. He'd given up on school when his teachers assigned him to janitorial duties rather than have him in class. Although on his way to becoming a prolific (and well-known) burglar, Mills in no way considered himself a criminal. He entertained notions of respectability in which he would someday be the one pulling up in the black car for gin and tonics before a day of golf. His plan for getting there was to be near the action. To David and George, it seemed logical.

"Everybody who has money plays golf," Bob Mills informed the younger boys. "If you're going to have money, you have to play golf. And tennis. But we'll concentrate on golf first."

David, still the youngest member of his group, had lied about his age to get the job. He was only eleven. He should have been twelve. Later, he would lie about his age to get into the Boy Scouts, an experience he would treasure even though he would eventually be expelled for cutting the ropes on a rival troop's tents during a camp out. And he would lie to the Marines about his age. They would reject him, too, but this time because of his extensive juvenile record. But the caddy master had only cocked his head skeptically, then signed him on.

As he would be his whole life, David was both fascinated and disgusted by the country club set. He admired their fabulous new cars, but was angered to think that some flunky like himself kept them slicked and shined. The people, too, he envied, all laughing and happy in bright clothes. They had an easy confidence that comes from knowing you aren't going to get screwed over by anybody in this lifetime—at least not without being able to retaliate. David didn't guess his mother had ever felt that way.

Bob Mills loved to tell and retell his story about caddying for Bob Hope once. Even though David couldn't help but be annoyed by the way the story grew every time Bob told it, it awed him to think that he knew somebody who had actually spoken to Bob Hope. David didn't figure the regular Wakonda clientele lived like Bob Hope, but he imagined their lives were pretty good. They probably always had meat in the refrigerator. Ice cream, too. They had televisions, no doubt, and new clothes they might not have even worn once yet. It was hard to imagine more than that, but he was sure there was more.

David had long since stopped caring about the superior looks he received from his teachers. In fact, he rarely attended school at all anymore. His report cards showed failing grades in almost everything but his physical condition, which was graded at Nathan Weeks for some reason. His teeth had stopped hurting, but he believed he had an overbite. No one else seemed to notice it, but it was a source of embarrassment and discomfort to David and being around the country club set made him more self-conscious about it. He practiced smiling so that it would not be so apparent.

"Grandstaff!" the caddy master shouted. "Front and center. You're going out with Mr. McBride.

Ray McBride was a prominent columnist with the *Des Moines Register.* Like all well-known journalists, he was courted shamelessly, even by the rich and powerful who might ordinarily think of reporters as vulturous scum. But a nice word or a timely mention in McBride's column could work wonders, either for your social status or an impending business deal. McBride rarely had to pay for his own drinks at the Wakonda Country Club. David was not sure if he was a member, or just a constant, underwritten guest.

McBride's fame had gone to his head. At least David felt it had. The man was always talking too loud and too often. David also felt disdainful of the flask that rattled around McBride's golf bag and the sneaky way the man would nip at it when he thought his caddy wasn't looking.

Still, David was determined to please. The caddies worked on three levels: honor level, grade A, and grade B. Each represented a different pay scale, with "honor" being the highest. The level times the number of holes played determined the salary.

To a certain degree, levels were obtained by the number of hours worked. But in addition, the players had to grade you at the end of each day as either excellent, good, poor, or unacceptable. David had achieved the honor category and this was an eighteen-hole game. If all went well, he stood to earn $3.50 that day—a small fortune by his reckoning. He would be in hamburgers and ice cream bars for two weeks without having to steal a single one of them.

David saw instantly that McBride had downed more than one gin and tonic before the start of play. That, coupled with the fact that he hadn't even taken his normal precaution of hiding his flask at the bottom of the golf bag, gave David a bad feeling. He shouldered the heavy clubs, determined not to react to McBride's bragging and bravado. But he knew you could not shoot a good game of golf while drunk.

McBride swung and chopped at the balls and was well behind his partner by the fourth hole. The dreaded question came.

"What kind of iron?" he mused. "Caddy, what do *you* recommend?"

No one answer would help. But he could not refuse one. David tried to evaluate the situation. A nine iron was the obvious choice, but not in McBride's condition. Based on his performance so far, he would swing too hard to make up for obvious lack of coordination and no telling where the ball would end up with a swing like that. Recommending a seven iron—a smoothly hit pitch with a seven—would make David look like an idiot to the other player and his caddy, yet it was the only one McBride had a chance with under the circumstances. David needed the money too badly. What's more, he needed his rating. He could not afford to have McBride blow a shot because he recommended the correct iron. David recommended the seven.

McBride made sport of the suggestion, drew out the nine iron, and whacked his ball into the trees to the right of the green. David had a very hard time finding it. As the foursome finally trudged back to the clubhouse, nobody had a word to say about McBride's game. There were a few remarks made at David's expense, but he wasn't listening. He just wanted his card and his money. When McBride gave it to him, he didn't even think to look at it.

"Here you go," the caddy master said, turning over David's pay.

"This is only two dollars and fifty cents," David said, thinking the caddy master made a mistake. "I'm owed a dollar more."

Frowning, the caddy master retrieved the card. "Says here you only did nine holes."

"The hell I did!" David said, lapsing into the language he tried to avoid at the club. "That was a goddamn eighteen-hole game."

The caddy master shook his head. "Mr. McBride signed this, Grandstaff. He put down nine holes. What's more, he gave you a bad rating. This may not affect your standing, but it's hard to say. There's been some serious competition in marks here recently. . . ."

"What bad rating!" David screamed. "That son of a bitch was drunk!"

The caddy master looked at the boy, shocked. David's eyes were dark, glittering with a hatred that couldn't match any experience the boy could have had. The fists were clenched, looking dangerously poised and steady. The caddy master actually wondered if the small boy would strike, and if he did, if it might actually hurt.

"You'd best go on, now," he said nervously. "Mr. McBride signed this. Maybe he made a mistake, but I can't change this without a say-so. You'd best go on home."

David whirled and fled the office in a rage. He didn't remember crossing the rolling greens toward the clubhouse—didn't even know why he was going there. Lowly caddies were not allowed at the clubhouse. Remembering that insult as well, David veered off, heading toward Fleur Drive, which he would have to cross to get home. There was a Coca-Cola plant nearby where the caddies would sometimes stop for a soda after work. He thought George and Bob might be there. The plant lobby was empty, but there was a door ajar in the corner.

David had never noticed it before. It led to the basement.

It was cool—cool and dark. Very dark. His eyes adjusted to the light slowly. His angry breathing slowed, replaced by a feeling of helplessness. He sank in the corner, sliding down the wall until his rump almost hit the floor, his back and his drawn-up legs supporting his weight. It wasn't a mistake, he told himself stubbornly. The man had been drunk, but it hadn't been a mistake. The son of a bitch had deliberately cheated him. He wanted to believe it was a mistake, but he knew. And he knew it wouldn't be corrected. The great Mr. McBride would not be confronted.

His breathing under control, he began to control his emotions. He shouldn't have yelled at the caddy master. Shouldn't have. It wasn't manly. He would have to plan something else. He would talk to Bob Mills about it. He would know what to do.

Gradually, he noticed a soft light across the dank, underground cavern. No longer angry, his curiosity brought him to his feet and he crept toward the glow, thinking he might see something illicit, as he often did in the unprivate houses of the Bottoms. But when he got close, he saw it was just a Coke machine. Realizing he was thirsty, he began fishing for the nickel it would take to get a soda—then saw the machine was open.

Gleefully, he helped himself to a soda. This was justice. He scanned the area, looking for a container in which to lug the rest of the sodas in the machine. He would make up his money here. There was a battered, heavy table near the machine with tools all over it but no boxes. They must have been working on the machine. Because it was the only semilighted area around, he looked again for a box. There were screwdrivers, hammers, and pliers. He put one of the pliers in his pocket, thinking it might come in handy with repairs on the pigeon huts.

Then he saw the thick metal ring. It was as big as his hand, glinting in the soft light, and it had what looked like ornaments attached to it. When he picked it up though, he saw the ornaments were keys.

David examined the keys with interest. Key rings were unusual to him, since most people in the Bottoms left their houses unlocked. He wasn't even sure if there were keys to the Bottoms' houses. But this key ring belonged to a giant and these keys looked funny, even to him.

They didn't resemble the keys needed to start cars. They were squat and fat and the ends were rounded instead of flat. He brought them closer to the machine's light. While bending to get a better look, his eye fell on the lock that had so fortuitously been left open. It also was round.

With mounting excitement, he placed one key after another into the open lock. It really did not surprise him when one of the keys fit and he was able to lock the machine. With another turn, he unlocked it.

David put the keys back on the table, although he had trouble taking his hand off them. It was as if the keys were magnetized and his hand a metal they attracted. He stared at them as he tried to back away, knowing that they probably opened other Coke machines and possibly the cash boxes in them. There was no saying what the ornaments on that ring opened. There was no telling where they belonged.

He backed away only a few feet before lunging toward the table again, snatching the keys up and into his pocket with the deftness he'd learned from shoplifting. There was no storekeeper to catch him here, but he didn't think of that. The keys were in his pocket and now he sauntered outside with the nonchalance he'd learned to affect in ice cream capers. Nobody said a thing as he hitchhiked along Fleur Drive on his way home. Nobody stopped him.

He didn't even bother to walk a few blocks before sticking out his thumb. He contemplated the possibilities of the keys. Lost in his thoughts, David barely noticed the gray sedan coming toward him until it got close enough for him to notice how expensive a car it was. Sitting at the wheel was Ray McBride. Defiantly, David stuck his arm out straight with his thumb up. Ray McBride looked just long enough to recognize his caddy before he roared past.

David watched him go, the keys jingling in his pocket like Spanish doubloons. In the months to come, the Des Moines Police Department would be baffled by vending machine thefts all over the city. The machines were never bashed in. They had all been opened with keys.

10

David Grandstaff and George Weir were arrested on the Wakonda Country Club golf course in September of 1957. Bob Mills, fifteen, was already in custody. David was thirteen. George was fourteen. The charge was residential burglary. About twenty of them.

A horrified caddy master fired David and George on the spot as the police put handcuffs on them. George's were put on too tight and he would have numbness in his hands for weeks after the arrest. Ironically, the police would never be able to arrest The Boys for the vending machine thefts. They had become too accomplished, sometimes committing the thefts while an accomplice distracted the business's owner with small talk. The thefts became so rampant, some owners just gave up and took the machines out altogether. Others tried changing the locks periodically, but The Boys always found ways to get the new keys.

The vending machines provided the pocket money necessary to court girls. The Boys went to the Val Air Ballroom each week for the teen sock hops. They became great dancers. Parents found them polite and respectful around their daughters, even though there was plenty going on in the backseats of cars outside the Val Air.

They wore tight jeans, T-shirts, and leather jackets with shiny zippers. The T-shirts' short sleeves were rolled up to accommodate packs of cigarettes; the slicked ducktail hairdos were carefully tended. Hanging around the south side pool halls smoking was the thing. The contemptuous stares from passing motorists were cherished as a yardstick of their success.

School was more or less a distant memory. Bob Mills had simply stopped going, choosing to burgle houses with Danny Davis, another older boy who would marry David's cousin. Idolizing the older boys, David and George proved themselves by going along on a few capers. Bob and Danny thought it showed a lot of moxie. They thought the younger boys showed promise.

Hoping to encourage that, David and George instigated a few capers of their own. These were thefts of bicycles and Coke bottles, which were stolen from the porches and garages of the folks David delivered vegetables to. The bicycles were usually given away to younger siblings or neighbor children. The return on the bottles often went to purchase Va-Lo, a nasal inhaler that contained amphetamine. It was the drug of the times.

For the beat cops and detectives who roamed the Bottoms, however, it was not difficult to identify the stolen bikes. Des Moines was still a small place. You could hardly drive down a street without seeing a half dozen people you knew. The police didn't need an artist to paint them a picture. David, George, Danny, and Bob already had reputations, along with Jack Kimes, founder of the "Bullet Gang." Although the gang confined itself mostly to petty theft and small robbery, Kimes, at seventeen, was showing signs of serious violence. In a few years, he would commit murder. Right now, the cops were just trying to contain him.

The police slapped David silly at the station. In 1957, the treatment was expected, especially since David had already come to the authorities' attention. He'd already spent a month in Myron Juvenile Hall for suspicion of burglary. Even if the police couldn't prove it, they believed he was involved in the vending machine ring. David made no sound as he banged off walls, absorbing the slaps to the face and head and hearing the demands for confession. He heard the demands, but didn't listen.

In another room, Bob Mills received similar treatment, although the questions were different.

"Which ones did Grandstaff and Weir do with you?" the police shouted again.

"I did 'em all my own self," Bob answered stubbornly. "They weren't involved in a fucking thing."

A harder smack did nothing to change the answer. Bob had already been to the Eldora Training School for Boys on more serious charges than David and George now faced. Bob knew that he would go again. The burglary charges from Fleur Drive ensured it. They were nice houses. People were angry. Bob accepted it. He would be angry, too.

But David was still small for his age. The moment he'd been arrested, Bob had decided he would accept responsibility for everything. He knew the younger boys would not be able to escape the smaller thefts. But there was still a possibility of probation there. True, David had been to Myron Juvenile Hall. But there had been no charge. It had been a detention. It was possible that David and George could walk away from this. Bob didn't want David to go to Eldora, especially not at his age.

Besides, Bob didn't want Sharon in tears. He was dating David's sister, was in fact fairly smitten and had dreamed about the possibilities of marriage and a picket fence. Recently she'd been picked up for truancy. Benny Grandstaff let her sit in juvenile hall for fourteen days before claiming her. Nobody, not even David, was told where she was. David had been inconsolable, as Bob knew Sharon would be, imagining her brother in far worse confinement. For Sharon, the experience had been a terror that would last the rest of her life. She would not get into trouble again.

At his guilty plea, Bob took the stand before Judge Harold Myers to again accept full responsibility for the burglaries. He refused to allow the majestic courthouse in downtown Des Moines to intimidate him. The handsome, dark-haired boy strode over the marble floors, making himself believe that this arm of the Gold Dome could not hurt him. He kept his shoulders back, his eyes fixed forward, and his face unlined. When he saw someone he knew, he gave what he hoped was a dignified nod.

To the infuriated prosecutor, the attitude looked more like arrogance. But Detective James Kellog was familiar with the expression. It didn't anger him. Kellog understood the psychology of it all. A big, blond man, Kellog lived near the Bottoms, close enough to view the social floundering firsthand. He had a certain amount of sympathy for it. In fact, his daughter would attend Lincoln High School with Mike See. Most of these people had their tickets punched at birth. Kellog was not a believer in the notion that anybody could make it if they tried. He'd seen too much evidence to the contrary.

Still, he was a cop. He was a taxpayer. He made it his business to watch The Boys closely and he'd lost count of how many times he'd arrested them for minor offenses. But he tried not to brutalize them, and had found that his good treatment of them was repaid. They did not curse or spit at him. George Weir even told him jokes. In a way, Kellog liked their spunk. It was much better than the sullen meanness he got off other petty criminals in the Bottoms. Those folks were going to surrender to liquor or worse eventually. Kellog was not at all sure that would happen to The Boys.

The prosecutor did not share Kellog's philosophical view of the situation. He'd noticed a disturbing trend rising from the swamps of the Bottoms. There seemed to be a whole cadre of young people who were bonding in crime. They didn't take jobs at the factory as their fathers had. They dropped out of school—that wasn't unusual. What was unusual was their communion with one another. Bottoms people often fought among themselves at the drop of a dime. These boys protected one another, worked together, and gave one another's families money when needed. The money, of course, was mostly illegitimate.

It was very alarming, this budding criminal society that didn't seem to hold to the traditional ethnic biases embraced in the Bottoms. They were creating their own society right under everybody's nose. It was as if they weren't part of the rest of the country.

Gary Breeze would plead guilty here today for his part in the burglaries, but it was small consolation for the prosecutor, who felt some responsibility to get all these boys off the street. Those vending machine hits had happened all over town, not just in their neighborhoods where it wouldn't have mattered so much. Bottoms businesses did not go to the authorities, but the rest of the city's small merchants—and even some of the larger ones—were screaming. It infuriated the prosecutor that The Boys could not be caught. Now, some young kids like Doug Brown were starting to act up, even though they'd not yet been accepted into the clan. In fact, the prosecutor didn't even think of the boys in front of him as children anymore. They definitely didn't act like children.

The effect this unholy alliance was having on the community was evident to the prosecutor when he walked into Myers's courtroom.

Normally, Bottoms people never came to court, unless it was in hand-cuffs. Sometimes a wife or a parent would show, but this courtroom was packed. Sisters, cousins, friends, aunts, uncles. It was infuriating that they'd all come to watch Bob Mills lie in open court, under oath, to protect those Grandstaff and Weir kids. The prosecutor reflected that his assessment of The Boys' characters was correct. They had no respect for the system. None of these others did either.

The prosecutor wanted Grandstaff and Weir to go to Eldora, but he knew Judge Myers would have no choice but to dismiss almost all the charges against them if Mills clung to his story. Looking at the boy's determined face, the prosecutor knew it would be an uphill fight. The gallery was almost a guarantee that he would not back down.

Bob watched the prosecutor circle him with aplomb. Trying to be a big man, Bob thought disdainfully, Well, take your best shot.

"Now, you don't really expect us to believe that you committed all these robberies by yourself!" the prosecutor thundered, whirling on Mills. He hoped his volume and sudden movement would startle the kid in the chair.

"All by my lonesome," Bob replied mildly.

The titters in the courtroom nearly drove the prosecutor to dis-traction. It was so *flagrant*. Judge Myers banged his gavel.

"Now, on the fifteenth you and Grandstaff were together, were you not? You did not go to work that day and you were seen together out-side a home on Fleur Drive that was burglarized that same afternoon! How do you explain that!"

"I don't know what kinda explanation you want. I did the house. David didn't. Anybody who looks at him can see he's not big enough to reach the windows we went in. He's a shrimp."

More muffled laughter. The prosecutor looked at Myers, who banged his gavel again.

"He's given his confession to the police, has he not, Counselor?" the judge asked.

"Yes, Your Honor, but . . ."

"Well," the judge lowered his voice, "I understand your sentiments, Counselor. But I don't see any changes occurring here. He's willing to plead guilty to the acts. Let's get him sentenced."

Wearily, the prosecutor sat down.

●

David and George did not escape the bike and Coke bottle thefts. They pleaded guilty and Ava Grandstaff got up to speak, the first time she'd ever spoken in a public place. Now, there were no titters in the gallery.

"Please, Judge," she said, breaking down into sobs. The gallery was now quiet. "Please. He's a good boy." The words were choked in tears and gasps for breath.

"Mrs. Grandstaff," Myers said uncomfortably, "your son has a very disturbing record. He's heading down a very dangerous road and I'm not really inclined to let him travel it much farther."

"It's not his fault, Judge. It's not! We couldn't give him nothin'. He's just takin' little kids' stuff because he ain't got nothin'. He'll change. I'll help him change."

Myers shifted in his seat. The woman in front of him looked as if her skin would shrivel up in the courtroom before his eyes. He could see she was a youngish woman from her bearing and coloring. But she was aging quickly. Her face was too anguished for him to guess an age. It could be anywhere between thirty and forty. The clumsily applied makeup had been cried over many more times today than just this moment and her hair looked frayed—as if she'd combed it a thousand times without achieving the desired effect. It strayed independently off her head, reflecting the courtroom's light, as if she were no longer concerned about it.

"Please, Judge," she said again, dropping her head. And Myers knew it was all she could do to keep herself upright. The courtroom hushed completely. There was a sea of faces.

The boy, David Grandstaff, did not make Judge Myers's decision easier. The boy seemed to sag. He seemed to drop his eyes halfway, but only to raise them again. He *seemed* ashamed, but Myers could not be sure if it was his own perception or a reality. If the boy had wept, if he had turned toward his mother, Judge Myers may have been able to do with a clean heart what he had already decided. As it was, he had misgivings. He did it for the mother. And maybe a little bit for the gallery.

Reluctantly, Myers sentenced both David and George to probation. David was not unhappy to get probation. But he was humiliated that he'd received it because his mother had begged for him, and had exposed a financial inadequacy he'd been trying to cover up for so many years. He wondered if it would hit the papers, the papers he couldn't read very well. Maybe Eldora Training School for Boys wasn't so bad. He envisioned a place where he'd have his own room and be around kids just like himself. He could escape his father's oppressiveness there. There might be classes about dentistry and such. And he did want to learn to play the clarinet. He'd heard that training schools let you do things like that. Six months later, after an abusive and volatile relationship with his probation officer, he found out about Eldora firsthand.

This time, there was no courtroom scene. Judge Myers sat dourly behind the bench, surveying the youngster he'd let go six months before, only to see him back on a car theft charge. He was more than happy to do what the law required, revoke the probation and sentence the boy to Eldora.

George had not wanted to steal a car, but David had been in one of his intractable moods. Both boys had been keeping pretty much out of trouble after their first visit to Myers's courtroom. But they couldn't get their caddy jobs back and were too young to work for any other businesses. David had lost his vegetable delivery route. Neither of them had money to go to the sock hops at the ballroom where their girlfriends were now amusing themselves with other boys.

David first suggested a gas station vending machine. He'd been in the station earlier in the week observing, and saw that the night attendant placed the evening cash receipts inside the vending machine, to be opened the following day. The caper sounded like a cakewalk to George. Vending machines were easy and the promise of an additional hundred or so dollars in cash was enticing.

David and George skipped school that day to plan. It was one of the few times when the school actually notified someone they weren't there. By evening, their parents had reported them missing to the police.

By that time, David had decided they needed to steal a car. The gas station was on the other side of town and they could hardly expect to run, hitchhike, or ride bicycles back. George knew this was not true. That's exactly how they'd always gotten back. But he heard David saying "And that's the end of that," and knew an argument was pointless. It was just like the pigeons. David had found a way to sneak into Old Man Smith's roost. He'd stolen a half dozen great birds with good markings and nice bearings to breed with their own scrawny crew.

The pigeons escaped the secret dell roost eventually, though, and flew back to their original owner. David had then tired of the enterprise. He and his cousin, Ken, started shooting the pigeons with BB guns instead, taking them down to the black section of Des Moines where they sold them for ten cents apiece.

George himself did not participate. He couldn't bear to kill things. In fact, it had taken him a while to get over the fact that David could. George didn't like that side of David. The hunting part. George was glad that the pigeon-hunting business ended after Ken got caught trying to steal some new rifles.

As far as George knew, David didn't shoot anything but BB guns. Now he was talking about stealing a car. David couldn't even *drive*. And stealing cars was a bit more serious than George cared for.

But David's face was immovable. Once again, he patiently explained the need for a car, how they wouldn't damage it and could even return it when they were finished. As usual, George began to feel stupid that he couldn't have followed this logic to begin with. By the time they began hunting for one with keys in it, George wasn't even worried.

The car they got was a late-model Ford, the kind David usually eyed on the street. It was dark blue—a "class" color, David informed him. He was euphoric driving it through the city streets, if you could call it driving. David had to bunch up both of their jackets to sit on so that he could see over the steering wheel. George was not sure how he was reaching the pedals.

The gas station temporarily forgotten, David suggested that they take their new treasure by Ricky Wycoff's house. Ricky had just returned from California, where he'd be sent after his mother had decided his father should have a hand in his upbringing. The arrangement had apparently not worked out.

David sat in the car while George walked up and down the street, trying to remember which house Ricky's mother had moved to. Suddenly recognizing it, he mounted the steps only to hear screeching tires and bullhorns.

"Stay where your are! You are surrounded!"

George whirled and saw that the police had not yet spotted him. David, he could see, was dead meat. They were dragging him out of the car by the hair.

George ran until he thought his heart would burst. Down the slimy railroad tracks and into a brickyard that covered his shoes and pants with clay. From a truck stop where he stopped for refuge, he saw the police cars driving by, with David in the front seat of one. He was shaking his head stubbornly. George knew he would never say who was with him.

What he didn't know was that the police had missing persons reports for *both* boys, whose association was well known. George slept in the garage that night, something he often did. He was arrested at school the next day.

"Where were you last night, George?" one cop asked.

"At the school rec yard," George said. "You gonna take me to jail for skippin' school? Is that a crime now, too?"

"Rec yard," the cop repeated thoughtfully. "That how you got all that clay on your shoes?"

"I musta walked through some somewhere," George said immediately.

"Wouldn't have been by the railroad tracks last night, would it?

Wouldn't have been at that brickyard near where we got your buddy?"

George felt the black anger rising. "Why don't you fools just do what you're gonna do. You don't have to set here chattin' with me. If you've got somethin' to do, do it."

He expected the yank to his feet. Expected the gratuitous slaps, jabs, and pushes. And expected to be thrown, not led, into a small holding cell. It didn't matter.

●

Judge Myers, apparently accepting George's lawyer's arguments that Grandstaff was a clear instigator, turned him over to his lawyer's custody. David was given a hard year at Eldora. George would not see him again for several years, due to some other unfortunate circumstances involving school.

After David was led away, George tried to go back to school. He was not a welcome sight. The boy who heisted Coke bottles, took stolen cars on joyrides, and terrified his enemies was not wanted anymore, if he ever was. He got into several messes, beginning with an altercation with a black teacher in the boys' bathroom.

The boys were lined up before the mirrors, carefully combing their ducktails in place, when a few of them began horsing around, slapping at one another's faces and shadowboxing. Things got a bit out of hand, someone lost his temper, and several bodies went crashing into a large metal trash container in the corner. It made a terrible noise and spewed paper towels, empty cigarette packs, and candy wrappers across the scrubbed floor.

The teacher, Joe Bowman, roared through the bathroom door when he heard the crash and went immediately to George, who protested he'd had nothing to do with the ruckus. George already had a reputation for fighting, though. Bowman smacked George hard enough on the back of his head to drive him forward, almost causing him to fall.

"You little son of a bitch," Bowman snarled. "Clean this mess up right now." And he walked out.

George also walked out, to the telephones. His eyes stung with pain and rage as he dialed his older brother Larry's work number to report the outrage.

Larry arrived at the school within fifteen minutes, charging up and down the halls, screaming that he wanted "to choose" the "nigger" who had accosted his younger brother. The situation was intercepted by Principal Tomilson, who managed to get everybody into his office before a full-scale riot erupted, not only at Nathan Weeks but possibly in the entire neighborhood. Racial tensions were running high since Arkansas governor Orval Faubus sent in the National Guard to prevent nine black students from entering Central High School in Little Rock. A full-scale riot developed and President Eisenhower had to personally chastise the governor, eventually sending in federal troops to enforce federal integration laws. Arkansas was only one state removed from Iowa and lots of people went there for vacations. The incident had everybody on edge, especially Tomilson, who had nightmares about similar explosions occurring at his school. No. He couldn't have it.

After pacifying Larry, Tomilson sent him back to work, turning his attention on the smoldering boy before him. George Weir puzzled Tomilson. He was a poor student, but that could be chalked up to upbringing and attention span. What Tomilson could not understand was the boy's violent mood swings. He was normally a sweet, if scholastically lazy, youngster, but Tomilson had already seen the damage he could inflict when angered. The anger didn't seem to be rooted in anything Tomilson could put his finger on.

"I'm sorry about what just happened, George," Tomilson said softly.

George continued looking at him defiantly. "It was wrong," George said sullenly. "I didn't do nothin'. It was wrong."

"Well . . ." Tomilson did not want to be in the position of indicting his teacher. He resisted the urge to correct the boy's grammar. "Now, naturally we would have liked to talk to all the boys involved. . . ."

"It was wrong!" George shouted stubbornly. "And I ain't tellin' you about no other people in there! I ain't no snitch!"

Tomilson sighed inwardly. Regrettably, this would have to be handled differently. "George, what happened in the bathroom was unfortunate. What happened afterward was equally unfortunate. Do you understand that your brother could be arrested for what happened afterward?"

The boy did not answer, but Tomilson saw that George instantly understood the threat. George's face had gone as passive as marble, if marble could look disdainful, the way George was looking at Tomilson. The anger seemed to have left, replaced by an expression that said: "I knew it. I knew you would resort to this all along." Tomilson promised there would be no repercussions for anyone if George would just forget the whole thing.

George weighed the words. The sons of bitches always came down to this, he thought. If it wasn't beatings, it was threats. If it wasn't threats, it was jail. And he hadn't even done anything wrong. Still, the offer—although not just—would at least keep his brother out of trouble. He agreed.

But of course it didn't end there. George remembers that in homeroom the next day, teacher Richard Scanlan gave a speech about what a hooligan George was. He also called him a coward as the rest of the class stared.

George left the classroom after the others, overturning a chair in the process. When Scanlan ordered him to pick it up, he did. George recalls hitting the teacher over the back with it.

●

When he returned to school, he was assigned another homeroom teacher. Tomilson had not been pleased with Scanlan's performance either. Although George continued to attend school, he failed every subject, including physical education, at which he was unquestionably superior.

George lost what little enthusiasm he'd had for school after that report card. Since nobody cared whether he stayed or left, he left and took odd jobs. For a while, it looked as if he might follow in his father's footsteps, but then he decided to go to the Golden State of California. He went there but couldn't get used to the life-style. So he tried Colorado. That was a little better, but he still got homesick and eventually returned to Des Moines and David Grandstaff.

●

David made two trips to Eldora before he had a guard bashed in the head with a lead pipe and got sent to a real prison. The real prison was a relief.

12

ELDORA

There were no single rooms in the Eldora Training School for Boys. There were barracks. They called them dormitories, but they were barracks, complete with steel bunk beds and guards who often called the boys by number instead of by name. Any illusions of David's craved privacy were put to rest by the living arrangements. Sixty boys to a barrack. No talking allowed after 8 P.M., when the boys were in bed. A boy who needed to use the facilities had to sit upright on his bunk and snap his fingers until a guard granted him permission to leave the room. If you snapped too much, you got a smack to the head instead.

There were plenty of Bottoms boys in Eldora. David's cousin, Larry Agee, was there. Charlie Watts, who would later contract multiple sclerosis and be caught robbing a bank with Mike See for money for a penile implant so that he could make love to his girlfriend in his final years. Rod Welcher, who would die after a car accident in which George Weir ran the vehicle off the road—an event George would never forgive himself for. Others who would die in prison or in shootouts with the police. And some who would get out and never return. And then there were the few who would prompt some of the more major manhunts in FBI history.

But then, they were all under the age of sixteen, with all of the immortal beliefs most teenagers share, except that they were accustomed to consequences more severe than losing an allowance or a weekend night out of the house. David earned the nickname Cue Ball because he was perpetually bald. Head shaving was a common punishment for minor infractions, such as talking back to guards or violating queue rules in the mess hall. More severe infractions were punished "across the road," the boys' euphemism for solitary confinement. David spent a good deal of time there. Each boy received a Bible, a blanket, and two meals a day, one of them consisting of two slices of bread and a cup of milk. On Sundays, the guards brought pencils and paper for letters home. David used the pencil to scrawl obscenities on the wall. He knew when he did it the retaliation would be painful. His stock with the older boys shot skyward. David was still small for his age and the beatings seemed worth the extra respect he could not accomplish with size.

The only decent thing about the "training school" was the fact that it ran a farm. Cows, pigs, chickens, and produce. The boys worked the farm after what passed for school classes as part of their rehabilitation. The farm was run for profit, but the boys were allowed to eat as much as they desired before the goods were sold. David had never had unlimited access to fresh produce, milk, eggs, meat, or bread. In grade school, he'd tried to compensate for a poor diet by exercising and developing what he thought of as "mental exercises" that would enhance growth. He would imagine himself "growing"—stretching his arms up as if they could pull his torso along with them. Now he had a diet—which would become a lifelong interest—to go with it. He tried to read about good foods with whatever sparse materials were available and ate accordingly. He entered Eldora weighing 90 pounds and left weighing 145.

●

David was released from Eldora the first time after one year. After three months, he was caught robbing vending machines. He was sent back, but this time he had no interest in staying. His "plan" for leaving ended his juvenile career.

Enlisting the help of two other boys, David told them he would say he needed to use the restroom in the middle of the night. Once in the lavatory, he would scream for the guard. When the guard came, John Branch—a huge seventeen-year-old—would hit the guard over the head with a pipe. The guard would go down and they'd walk out.

The plan was based on television shows in which anyone hit in the head was lights out immediately. The only problem was it didn't work that way in real life. The guard did not go down. He screamed, yelled, and bled—a lot. Blood flew everywhere, splattering walls and everybody's clothes. The guard also tried to fight in a dazed way. Panicked, Branch continued bashing him until David was almost certain the guard would be killed.

Hearing the running feet in the halls, David dragged Branch off the now unconscious guard and pushed him toward the bathroom door. David stripped off his bloody clothes and tossed them. Running back into the dormitory, he grabbed clean clothes off another boy's bunk and slammed into his bunk just as the dormitory's doors burst open. The administration first arrested the innocent boy with the bloody clothes on his bed. Eventually, they took David away. He made no denials.

●

Because he had not struck the actual blows, David did one year in the Polk County Jail. When he was released at age fifteen, he worked sporadically, moving between Chicago—where Mabel Agee now lived—and Des Moines, where he was no longer on speaking terms with his father. It didn't matter that much because his parents had divorced.

The Chicago days were good times. Ken and David outdanced, outpoker-played, and outromanced the locals. It gave them both a certain kind of pride. The Chicago boys had first ridiculed them as hicks from the backwater. David liked stealing their girlfriends.

What he did not like was the inescapable conclusion that he would never rise above the level of an unskilled laborer, subject to the whims and orders of men he respected no more than the guards who had so gleefully shaved his head. He became angrier by the day.

He did six months on a stolen car charge. He and Ken took the car in Des Moines and drove to Chicago. The file landed on the FBI's desk because the vehicle had been taken across state lines. This was pretty small time for the FBI, though, and they let local authorities handle the case and filed their own reports. It was the beginning of a long relationship.

David and Ken turned back to their old standby—hitting vending machines. Again, they were never caught for the thefts, but David was nailed after he and four other youths slapped the son of a prominent Des Moines businessman silly and took his wallet. One of the boys had a knife. The charge was armed robbery. The judge sentenced David to ten years at Fort Madison State Prison, the worst penitentiary in the state. He was seventeen.

At the sentencing, Sharon was horrified. She clapped her hand over her mouth to keep from hyperventilating. Ava burst into tears. David was no model citizen, but no seventeen-year-old should have to go to Fort Madison. Sharon believed it was just plain spite. She'd seen all the cops show up for David's sentencing, along with the father of the kid who had been robbed. He and the judge seemed to know each other, Sharon thought. And there were plenty of cops in the gallery who didn't need to be there. They had only come to see David hang.

David didn't hang in Fort Madison, though.

He knew that when he entered the prison for the first time, older inmates would start to salivate. He was young and still small. He'd never had much hair on his body. He was prepared for the worst and fashioned a shank his first day there.

Charlie Watts, Don Cady, and several other, older Bottoms boys had graduated to Fort Madison, too. Watts had beat the hell out of the first "old wolf" who approached him and had earned a reputation as a crazy motherfucker who would get you any way he could. Now he told the wolves the same held true about David Grandstaff. And if David didn't get them, he would.

For his part, David would have welcomed an attack. It was the one sure way to put an end to the whispers and the worries about the shower. But none ever came. And after a month, sombody in the administration realized that this kid shouldn't have been sent here to begin with. It was a terrible precedent—not so much for the inhumanity of it, but because youngsters like this could cause huge fights among the older inmates. He was whisked to Anamosa overnight.

●

In his first stint in Anamosa, David learned about crazy people. He was assigned to work in the mental ward with Bob Mills, who had also graduated to Anamosa on burglary charges.

It was a marvel to David that these people were in a prison at all. Some of them banged their heads against walls and slept in their own excrement. Some of them didn't stop at sleeping in it, but smeared it all over everything. David had to clean it up.

There was one guy who'd been there for something like thirty years. It was said that he'd killed his wife, ground her up, and fed her to his children and in-laws. It was supposedly the worst crime in Iowa history.

The man's name was Bill. He carried dozens of mice around in his pockets. He'd caught and tamed them and they ran all over his body like a rainstorm. He carried other things in his pockets. Scraps of paper, clips, pens, and anything else he could find that wasn't nailed down. He looked like a fat, walking scarecrow, his clothing was so stuffed. Every so often the guards would come and make him empty his pockets and he'd scream and scream at the top of his lungs.

Bill also hated to lose at cards. Every time he did, he'd go into the bathroom, stick a pipe or hose up his ass, and scream, "I'll make a punk out of you yet, Billy boy!" Some of the other inmates would remove cards from the deck and then invite Bill to a game, just to laugh about his antics when he lost. He was inconsolable after Bob Mills hung all his mice. The sane inmates were tired of the filth they generated.

Some of the inmates were violent, but David didn't worry about it too much. He kept close to objects that could be wielded as blunt instruments, the plan being to bash the first one who attacked him in the head. It never happened, though, and working in the nut ward had other benefits. There was a little more freedom, and with some ingenuity, you could sometimes get to the medicine cabinets. Some of those pills provided a nice checkout from the screaming and banging around in the place. And they were better than shooting up Va-Lo, the nasal inhaler still popular with the out crowd of the 1950s.

●

Paroled after two years, David was soon arrested for stealing paychecks from the Colonial Bakery. He was acquitted of the charge, but
knew his parole would be violated anyway. Ken, meanwhile, had been
caught with a bunch of vending machine tools and socks of money.
Just as Bob Mills had done for him years earlier, David decided to
take the rap for his cousin. He was going back anyway.

It was tricky. David had no information about Ken's caper or his arrest. He didn't know where the tools had been found, for instance, or
even what color the car was. The socks containing the change were
all different colors, too.

But through a series of jail house communiqués involving notes,
clandestine newspaper clippings, and visits from total strangers, he
found out. And when the prosecutor tried to shake him, he was ready.
He said the car and everything in it was his. No amount of grilling
about the color of those socks shook him. He had it down and the
prosecutor had to give up in a rage again.

●

During his second stint in Anamosa, David learned about crazy people who weren't necessarily in the crazy ward. This time, he was assigned to work in the dairy. He was in charge of the calves.

There seemed to be something wrong with them. David had not
been around a lot of calves in his life, but it was hard to escape them
altogether in Iowa. These just didn't seem right. Skittish or something.
And then one day he was coming around a corner with a bag of feed
and saw a bunch of guys fucking them. They were inmates who
worked in other areas of the farm but had sneaked off to get to the
calves. Three or four guys, standing with their pants down around
their ankles, whooping and jeering, grunting with effort as the calves
bellowed in terror. The animals were tied in their stalls, preventing
even a token resistance. It enraged David. What's more, they were *his*
calves.

He picked up a stick. Holding it like a baseball bat, he walked over

and said, "If I ever catch you around my calves again, I'll kill you."
He meant it, and he could see from the looks on the other inmates'
faces that they understood that. They backed away, first zipping their
pants and then holding their hands up in surrender.

The calf incident was only one reason that David was considered a
leader in Anamosa. Bob Mills was glad he had a history with David.
He saw how David took command of situations. He could get the other men to do things without raising his voice or making a threat.
There was just something in his eye and bearing that the other men
respected. Far from resenting David's organizational demands, they
went out of their way to please him.

Not that David was opposed to violence. He'd use it if he had to. He
was a pretty fair boxer and a star player on the Anamosa football
team. That team was beating semipro teams who came to the prison
to practice. It was David who had convinced the administration to
give the prison team more protein, like peanuts, so they could be more
competitive. David had always been a nut about diet, Bob reflected.
It was bewildering the way he'd go on and on about proteins and fats
and vitamins—like he'd read books on it or something. But Bob had
to admit David's obsession with the subject had gotten the football
team, at least, better food. The prison administration liked winning
the football games.

Just having everybody know David and he were old friends gave
Bob standing he might not have had without it. Bob enjoyed it, even
if David had horned in on Bob's profitable cigarette business when
he'd come back after the Colonial Bakery thing. But there was one request Bob had really balked at. David came by his cell one afternoon
and sitting real casual on the bunk had told Bob he wanted to get all
the guys in the cell block to enroll in school.

"What for?" Bob asked, amazed.

"Well," David said nonchalantly, "they won't bring the classes in
here unless enough guys sign up."

"Shit, David. That's sissy crap. Nobody wants to waste their time
sittin' around listening to some college punk tell us stuff." In truth,
Bob was getting concerned. He could see the intractable expression
on David's face. He expected to hear him say any minute, "It's as simple as that." And Bob had more problems than his image to consider.

He couldn't read. How was he supposed to enroll in a class when he couldn't read? He couldn't say that. Nobody knew. "Jesus, David," he pleaded. "Why? Why do you even want classes in here. Let's just do our time and get out."

"I want to learn to play the clarinet," David said without embarrassment. "I seen in this catalog that it's a class they have and I want to learn to play. I can't do it unless they bring other classes in."

Bob was stunned. The clarinet, for Christ's sake. Who would have thought it. But he knew a desire that weird was something David must have been nursing for quite a while. He knew there was no way out of school.

"Let's go get the other guys," David said, standing. The conversation was closed.

Twenty years later, Bob would sit at a kitchen table in Tucson, Arizona, and say that was the best thing David ever did for him. He'd gone straight after he'd learned to read. He never would have been able to do it if that teacher in Anamosa hadn't discovered his handicap and taught him.

●

David did not let on how much he despised prison. To everyone there, he was a part of the fabric. But he hated the strutting guards. He hated the mindless rules. Most of all, he hated the mire the other inmates wallowed in. They had no vision. He got out in 1966, swearing he would never come back. Not that he would go straight. That he would never be back. When he was paroled, he went to live with Sharon and her husband at the time, John Oliver.

●

Sharon heard David screaming for her upstairs. What now? she thought wearily. David had not been the same since he was released from Anamosa. He was moody, quiet, and—if possible—more intense. He didn't laugh very often. He insisted on sitting with his back to the wall and jumped if someone came up behind him unexpectedly. He seemed to relax only with her husband and although she treasured their good relationship, she was not fond of the many demands he put on her. The jeans pressed just so. The food he had to have. It was as if he had forgotten how to do anything for himself. But when she heard him calling, she hurried away from her ironing to tend to him.

Over the years, David had acquired several tattoos since the days when he and Sharon used india ink to join the out crowd. He'd gotten one—a pair of women's legs—on his right calf in Eldora. The rest had come from Fort Madison and his first stint in Anamosa, inked mostly on his arms and shoulders. But he'd come to despise the tattoos as symbols of failure in life. The magazines he'd been studying for hints on fashion and food showed no people with tattoos. So during his parole, before the Colonial Bakery robbery, he'd had all but the legs scraped off. The women's legs could not be removed because it would damage his calf muscles.

The scars became infected during his second stay in Anamosa and had never healed properly, even though the prison sent him to a hospital every week for treatment. Now free again, David still wrestled with the festering wounds that, finally, looked like they might heal someday. It was hard for him to move, though. Hard for him to dress. Sharon had been helping him. She'd watched in quiet admiration as David sat chatting with friends and family in the living room, shifting his weight but refusing to complain about the pain when his clothes stuck to the puss seeping through his bandages.

"What's David yelling about?" John asked casually. Her husband stood behind her, eating ice cream out of the carton. She suppressed the urge to remind him that the ice cream was for the children. She'd just have to get some more.

Sharon went to find her brother upstairs. She checked the bedrooms but finally found him when she heard him bellow again—from the bathroom. Knocking on the door, she hoped this wasn't going to be some really weird demand.

"Well, come *in*," David said, exasperated. "I didn't call you to stand jiggers at the door." *Stand jiggers.* The prison slang was getting to her.

Sharon opened the door to find David standing calf deep in bathwater, the terrible wounds on his arms still smoldering. He stood with his arms out from his sides so no skin would touch. His legs were similarly positioned. He was wearing his boxer shorts.

"I was wondering if you could wash me off," he said, lowering his eyes. "It hurts for me to move. But I hate bein' dirty."

Sharon was having a hard time suppressing her laughter. David taking a bath in boxer shorts. "Get them shorts off, boy," she ordered with a straight face. "You can't have a bath when you're all dressed up for dinner."

David looked at her incredulously. "Have you lost your mind?" he demanded. "Have you gotten perverted in your old age? I ain't takin' these shorts off."

"You don't have nothin' I haven't seen before. Even on you." Sharon was starting to enjoy herself.

"Work around them!" David shouted. "And I'll thank you not to involve me in your sick little daydreams."

Suppressing a giggle, Sharon started washing, making sure to only dab at the wounds. There were two massive ones on each shoulder and several smaller ones on David's wrists.

David's surgery, however, had not stopped what Sharon viewed as an unhealthy pursuit of women. It was like he was making up for lost time. He never went out with any of them more than a few times, usually dumping them as soon as they showed signs of affection. A few had displayed more than affection, and these David avoided like the plague. Sharon was worried that her brother's prison experiences had made him unable—or unwilling—to fall in love, which in Sharon's mind would have been the best thing for him. It would get him some emotional stability. David just brushed her away when she mentioned it.

At least David was benefiting from his relationship with John. They often went out to the countryside to hunt and fish and Sharon approved. The quiet was good for David and maybe he felt more comfortable talking things over with a man.

Besides, David loved to cook up the squirrels, rabbits, and other game he shot. It was really pretty endearing. He'd get out a Crockpot and carefully cut up his ingredients. He was pretty picky about it. Onions, carrots, potatoes, and the other fresh vegetables he craved. Then he'd add the meat and let it cook all day. It really was quite delicious. On the days he cooked, the bachelors David worked with would all seem to happen by the house at the same time. Supper time.

It didn't bother Sharon because it didn't bother David. He seemed pleased that his concoction was so well received. She thought she saw a little hope for a domestic side in him. Years later, a disappointed girlfriend would receive a Crockpot for Christmas without understanding the significance of the gift for David.

●

One day, David came home and put his hunting rifle away. He never got it out again. He never went hunting with John again. Later, Sharon found out he'd shot a rabbit but hadn't killed it. It was winter. Snow was on the ground, making the blood trail easy to follow. David went stalking the wounded animal and found it trying to slither across a frozen pond. It was too weak to walk. It was squealing an eerie, high-pitched banshee shriek that cut through his mind like sharp ice. He didn't know rabbits could make such a noise.

Its entrails had come out and were caught on a branch. The more the rabbit moved, the more came out. David thought the rabbit turned and looked at him with hatred. For a moment, David thought the animal's eyes were actually human, like some reincarnated thing living out the worst nightmare of another life and he was it. Then the expression faded, replaced once again by wild, animal fear. The rabbit crawled harder and harder, pulling its own guts out in the process. David dispatched the animal and buried it instead of taking it home to eat.

"I'm never going hunting again," he said. "Anything that wants to live that bad ain't gonna be killed by me."

When George heard the news, he was happy. That hunting business had been the one thing about David's character he hadn't liked. Now maybe the men could spend more time together.

13

GEORGE

When George Weir got back to Des Moines from his travels, he hadn't wanted to do anything but get a job and put some money together. He'd been unable to stay away from women in Denver, they delighted him so. But they'd also kept him broke. All that hard work at Martin Marrietta and he had nothing to show for it.

The work he'd done in Denver had been unskilled labor and that's what he was looking at now. He got a job welding. It was nasty work and he came home filthy, but there were still unions in Des Moines. You could say that much about the place. Nobody could even think of a time when there hadn't been unions and a man couldn't earn some kind of money.

He got a small apartment, hunkered down, and stayed out of sight. He didn't even see David that often. David seemed like he needed some time to himself. George was learning to enjoy his own solitude.

Watching television one afternoon, a buddy of his called, dangling the prospect of a pretty girl before him. George had been trying to stay away from his weakness—women—and besides, he smelled a catch.

He was right. His friend wanted him to help move his girlfriend. Out of friendship, George agreed. But his friend's girlfriend did have a sister.

George married Patti after six months. Within two years Patti, who already had a child from a previous marriage, had given birth to a son and twin boys. The family lived in a run-down house that was way too small for them. George's beat-up car was unreliable to take him to job sites—when there were job sites. Construction was slow that summer. With two infants and a toddler in the house, Patti could not work at all.

On a hot, dusky night in July, George came home from one job site hungry. He hadn't eaten during the day. The Iowa summer day had been humid and the work dirty. The damp air combined with his sweat had caked every piece of dirt to his skin. He felt miserable.

Opening the refrigerator door, he saw only a carton of milk. That was it. He couldn't believe it.

"Patti!" he yelled. "What the hell am I supposed to eat here?"

"Same as me, honey," Patti said mildly. "Nothing."

Incredulous, George walked into the living room where Patti sat, her legs tucked underneath her, reading a newspaper. She looked up and smiled at him, a weak smile intended to cheer him up, but he could see the misery in her eyes.

"I'm sorry, honey," she said. "But the twins are gonna be hungry soon. We'll have to go to the store and get some formula. I just didn't have any money."

George had $6.00 in his pocket. The formula cost $1.50 for six bottles. They would have to buy at least three to just get the twins past breakfast. He sank onto the couch, covering his eyes with his hands.

"We're just going to have to borrow some money again," he said after a while.

"George," Patti said, laying her hand on his arm, "we can't. You know we've borrowed too much already. Even if you get steady work, it'll take all year to pay it back. Besides, I doubt anybody will give it even if we ask."

"What about your grandmother? We haven't gone to her yet."

"Honey, she's sick. She can't hardly move about the house. What little money she has, she needs for medicine. George, I just can't ask her."

George nodded. Patti was right. He couldn't take money from a sick old woman who might get sicker without it. He could feel the dark anger coming up again. This just wasn't right. It wasn't right that he slaved for ten hours without food and still couldn't eat when he got home.

Patti said nothing. She knew her husband's moods. It was better to let him think it through. She felt no anger toward him. She knew he was trying. Presently, George got up and went to the front porch. He collapsed in the rickety glider, staring at the bright summer sky. He started to sweat, despite the fact that the evening was cooling rapidly.

After a while, Patti got up, packed up the twins, and left the house. He supposed the girl, Shana, was with Patti's sister. He supposed Patti was going out for the formula and didn't want to interrupt his musings. As soon as he heard the old car start, he went to the bedroom. She returned a short while later and quietly dealt with the kids in the kitchen.

On the top closet shelf was a .38 he'd bought for protection. He checked to see that it was clean and loaded and laid it on the bed. Then he went to the bathroom and cleaned off his face, neck, and arms. He returned to the bedroom and rooted through the closet for suitable clothing. He decided on a long cotton coat. It might look a little strange this time of year, but what the hell, he was going to look strange walking into a store with his inch-thick, yellow welding glasses on, too. He didn't want people to be able to describe his build.

He checked the glasses in the mirror. It wasn't a mask, but he doubted anybody would be able to accurately describe him with them on. He topped the ensemble off with a hat and walked back into the living room, where he picked up the phone.

"Sharon," he said when David's sister answered, "let me talk with David." Sharon handed the phone to her brother, dreading what the call, coming this late in the day, would mean.

"Can you get a gun?" George demanded when David answered the phone. The question—and the urgency in George's voice—took David aback. George was never this hyper. But he remembered that John still had his .38 from his military stint. David said he could, but why?

"I'm gonna rob somebody," George announced. "I don't care who it is. I don't care if it's the governor. In fact, I hope it is the governor. Goddamn son of a bitch can't even create a state where a man can feed his family."

David understood right away that George was not just talking. He meant to do it. "I need a lookout," George said. "I thought of you right away. You're the only one with enough balls to keep calm. Fifty-fifty. What do you say?"

"All right," David said, looking at his worried sister. "I'll meet you at your place." Hanging up, he told Sharon, "I don't know what you're so upset about. Is it better to live like a bum your whole life?"

"God, David. Please . . ." she began, but he'd already gone downstairs to get her husband's gun.

●

Driving around, George said, "What about that place?" It was a gas station on an island on Army Post Road. Since it was late, the traffic was scarce, but David said no. Looking at him, George saw his face was fixed and his eyes were scanning every bush and curve.

"Too well lighted," David announced. "And the street is too busy. The bars will be letting out soon and this is a main thoroughfare. People might stop in to fill up or puke up their beer. Let's try a side street."

George was getting frustrated, as usual. David always took so long to plan things. It seemed like a waste of time, but George knew better than to say that. David would give him a look that could wilt metal. George would feel dumb again.

Finally, David suggested the Superior 500 gas station across from the Pittsburgh Paint plant. David was working there now under a parole program and he hated it. But that wasn't the reason he wanted the gas station. He'd noticed that the station cashed checks for the laborers who worked in a variety of plants in the area. That meant they must have a lot of cash on hand.

Only thing was, the checks generally were cashed on Friday. It was Tuesday. David suggested they wait. The score would be bigger in two days.

"Can't wait," George said stonily. "Kids ain't got nothin' to eat."

David shrugged. He also knew when to hold his tongue.

The station looked ready for closing. An older man stood behind the cash register, counting receipts. A young man mopped the floor. George parked his car a block away and they walked up. George was real scared. "Get a grip," he told himself. "You don't want to hurt anybody because you're shaking hard enough to blow someone's prick off."

"Put a lot of authority in your voice," David advised him as he took up his position behind the station's door. From inside, the attendants couldn't see David. He was there to waylay any late customers.

But as soon as George pointed the gun at the older man's face, he could see an authoritative voice wasn't needed. The guy nearly fell over with fear. It startled George. Here he was, nearly dying of fright himself, and this old man thought he was in complete control. It was weird, but it kind of gave George a sense of responsibility. He had to live up to this guy's expectations so that nobody would do anything stupid. But it surprised the hell out of him that the mere presence of a gun would change a regular guy into a quivering maniac. Years later, George would never have anything to do with people who committed gratuitous physical violence. "It isn't necessary," he'd say. "Most people just fall apart when they see a gun. It isn't necessary to hurt them."

The young guy mopping the floor came over quaking when George told him to. There was no trouble and no conversation. George backed out of the station telling the two men not to call the police for ten minutes. They actually didn't.

Outside, George and David ran like maniacs. They ran away from the car, which they now realized was a stupid move. They shouldn't have driven their own car.

They ran down the back streets, across parks, through deserted intersections, and finally, along a railroad track. They ran without speaking, their breath coming in great gulps and the sweat soaking their clothing. George noticed David was not tiring as quickly. Working out again, George thought. In this line of work, that seemed like a good idea now.

They hit the Des Moines River, miles from the gas station. There was a large embankment to climb up to the bridge. David started scrambling, clawing at the slick mud. George sank to his knees, gasping.

"I can't go any farther. I don't care anymore. I don't care if they catch me. I hope they do."

David stopped climbing, jumping down from the embankment like a cat. He no longer even seemed winded. George noticed there was a look of curiosity on his face as he sat down opposite. George just kept trying to get his breath. David seemed to be studying him, looking for some clue. About what, George didn't know.

"Why don't you count it up?" David suggested after a while.

He'd almost forgotten he had the sack. A brown paper sack. It was the only thing the attendant could find to put the money in. George hadn't thought to bring his own and the fumbling for a container had been the only hitch in the process. It had wasted time. He wouldn't make that mistake again.

"Right," he said. He was stunned when he opened the bag. There were piles of bills in it. "Jesus Christ," he said.

The split came to $1,800 each. It was a fortune.

"I ain't runnin' back to that car and we'll get stopped this late if we walk," George said. All that money made him feel a lot better.

"I'll call Ken," David said. They went off to look for a phone.

●

Ken Agee was at home asleep when he got David's call. He and his wife had a newborn and a toddler. He was breaking his back trying to start a painting contract business. In fact, he'd been the only painter in the city who had agreed to take the contract for the slaughterhouse. Nobody else wanted to be around the stench of blood, shit, and guts as they ripped the cattle apart. Nobody wanted to listen to the screams.

Ken took the job because he figured he could prove himself. It was a way to get started. If he were willing to work that hard, maybe people would notice and give him a chance. It was a concept, he'd noticed, that David didn't seem to grasp.

But that was all Ken wanted. Unlike David, Ken had not adjusted to being caged like a zoo animal. After David had taken the rap for him for the vending machine tools found in his car, he'd continued hitting vending machines and doing a little burglary on the side. He'd finally been caught with Larry Agee, and sent to Anamosa himself. The experience scarred him. He'd concluded that working for a living could not be any more humiliating than prison.

Ken knew that David was still itchy and he wanted to steer clear of him. Still, David was his cousin and when the call came, he could hardly refuse to go get him. David didn't say why he needed a ride in the middle of the night from downtown. But Ken knew. He knew David wouldn't call unless he really needed him. The look in his wife's eyes told him she knew, too. Joann begged him not to go.

"What if they arrest you with him?"

Family was family, Ken told her. And David had helped him in Anamosa. Made things a little bit more human.

"I don't want to know nothin' about nothin'," Ken told David and George when they got into his truck. When they didn't answer, he said, "You guys are some real morons. Why do you want to fuck up your lives this way? I don't want you involving me anymore."

Years later, he would soften that position.

●

George walked into his dingy house, stowed the gun, and threw the now muddied coat on the couch. Patti was in the bedroom, again reading the newspaper. He assumed the children were asleep. When he walked in, she looked up at him, questioning. He didn't say a thing. He took the bundle of bills out and scattered them over the bed. They covered Patti like a crazy quilt.

Patti didn't say a thing, either. She picked up the bills and began counting. She put them in neat piles and looked back at her husband.

"Where did you get it?"

"Does it matter?"

She looked back at the bills, considering. "No," she said finally. She knew anyway.

George called Patti's sister to come right over and baby-sit. Then he and Patti went to an all-night grocery store and filled five shopping carts full of food. The next day, George put down a deposit on a nicer home across town. Far away from the Bottoms.

PART III

GRADUATION

VIRGINIA FRY

Virginia Fry prided herself on her good sense and steadiness. She'd made a mistake with her first marriage. They had both been too young. Now she was going forward with her life, leaving Kioac, Iowa, for the Emerald City of Des Moines, where she would put her life together again with her two small daughters.

Virginia knew she was not beautiful. With her raven hair and creamy complexion, she was more like a plain Snow White. But she was proud of her eyes, which were wide and compassionate. And she knew she had a nice figure, even after two children. In addition to that, she had a trusting, open nature that people seemed drawn to.

Virginia was adopted, but she had a terrific relationship with her parents. She embraced all of their Protestant values and work ethic and had been very involved in her church. She was hard working and accepted responsibility easily. Her parents never had a moment's worry over her. She never lied to them.

Arriving in Des Moines, she was determined not to become overwhelmed. She rented a small apartment and immediately went looking for work. She ended up with a modest secretarial job in the state-house, under the Gold Dome.

The secretarial job was fine, but it didn't pay much and it wasn't the reason Virginia had come to Des Moines. What she'd really wanted was something more exciting with better money. The data input job at *Look* magazine wasn't exactly a career as a top model, but it had better possibilities than typing forms all day. She took it.

The girl sitting next to her at the input machines was named Cheryl. Cheryl Agee, the wife of David's cousin, Larry.

"You know, Virginia," Cheryl said casually one afternoon. "You could stand to go out more."

Virginia looked up, somewhat surprised. "Well, you know, I have the girls and they keep me pretty busy."

"Nobody can just be around kids all day long, honey. I know just the guy for you. He's a little rough around the edges, but he's really sweet inside."

"Oh?" Virginia was interested despite herself. She hadn't been getting out much. But there was something in Cheryl's tone she didn't like. Her friend was being too nonchalant.

"Yes. Well, he's had a few problems. But mainly just bad luck is all. He's been railroaded quite a bit. The police just hear his name and suddenly David has done everything bad that's ever happened in this town."

"The *police*?" Virginia was horrified. She'd never known anyone in trouble with the police for more than traffic tickets. She was stunned that Cheryl would even suggest meeting a man who had problems with the police.

"Well," Cheryl went on, oblivious to Virginia's reaction. "He just got out of prison and he's really looking to clean his life up, you know. . . ."

"*Prison!*" Virginia gasped. This time Cheryl did turn around. "Oh, my God, Cheryl. Prison? I couldn't possibly deal with someone like that. I don't want to know anybody like that."

"Well, for goodness' sake, honey." Cheryl seemed surprised at Virginia's outburst. "It's not like he murdered anybody. It's like I said. He's had some terrible breaks. Prison isn't so strange. My Larry has been in, too."

"Larry has been to *prison?"* Virginia couldn't believe what she was hearing. She looked at the woman across from her as if she'd never seen her before. Cheryl actually *slept* with a criminal. It was too much to assimilate. Never mind the fact that now Cheryl wanted her to go out with the same kind of man.

"Excuse me," Virginia said. "I need to use the ladies' room."

Cheryl kept after her, though, and Virginia realized that through Cheryl she knew Sharon Oliver and Ava, Sharon's mother. She liked both women a great deal and started to think that maybe David Grandstaff couldn't be that bad. After all, Sharon was a hard working girl raising two kids. John Oliver, her husband, seemed attentive and committed, and Ava was an absolute sweetheart. So Virginia started to rethink her position.

But her additional questions revealed that David had been to Anamosa not once, but twice. Once for stealing a car and driving it to Chicago and the second time on a violation of his parole. He'd been tried for stealing a bunch of Colonial Bakery paychecks and cashing them around town. He'd been acquitted, but they'd sent him back anyway. Maybe if he hadn't done the paychecks, Virginia thought. A jury did find him not guilty. But when you added everything up, including the two stints at Eldora before he was seventeen years old, things didn't look right. She decided against a meeting.

Then Cheryl picked her up one day to go shopping. They often went shopping together, so that wasn't unusual. It wasn't even unusual when Cheryl said she had to make a quick stop at Sharon's house. Virginia hadn't seen Sharon or Ava for a while anyway. She didn't mind the extra half hour. Of course when they got there, David was there. Virginia was peeved.

David had this obnoxious friend with him. Virginia didn't catch his name. She didn't want to. The guy was loud and profane and dressed like a creep. He was everything Virginia imagined a criminal bum to be. Anyone who hung around with him couldn't be much better. She ensconced herself in a corner chair, waiting for the episode to end.

Cheryl kept jerking her head toward Virginia in a very obvious way, telling her to go over and talk to David. It was embarrassing. But it did seem strange that the man hadn't made a single effort to talk to *her* when it was clear why she was there. She looked him over cautiously. He was very handsome in a brooding sort of way. In fact, he reminded her of James Dean. His hair wasn't quite blond, but looked like it would lighten considerably in the sun. It had nice highlights and it was immaculately combed. Also, he was well dressed. Not at all like his awful friend. Understated and kind of dignified. And he was quiet. He just seemed to be taking things in as if to size the situation up before saying anything foolish or unfriendly. Virginia liked that. She liked introspective men. They were gentle.

When their eyes finally locked, Virginia saw quite a bit of pain there. There was a kind of confusion, too. As if he didn't really know how to proceed. This was not the cockiness she'd expected. She saw a lot of depth in his brown eyes. She wanted to get out of the house before she wavered.

She left the house first, but when she turned to chastise Cheryl, she found it was David who had followed her out.

"I don't know what you've heard about me," he said directly. "But I wonder if you'd like to go out sometime and give me a chance to prove it wrong."

His expression was so frank, it took Virginia aback. And his voice. It was a husky, gravelly voice with a sweet, country lilt. The combination proved irresistible. She relented.

●

They did small things at first. On one of their early outings, they went ice-skating. He wasn't that good and kept grabbing her scarf to break his falls, which naturally brought her down with him. She didn't mind. They giggled on the ice like school kids, got up, and tried again. She got cold, though, and wanted to leave. David asked if she'd mind sitting in the car awhile so he could skate some more. It was a little annoying, but she didn't want to ruin their day, so she agreed. Watching from the car as David practiced, Virginia could see that his expression was intensely focused. He was not going to leave the rink until he got it down, she thought. She liked that, too. Determination was good in a man. She didn't mind sitting in the car the extra half hour while David mastered a few turns on the ice without falling. Then he took off his skates and came back to the car. She did, however, notice that there was no apology for the wait.

They would take her children to the park. He was wonderful with the girls. He never raised his voice to them. He bought them things without spoiling them. Virginia's heart would melt, watching him play with them on the floor or guard them from possible danger. She liked it that most children were attracted to him. She believed that children had radar when it came to detecting goodness in people. Soon, he moved in with her. They toyed with the idea of marriage. David said he wanted a family. A real family with a nice house and a fenced-in yard. He wanted children. Ava couldn't have been more ecstatic. Virginia was pretty happy, too.

At the time, David was enrolled in a prison work program. He worked for Pittsburgh Paint and was painting in a small, cramped room with little ventilation. She drove him to work every day. He hated the fumes and complained that the room he painted in reminded him of a prison cell. He felt that they'd assigned him this work deliberately, to continue his punishment. He said they probably didn't want him to succeed.

"Well, David," she told him, "it's a job." She didn't like her present job either, but she tried not to complain about it. His complaints made her nervous, but she figured it might take a while for him to lose his bitterness. He'd been locked up for a very long time and God only knew what had happened to him inside. He never talked about it.

He wanted to go out more and more at night. She didn't mind that, either. She was twenty-three. He was twenty-two. There was no reason not to kick up your heels a little. But some of the episodes were disturbing. For one thing, there seemed to be more money available than there should have been. David complained often about his "convict wages," so she had an idea what he brought home. She certainly knew what she brought home. They were just spending more than that, plain and simple. Yet the bills always got paid.

Then there was "the group." George and Patti Weir, Mike and Joanne See, and Larry Agee, and a dozen others. It wasn't that there was anything wrong with them. They were perfectly fine. They had a good time. They paid the rent and their children were always clean and well dressed. Virginia couldn't really put her finger on it. Maybe it was the way the men would sometimes go off in hushed conversations while the women pretended it wasn't happening. It was like everybody was in on something but her.

One night, David blew up at his sister Sharon. They'd gone to the 505 Club and David found Sharon there without an escort. She was separated from John, so it wasn't as if she were cheating. She'd come with a couple of girlfriends and they weren't doing anything. Just sitting around talking. David scowled and became upset, but the lid really came off when two guys walked over to the table and struck up a conversation. They were unusual guys for Des Moines. Latin looking with obviously expensive clothes that could not have been bought anywhere in the Midwest. Enraged, David walked over to Sharon and ordered her out of the club. He told her to go home to her children. She looked shocked and began a sputtering protest, but he yanked her out of her chair.

"If you act like a whore, you're gonna get treated like one!"

"My God, David," Sharon said, still stunned, "you've been out with all these women. Do you think we're whores?"

"Get home!"

Sharon left. Virginia felt sick. She felt sicker when she found out the two men were drug dealers from the East Coast and that David knew them. He didn't like them, but it didn't help matters that he knew them at all.

Now completely in love, Virginia tried to ignore all the signs. She couldn't ignore them completely, though, and made small noises once in a while over dinner. David looked at her and told her not to worry. Neither she nor her children would ever be placed in jeopardy.

Then one morning David announced that he was not going back to work for Pittsburgh Paint. He simply couldn't stand it anymore. Virginia was more frightened than angry. What could it possibly mean? Not to worry, David said. He would work for his cousin, Ken Agee, who was coming along with his business. This also left Virginia with a sinking heart. She really believed that David had to get away from "The Boys" to make their dreams work.

She caught David looking at her, not with love so much as a kind of chilling understanding. She never knew whether she liked that look or not. On the one hand, it said, "I know your exact thoughts. I know your exact feelings." On the other, it said, "I will never feel the way you do."

"I will never place you or your children in jeopardy," he said. "I will never do anything to hurt you."

She believed him. What was tearing her apart was that he didn't seem to have the same regard for himself.

15

Virginia was only guessing about The Boys. The Des Moines Police Department was not.

For the next two years, no gas station or grocery store was immune from what appeared to be indiscriminate and increasingly sophisticated attacks. The Boys never kept track of how many places they hit, but they estimated it at well over two dozen, maybe three, with takes ranging from $10,000 to $50,000. Grocery stores all over the city remodeled, placing managers' offices and safes in obscure places, hoping to avoid attack.

But it didn't deter. The robbers always found other ways and never were they in the store for more than a few minutes. The hits were always made within a few minutes of the armored car cash deliveries. The getaway cars described by stunned customers were always found within a few blocks of the scene. They had always been stolen and usually the owners hadn't even missed them yet. The Boys would then switch to "clean units"—cars that had been licensed and purchased legally—that had not been seen anywhere near the holdup area. The police could not catch them.

One Des Moines officer, who was a rookie at the time, remembered several high speed-chases that ended when the quarry vehicles seemed to vanish. He spoke about them with near admiration.

The Boys did nothing untoward in their daily lives. They went to concerts and movies, lived in well-maintained homes with their wives and children and, for the most part, held down some kind of job. But the police couldn't help noticing how their life-styles, and those of their relatives, improved steadily. David now owned a nice duplex on the east side—nothing fancy but still well away from the Bottoms. Sharon also had managed to escape and was renting a neat little three-bedroom house in a decent neighborhood. There were Las Vegas vacations as well as the standard water-skiing camping trips. Everybody seemed to be dressing well. There was never a shortage of groceries in the refrigerator.

●

None of them felt bad about robbing the stores. They felt they'd been cheated plenty in the markets. But eventually, David became concerned that an off-duty or even an undercover policeman might be around during a score. Policemen, he felt, would not be able to excuse inaction among their peers by saying that they didn't realize what was going on. Even if a cop didn't *want* to pull a gun, he might feel compelled to do it. It could be very bad. The cop would not stand a chance and what's more, tongue-tied shoppers could get caught in cross fire. David called a breakfast meeting.

"I think we ought to think about something else," he said, after they'd ordered their coffee and eggs. "As long as we might get killed, we might as well make it worth our while."

"This is working fine for me," Mike See groused. "I don't see why we should mess up something that works."

David looked at Mike disapprovingly. Mike had a ton of balls, once you got him going. But he had less vision than George and was worse with his money. Mike had a gambling jones. Sometimes he did just fine. But like most gamblers, he lost more often than he won. He seemed content to grab $10,000, blow it in Vegas, and then come back to the breakfast meetings looking for more work. David had serious doubts about people who could not control their impulses. They were dangerous on a job. He especially disapproved of unchecked gambling. It was a stupid way to blow hard-earned money.

"Maybe you should find another crew then, Mike," David said evenly.

Mike looked up, hurt. David was always hurting his feelings. He was completely devoted to the guy. Would have done anything he asked and he comes up with that. "I'm just giving my opinion," Mike muttered.

"You ain't heard enough to give an opinion."

George stirred his coffee thoughtfully. "Whaddya have in mind, David?"

David gave one more look at Mike. "Banks," he said finally. "I think we should think about banks."

George felt a little weak, like the night David wanted to steal the car. "Banks?" he asked quietly. "That's pretty serious. That's federal."

"So what?" David demanded hotly, forgetting that George had never done time. "Do you think the feds could be any worse than these state fuckers? A gun is a gun. Besides, there's less risk in a bank if you do it right. There's not as many people. There ain't as much risk of injury, gettin' stuck with an assault or even a murder rap."

"Shit," Mike said. He really did not like the sound of that last remark.

"All right. All right," David said. "What do *you* guys suggest? We can't go on like this. Sooner or later they're gonna put cops in these stores and a lot of people, including us, are gonna get wasted."

Mike, still smarting from the earlier remark, had been twisting an idea around. He was not sure now if he should bring it up.

Mike See didn't grow up in the Bottoms or anywhere near it. He grew up on the west side of Des Moines where the houses were comfortable and everyone had a car. He wouldn't learn he was adopted until he was twenty-six. Only then would he be able to assign a reason to his feeling that, somehow, he never belonged anywhere. It seemed to him that people were always looking at him funny. It was nothing he could get a hold of. He would be sitting at the table minding his own business when he'd get this *feeling* that he was being watched. He'd look up and sure enough, his mother would be looking at him as if she were *curious*. It was unnerving. He didn't understand it at all. Later, he didn't care, although he tended to drink heavily.

"What about a bank burglary?" Mike suggested nonchalantly, hoping to redeem his earlier gaff. "I know safes."

Nobody said anything, but Mike knew this was because they were thinking about it. That was pretty good success in itself.

"What kind of burglary?" David asked, chewing his food. George seemed interested, too. It was a good compromise. If abandoning grocery store heists would remove them from a possible assault charge, a bank break-in would remove them from armed robbery and the feds. Everybody knew the feds picked and chose their bank cases. Bank burglaries were not something they'd pursue.

But the damned thing came off badly. They'd cased a few places around the state, arriving at a tiny little bank in Minas. They'd checked out a half dozen towns before settling on this place. Everybody had been a little surprised at how David kept referring to the farmers in vicious terms. He was the one who never failed to tell outsiders he was from Iowa.

In any event, they'd landed on this bank because there were apartments above; one of them was empty and the one next door was occupied by a deaf woman. They decided to cut through the ceiling of the empty apartment, which led into the bank. Who would hear?

They set out on a Saturday. The ceiling part went fine, and they were able to get to the flimsy safe deposit boxes, but the safe proved much harder to handle. Mike couldn't seem to quite get it, so George, with his welding experience, got annoyed and went for equipment. George and David labored with welder's glasses and blowtorches. Mike was supposed to keep watch, but it was boring. David and George had put up a canvas tent around their activities to shield the light, and every once in a while they'd come stumbling out, coughing and choking on smoke and soot, their faces black and their hair singed. They weren't getting anywhere and George definitely looked angry at Mike. Well, hell, thought Mike, he was only amusing himself with the things in the open safe deposit boxes. A little jewelry. A few coin collections. Nobody was going to come anyway.

"That motherfucker isn't doing his job," George told David. They were once again under the tent and their faces looked like wax masks in the glow of the torches. "I don't want him around again. He wouldn't know the law if it slapped him upside the head."

"Take it easy," David said steadily. "Let's just get done here."

But they didn't get done. The oxygen in the blowtorches ran out and they still hadn't gotten the safe open. Coughing and spitting up soot, David and George stumbled to a hotel, then took a look the next morning. Nobody had noticed the break-in, so they went back.

This time, they finished the job, but George was furious.

"If I'd wanted to work like a fucking slave, I would have stayed with the construction work!"

"Take it easy," David counseled again. "We'll come up with something better."

"I don't want that asshole around me at all anymore."

"We'll see."

George spit up black bile for a few weeks. Patti never asked what it was about.

●

Despite increasing arguments over David's unexplained absences, Virginia went shopping for David's Valentine's present. She thought it might mend things over and even change his mind. She thought she might be able to convince him that there were worse things than listening to a woman who loved you.

She decided on a nicely tailored white shirt and it cost more than she could afford, but that hardly seemed important, under the circumstances.

David did not come home on the evening of the eleventh and she spent a sleepless night. Too excited to wait until Valentine's Day to give David his gift, she'd left the shirt with a nice card on top of it, draped over a chair where he could see it as soon as he came in. In the morning, she went to work exhausted.

David saw the shirt when he came in later that morning to collect his equipment. He touched it gingerly, not wanting to soil it. He couldn't bring himself to look at the card. It would only make things harder.

16

Even before the Valentine's present, Virginia was beginning to understand that she would be unable to push David on anything. It left her with a bad feeling. They were talking about getting married, but he wouldn't discuss anything with her. He listened, or seemed to. But then he just did exactly what he wanted.

Still, he was impossibly kind to her. Just when she thought she might have to begin an argument, he would show up with a beautiful (and desperately needed) blouse or a kitchen item she'd wanted but couldn't afford that month. She'd never even been aware that he'd noticed what was lacking around the house. She never complained about anything because he didn't. David did not believe in complaining. If you couldn't fix what was wrong, shut the fuck up.

"Don't have a breakdown," he'd say after he had bought her something. She'd smile and find a conspicuous place for the gift so he could see it, at least for a few days. She noticed the pleased, covert looks he'd put in the gift's direction.

"You know," she'd told him once, "I love flowers. You could just bring me some flowers if you liked."

"Flowers die," he'd answered abruptly. "It doesn't make any sense at all to spend money on something that's gonna be dead in three days."

●

Virginia did not know about the first time. She did not know about Minas. She did not question the lavish nights out—the steak dinners and such. She did not know where the money came from to buy the presents or her girls' clothes. She didn't think about it. David would later say that she surely knew. Who was she kidding? Only herself.

●

On the twelfth of February, Virginia came home from work to find George and Mike See sitting with David in the living room. It was a bad sign. The two men had never shown her anything but the most knightly respect in the past, despite the fact that they knew she did not wholly approve of their association with David. In return, she had been a perfect lady with them but had put her foot down when it came to any of them influencing her children, especially in her own home. David had never questioned her request that The Boys congregate somewhere other than their home, but here they were and David had done nothing about it.

George and Mike rose politely when she entered, but David remained seated, looking off through an open window as if he were too hypnotized to realize she'd walked in. It angered her. He knew she was there. George and Mike gave each other sidelong glances, which drove her to the kitchen in a fury.

" . . . won't let you make a living," she heard George say . . . "can't get ahead no matter how hard I try and Patti is pregnant again. . . ."

Virginia sagged into a chair. It was one of The Boys' most common discussions. Rich versus poor. Capitalism. Politicians. Banks. She felt hot tears coming.

" . . . girl works there and says it's a perfect score," she heard Mike say. " . . . been working there about two years. She says the routine never varies. . . ."

" . . . couldn't hurt to look . . ." she heard David say.

Then he stood in the kitchen, looking at her. She heard the front door slam.

"I'm gonna be gone for a few days," he said.

"Why?" she screamed. "What are you going to do?"

He looked at her.

"Don't do this!" she said hysterically. "You don't have to do this! You *can't* do this to us!"

"Don't you ever tell me what to do," he said without inflection, and left the house.

No blows had been struck, but it was the worst argument Virgina and David had ever had.

It wouldn't be their last.

17

On February 14, 1967, Kellogg, Iowa, didn't look like a midwestern town. It looked like something out of the Old West. A movie set with latticed storefronts and broad sidewalks that looked like Bat Masterson could come clomping over at any minute. The First National Bank sat on a prominent corner of Main Street just as it could have in the 1800s, waiting for the boys in the long coats to relieve the vaults.

The James/Younger gang sometimes rode racehorses on their jobs, a choice that might have afforded good getaway speed but had the drawback of attracting the attention of the townspeople, who owned plow horses. In 1968, George, David, and Mike made a similar mistake, pulling into town in a sleek, black Buick sedan. The people in Kellogg wore coveralls and were inclined toward pickup trucks dented up from having bags of heavy feed miss their marks. A shiny black sedan made an impression on folks like that.

Still, the car at first was just a curiosity and when they pulled into a downtown gas station, the plan worked fine. David got out and picked up a pay phone close enough to the attendant to ensure that he'd hear every word.

The Boys had learned that people would supply them with the

damnedest information if they got them involved enough, flattered them enough, or made the scene mysterious enough. The plan was for David to loudly announce that he was going to look up a girl he'd known briefly, no matter what. George and Mike were to dissuade him, saying that they didn't even know the girl's last name, only where she worked—the bank.

Kellogg was a small town and the station attendant was having a hard time controlling his curiosity. A hometown girl had made a date with one of these guys, who, with their big black car, were probably from someplace exotic like Des Moines, or maybe even Chicago. He had to know who it was. It would be good barter at the tavern that evening.

"God, I wish I could remember her last name," David said, smacking himself on the forehead.

"Goddammit, let's go!" George yelled. The attendant had now ambled over, looking nonchalant.

"Maybe I can help you boys," he told David. "Most everybody in town buys gas here. I know most everybody."

David smiled inwardly as he hung up the phone. He explained that he was looking for a girl named Nancy. She had worked at the bank, directly under the bank president. He couldn't remember her last name, but she had gorgeous blond hair and long, long legs . . .

The attendant shifted uncomfortably. It would prove embarrassing if he didn't know this remarkable Nancy girl.

"Nobody like that at the bank now," he said tentatively. "But I think there's some folks named Kissen outside of town had a few daughters might fit that description."

"You know what?" David said brightly. A wonderful solution had just occurred to him. "Maybe if I could find the bank manager, he could tell me where she is."

"Well, that's right," the attendant said. It *was* a great idea. "Ray would know. Ray and Pauline Welle. They run the bank."

When David said he didn't want to bother the man at work, the attendant supplied him with the Welles' home address and telephone number. George was having great difficulty keeping a straight face.

Mike went to the Welles' door without a mask. You couldn't very well claim a car breakdown and ask to use the phone wearing a mask. It was almost dark, though, and he hoped that would help.

When he knocked, the door swung open. It was unlatched. When would people learn, Mike thought incredulously.

●

Pauline Welle came out of her kitchen, wiping her hands on a dishrag. Standing in her foyer, she saw the front door swing open. What on earth, she thought, and then saw a tall, good-looking young man standing in the entryway. She couldn't understand why he was wearing sunglasses at this time of day. Young people.

"What do you want?" she asked, not unpleasantly.

"What I don't want is to hurt you," the man answered. And then she saw the gun. He quickly put on a mask.

It was the first time Pauline had ever seen a pistol before. Hunting rifles, yes, but not pistols. She wasn't sure what to make of it, but before she could decide whether she should be terrified, two other strong-looking men pushed in behind the first. They, too, had pistols. They were also wearing masks. Now Pauline was terrified.

"Please don't be alarmed. Stay calm. We are not here to harm you."

The man speaking delivered the words firmly—almost like an order and also as though he were accustomed to doing it. But there was a lilt to his voice, a kind of soft drawl that made Pauline feel calmer, if that was possible. She felt the man was in control. He was not crazy. And for some reason, she believed him.

George felt admiration as he watched Pauline Welle compose herself. It took some real character to pull yourself together in the face of all of this without even screaming once. He liked the woman. He felt bad when she said she had to use the bathroom and David jerked his head, indicating that George should go with her. How embarrassing for the woman. It didn't do much for George, either. But then she just might have enough moxie to open the bathroom window and start screaming bloody murder. It couldn't be risked.

Later, when they were all seated in the living room, David went through the routine. When would her husband be home? What was the combination to the vault? He warned her not to lie, promising that when her husband came home, he'd ask him the same questions and if the answers were different, there would be problems. Pauline Welle answered the questions and George hoped she'd answered them correctly. He felt like a shithead when he had to intimidate people.

Suddenly Pauline asked if she could get anybody coffee. The gesture clearly took David by surprise, but he said sure, coffee would be nice. Maybe everyone could relax a little more while they waited. Mike See asked if he could have a glass of wine. He said he was a little jumpy. The request certainly made Pauline jumpy. She turned immediately to David.

"Will he be all right if he drinks?" she whispered. George thought it odd that she trusted David. She was talking to him as if he were *her* conspirator.

"You have my word that he'll behave," David said solemnly. Pauline nodded as if that were enough, and fetched the coffee, cookies, and wine.

●

George played a little gin rummy with Pauline, but the waiting was really dragging out. There had been a snag no one could have anticipated. It was February 14, near income tax time. The bank manager and his accountants were working late on forms for some of the better customers. David had made Pauline call several times, but she'd been unable to convince her husband to come home. Too much work to do.

Finally, he did come around 11 P.M. George went to intercept him at the back door, where he always entered his home. Pauline begged George to be gentle. Her husband had a bad heart. George patted her knee and told her not to worry. He'd be as gentle as a lamb. It was the first time he'd seen Pauline look anxious in hours and George was determined to put her mind at ease.

But when Raymond Welle came in, the guy just simply went to pieces. George couldn't believe it. He'd stopped Raymond at the back entryway, telling him to turn off the light he'd just turned on. His gun was visible but not particularly pointed anywhere. Just in Welle's general direction. Welle fell against the wall screaming and blubbering. He was clutching at himself like an animal in a trap. George had to grab him around the throat and practically shove the gun up his nose to make him stop. In view of the way Pauline Welle had handled herself, this was a pretty piss poor showing for a man, George thought. He was actually disgusted.

"Are you trying to give your wife a fucking heart attack?" George hissed. "Shut the fuck up!"

"My wife," Raymond Welle blurted, forgetting the gun. "Where is she? Have you hurt her? Is she all right?"

Seeing that Welle had come to his senses enough to realize he had more than one concern, George lowered the gun. "She's in the living room playing cards and she's fine. Nobody's touched her. Nobody is going to touch her. Now try to get a grip on yourself so you don't scare her to death."

Raymond Welle was allowed in the living room long enough to assure himself that his wife was unharmed. Pauline Welle rose when he came in and calmly instructed him to tell the man with the drawl whatever he wanted to know.

"Tell the truth, Raymond," she said. "I've already told them the truth."

●

David talked it over with Raymond Welle in the kitchen. Yes, Welle said, the information they had was correct. There was approximately $50,000 in the vaults. But he could only get to $15,000 of it tonight. There were two vaults and the inner one was on a time lock system, newly installed. It couldn't be opened until 8 A.M. the following morning. It was the God's truth. "Well," David said, "we'll go down and have a look."

At midnight, Welle opened the first vault, handing over $15,000. David inspected the second vault and decided that Welle was probably telling the truth.

"We're not greedy," David said. "We'll get out of your way now."

There was another reason to leave now. David was worried about Welle's color. The man was not looking well at all and David was worried that whatever heart problem he had was kicking in. He did not want a dead man on his hands for an extra $35,000 he could pick up someplace else.

For that reason, he tied Welle loosely when he got ready to leave. It wasn't that he'd tied Pauline up so that she'd be uncomfortable, but he was even more lenient with Welle. He didn't want the guy struggling around, going into a panic, and having a heart attack. It was the reason Welle got loose in twenty minutes.

●

The Kellogg bank robbery made headlines from coast to coast. No one had ever taken a bank manager hostage before. No one had violated a person's home since Charles Starkweather's murderous rampage, when he and his fifteen-year-old girlfriend killed her entire family and a half dozen other hostages in three midwestern states. The midwestern papers were still in shock over that. They played the Kellogg story front page day after day. No detail from Pauline or Raymond Welle was too small to report. Even though no one had been hurt, the potential for another Starkweather loomed. The FBI promised swift, brutal justice.

●

Virginia picked up the *Des Moines Register* on February 16 and went numb with horror. It was as if she were evaporating into air. She couldn't even feel the newspaper between her fingers. It couldn't be true. He couldn't have done it. But he wasn't here. He certainly wasn't here.

●

David picked up the *Las Vegas Sun* several days running and became more amazed every time he read it. What on earth was everybody so excited about? The woman—Pauline—herself was quoted as saying they were perfectly polite. Nobody was hurt. Certainly they'd gotten more than $15,000 in a score before. David was bewildered.

He'd decided not to stay in Des Moines after Kellogg. Better to get some rest and relaxation before facing Virginia. Mike had come along for the ride. George had planned to go out to California anyway. He was still trying to put some sort of legitimate plumbing business together and he thought he had a good supply contact near San Francisco.

"Jesus," David told Mike. "People are having a breakdown over this Kellogg thing. We could be in some soup here." The prostitutes sitting at the breakfast table giggled. Mike just shrugged.

"Only person they saw was me and that was only for a moment."

But David was concerned about that idiot John Cline, who had been at George's house when they'd gotten back the night after the robbery. David didn't trust the guy. He looked like a lightweight and the others thought he was stupid, too. David had been strongly angry at George for having him there, but George said the guy had just shown up after his wife kicked him out. Patti had let him in to be hospitable. David remarked that both Patti and George were far too trusting.

David insisted on giving John Cline the one-dollar bills from the robbery—about $500—just to ensure some silence. It didn't work. The FBI, completely certain of the identities of their quarry, tapped John Cline's phone. George, unable to stay clear of any of his Des Moines friends, had called Cline from California and mentioned the robbery.

Now David picked up the paper to read George had been arrested in California. There was no mention of his name. He did not know that had not stopped the FBI from getting warrants to search his relatives' homes.

●

All Kelly really knew about his brother David was that he was often "away at school." Kelly didn't think much about it, being only nine years old in February of 1968. Nobody ever elaborated on what "school" was. Kelly had a vague notion that it might be some kind of college, but he never asked, even when David was home. The age difference precluded any socializing between the brothers and David often stayed at Harold and Mabel Agee's home.

But when David was over, Kelly saw the light in his mother's eyes as she cooked a favorite meal the family could only seem to afford when David was around. He saw the way David would pretend to sneak food and his mother would slap him playfully, clowning around with David in a way she never attempted with the other children. When David and his mother huddled in a corner of the kitchen talking in hushed tones, it was clear to Kelly that there was some understanding going on there the rest of the family could not share. They'd stand there together, their heads barely touching, until David would place his hand on her shoulder and she'd look at him, eyes bright with tears of happiness. Kelly did understand the relationship to be special. Nobody else could make his mom look like that.

On that day back in February of 1967, Kelly hadn't seen David for a couple of weeks. As usual, he hadn't thought anything about it. He was alone in the backyard, which bordered an open field. The yard was like a jungle, with tall lush grass high enough to conceal deer and little boys who wanted to hide.

Kelly had a stick. He was playing army and the stick was his weapon. He stalked through the weeds tensed to spring upon his imagined enemies, his mind keen and alert. He kept in mind his father's lessons about hunting. Being very quiet and staying low.

When he first heard the commotion in the house, the noise went through him like a shot. He thought his father might have dropped over for one of his tirades, but on second thought there were too many male voices and way too much shouting. He heard his mother screaming something about "him" not being there and to please not frighten the children. Kelly was torn between running to his mother's aid and taking to heart her belief that he—a child—was somehow in danger from whatever was happening in the house.

He didn't get a chance to decide because what looked like a small army of men came charging out the back door. They had guns and they were pointed at the yard. Kelly felt his stomach contract in fear. Hardly able to command his frozen limbs, he hunched low and started running, trying to stay wherever there was cover.

"I've got the son of a bitch!" he heard one of the men scream. "The son of a bitch is getting away! Get over here!"

In complete desperation, Kelly realized the men were talking about him. They were after him. They meant to shoot him. They had probably killed everyone in the house and now they would kill him.

He did not realize he was sobbing until he was knocked to the ground. A cold, hard thump from behind that may have come from the butt of a gun. The ground was as hard as marble and hurt. He thought maybe he had been shot, but when he rolled over, he found himself staring up at a giant of a man with cold blue eyes. The man looked disgusted, as if Kelly had done something terribly wrong.

"That's not Grandstaff," said another large man, who'd come running up. The first man spit irritably in Kelly's direction.

"It's not the one we want anyway," he said dryly. "At least not yet. This little bastard probably has the same blood. Where's your brother, huh?" the man taunted. "Where's your brother, kid?"

Kelly hated them as they turned back to the house, leaving him where they'd knocked him to his knees. He hated them again when he crept into the kitchen and found his mother crying silently at the kitchen table.

●

Virginia watched the scene from the street in disbelief. She'd come to Sharon's house after getting a hysterical phone call from Ava Grandstaff, whose house had just been wrecked by FBI agents. Apparently, they'd also run little Kelly down in the backyard and scared the wits out of him.

When Virginia arrived at the house to visit, agents were already holding curious spectators back. She did not attempt to break their lines or say she was a friend of the family. The activities of the agents were unsettling her picture of the world. The one her parents had painted, the one she'd learned in church and school.

She could hear Sharon screaming—crying, actually, or maybe it was closer to begging. She wanted the agents to at least give her a chance to get her children to a neighbor's house. There were sounds of furniture splintering and overturning. The children wailed, but the agents would not let them out of the house. She learned later they weren't actually hitting them, but there was shoving and manhandling. Virginia was shocked. She had never seen either Sharon or John raise a hand to those kids, and their terror was evident.

Virginia did not count the agents in and around the house, but she guessed there were around twenty. Finally, there was an enormous crash. It sounded like a wall was being ripped out with sledgehammers. It was only after the agents roared off in a cavalcade and the crowd began milling away that she found out Sharon's living room ceiling had collapsed. There were so many agents rooting around in the attic, the supports had given way.

Seeing the agents were preparing to leave, Sharon gathered all her strength and demanded that the agents pay for the damage to her home. They thought the request amusing and advised her of the location of the nearest courthouse. She could sue, they told her. They also told her that they would shoot her brother on sight if he did not turn himself in. If she knew what was good for him, she'd find him.

When Virginia burst into the house, Sharon was sitting in a cloud of dust and plaster. The floors were littered with the contents of emptied drawers; clothing lay everywhere. Furniture had been tossed around as if by some angry giant. The children whimpered. A few of Sharon's friends, who had been at the house when the raid began, walked around in disbelief. Sharon looked at Virginia with dull eyes.

"My God," she whispered, "David is right. They aren't any better than he is."

18

Virginia fared better with the agents. They were civil, but they still frightened her. She'd never even gotten a traffic ticket. They had no reason to know her—except that they must have been watching The Boys.

Then one of the agents told her that they would shoot David on sight if he did not give himself up. If he contacted her and she did not help them bring him in, his fate would be on her head.

When David finally contacted her from Las Vegas, Virginia became hysterical. He *had* to turn himself in. He had to explain what had happened. He would die if he didn't. They would come and kill him. She loved him. If he had to go to jail for a while, she would wait. She begged him to meet her at McKarren Airport, realizing only later that she could have been followed. She could have had her children removed from her custody. The thought never failed to chill her afterward.

David hung up the phone with Virginia, sighing. The very things he cared for in her—her honesty and goodness—were double-edged swords. She could not possibly understand this situation.

He had never even attempted to explain to her that the justice system was not just and that the American Dream was just that—a dream. He was beyond it all now. He had gone—or they had pushed him—too far. They would only be interested in revenge. He clenched his fists, thinking how they had forced him to work in that tiny room at Pittsburgh Paint when he'd gotten out of Anamosa. A tiny room, just like the one in prison, where he breathed fumes and was covered with plaster and filth all day long. Just like it had been in prison where the guards would come by and smirk, knowing how much he hated it.

He forced himself to relax. There might be some way to get clear of this yet. His name had come up in relation to Kellogg, but only because his partnership with George was well known. They had George only because the idiot had called John Cline from California, and Cline's phone had been tapped. Mike See's name had not even been mentioned. David felt sure they were guessing. He hadn't been in the system all this time without knowing something about how to manipulate it. *They* had taught him that.

Leo Ballard, Des Moines attorney-at-law, took David's call immediately. "Well, well," he said. "You certainly have stood this country on its ear. I'm getting to be on a first name basis with half the FBI agents in the nation."

"I didn't have nothin' to do with that robbery."

"Oh, I know that," Ballard said easily. "Of course you didn't. The problem is convincing them. However, I think we are in a good position there. They haven't a lick of evidence against you. George adamantly denies you were there and so far, John Cline has not said a thing."

"John Cline?" David was confused.

"Sure. Didn't you know they arrested John Cline for the Kellogg robbery? The Welles have made a positive identification. They say he is definitely the man who came to their door without a mask. They say they will never forget his eyes."

David's head swam. Mike See had brown eyes. Cline's eyes were blue. It was too much. "Where are they holding him?"

"Polk County Jail. No bond. Clearly, they want him to talk."

"How can they hold him on no bond on a damned bank robbery? He didn't kill anybody."

"David, please. This case has scared the wits out of half the country. Some bankers have hired bodyguards. The FBI is in an uproar and when that happens, they can get any bond they want. You know that. Now let's talk about getting yourself turned in. I think it's the best policy. If you do it, I can keep you out on bond. I don't think there's a chance in hell that they can indict you and they know it. Unless, of course, somebody can identify you."

"I told you I had nothin' to do with that robbery."

"Very good. When can you get back to Des Moines?"

●

David returned to Des Moines in early March and immediately posted a $10,000 bond for the charge of bank robbery. The bond was low because he came back voluntarily.

He visited Sharon, surveying the damaged ceiling, walking round and round in the living room staring at it as if each little crack and dent were strokes on an important painting and he wanted to study the technique. John Oliver had attempted to patch the thing, but John was a hairdresser, not a carpenter. Sharon watched David's expressionless face with growing alarm. She knew how he looked when he nursed anger.

"We'll get it fixed," she soothed.

He looked over at her as if he'd just realized she was there, nodded slowly, and left the house without a word.

At his mother's, he comforted Ava, but did not speak with Kelly. Ava felt it was best to let the boy forget. David did not argue.

At Virginia's, he listened as she cried and told him over and over through her tears how she had warned him and warned him and now look what had happened. They still had a chance, she pleaded. Come clean. Tell them what happened. They would give him some kind of leniency. Just tell them about the others. David shook his head quietly, marveling at how little she understood him.

Then the bad news came from Ballard. After a few weeks languishing in the county jail facing twenty years for robbery, John Cline had decided to talk. Cline, who had been at George's house the night after the robbery, claimed he knew who had *really* been involved. Could you believe it?

The crazy thing, Ballard said, was that the bastards weren't even going to give Cline a deal for his cooperation. They were still going to take him to *trial*. He was still facing the twenty years, even with his cooperation. It didn't make any sense at all. It did to David, who knew Cline was suspected in a number of punk gas station robberies. If they couldn't get him on those, they'd get him on this—even if he didn't do it.

Cline told the authorities all about Mike See, but they made no attempt to arrest him. They didn't even interrogate him. David had to smile about it. The bastards were so interested in convicting him and George, they were willing to risk an innocent man's freedom—and let a guilty one go. They knew he, George, and Mike would never admit to anything, much less testify against one another. Cline was all they had. Cline and Pauline Welle, who said she'd never forget Cline's eyes, though he'd been asleep on George's couch 200 miles away.

He listened to Virginia's steady breathing in the darkness, mulling it over. Virginia had been acting very cheerful, as if everything would somehow work out. She did not understand what the Cline development meant. He and George would be going to prison. The only question was for how long.

Cline's trial was scheduled for May. He would testify and then they'd have the record. It would be pointless for him and George to go to trial with that kind of record, even if Cline were acquitted, although their chances looked better if he were found not guilty. Still, David thought Pauline Welle's identification pretty much sealed it. He had a month to get things in order. Ballard had told him he could probably swing a sentence of twelve to fifteen years. In the federal system, he could be out in as little as four years. Time had long since lost normal proportions for David, who was willing to do four so that he could always come back to Des Moines without fear of arrest.

But there was Virginia. She would not be able to handle it. He decided the best way to help her was to hurt her so badly, she would not feel bad when they took him away.

●

Nancy Lynch was an exotically pretty, petite blond who had known David since she was twelve. It was more like she'd known of him. She'd never actually socialized with him. Like droves of other young women who came to Des Moines, she worked as a secretary. Like Virginia, she'd married young and had two young children. Like Virginia, she had divorced early and was determined to get a good life.

Nancy and her friends went out at night to the prominent Des Moines clubs. It was exciting. The lights, the chatter, and the constant promise of something good about to happen. From her times at the 505 Club, the Brewhaus, and other places, she knew most of The Boys, some well enough to talk to. She'd often noticed David and thought him terribly good-looking. There was an intensity to his face that drew her, but also when he laughed, he could light up a room. When David laughed, other people couldn't help joining in.

He almost always sat with his back to a corner, surrounded by a group. Even when the table was round, he seemed to be at its head. Sometimes people came and whispered things in his ear. He'd nod without changing expression—without even taking his attention from whoever was speaking at the table. For some reason, it impressed her.

He was always very well dressed, too. Nancy wondered how he afforded the clothes. She could certainly tell that he took pains with his appearance. Everything was always pressed and immaculate. His hair was always perfect and his shoes always shined. She supposed it had something to do with the dark-haired, creamy-complexioned woman who almost always accompanied him. Nancy guessed the woman took good care of him and he looked satisfied, so Nancy never seriously entertained the notion of dating him.

She'd noticed that he was usually excruciatingly polite, but there were a couple of times that made her wonder about his temper. The one that really hit her was the time he cold cocked a guy that looked to be twice his size. The guy had been loud all night, bothering the waitresses and such. He was sloppy drunk. By closing time, he'd taken his attention off the women and was looking for a fight. Typical Iowa bumpkin behavior, Nancy had thought. She'd been trying to get away from it.

David was directly behind the guy as everyone filed out at 2 A.M. In those days, the bars were open late and gambling was even legal. David had been in a card game across the room. The dark-haired woman was not with him.

Nancy thought he'd gotten behind the guy deliberately, but his movements were so fluid, she couldn't be sure. David's eyes were at the guy's neck level. The guy was a good head taller. Suddenly David raised his mouth and spit full force on the guy's neck. Nancy couldn't believe it. When the guy turned around, David hit him full force in the face. The guy went down so fast, it looked like he'd never been standing there at all.

The noisy crowd was stunned to silence. People stood there blinking, looking from David to the unconscious man on the floor. He wasn't moving at all. The crowd muttered, wondering what to do.

"Pardon the disturbance," David said. Then he stepped over the guy and walked outside. His hair wasn't even ruffled.

When Nancy got outside, he was still in the parking lot, leaning up against a shiny black car and watching the doorway. Mike See and George Weir were milling around near him, laughing. But he wasn't paying attention to them.

She thought at first he was watching to see if the guy would get up and come back out after him. She was thrilled when he approached her instead.

"Let's you and me go get something to eat," he said.

●

Though she now knew David was living with the woman named Virginia, Nancy dated him anyway. He was terrific fun. He always wanted to go places, do things, and laugh a lot. Nancy thought it odd because she also knew that he expected to go to prison. That didn't bother her in the least, nor did his reputation as a gangster. He was too wonderful, always pulling out chairs for her to sit, never raising his voice, and always picking up little trinkets. It was a far cry from some of the roughnecks she'd known.

It was uncomfortable when Virginia confronted her in the bathroom of the 505 one night. Nancy wasn't with David and neither was Virginia. Apparently, the woman had come looking for her specifically.

Virginia was pretty upset, alternating from screaming to crying but Nancy could see she was not going to do anything physical. She looked too refined for that. So Nancy just tried to keep her cool. She wasn't about to give David up and she was prepared to wade through almost anything to stay with him. She felt a little bad for Virginia. It was hard to be two-timed, but Nancy had her own priorities and Virginia's feelings weren't among them. She calmly told Virginia that she was yelling at the wrong person. Her gripe was with David. Nancy never knew whether Virginia ever talked to him about it.

Then came the time when Nancy got a firsthand look at David's rage. It would come out of nowhere, and he'd raise his voice and rant about people and things she'd never heard of. He'd speak of politicians and various legislation in progress. He'd rail about the hypocrisy of the justice system. Nancy just tried to be attentive during these sessions, even though she couldn't participate. She just had no idea what he was talking about.

John Cline's trial had just gotten under way and Nancy figured that accounted for the increase in David's outbursts. She was determined to be supportive, although it was wearing on her. But the day David suggested a group horseback ride, he seemed back to his old self. He joked as he marshaled the group together and made arrangements to borrow the horses and tack from friends outside of town. Nancy noticed that he really liked planning things. He was good at it, too.

He could also ride like a demon. It was almost scary the way he urged the animal up to a frenzied speed. David always gave the horse free rein. He bent forward to keep his weight off the hindquarters and stared straight in front of him, as if nothing mattered but the animal and the wind. No one could keep up with him. No one wanted to, although some of the men in the group looked embarrassed that they didn't.

There were about fifteen people there that day, but David and Nancy cantered off together after a while. David seemed relaxed, as if the crazy riding had purged something.

They lay on the grass and ate the sandwiches they'd bought. David talked about dinosaurs and constellations and many other things Nancy hadn't thought about since high school.

Afterward, everybody went to the Brewhaus—Clyde Brown's bar—for a party. They were a couple of cases of beer into it when the police came crashing through the door.

Nancy had never seen such pandemonium. People screamed and ran blindly, knocking over furniture. Some of the cops had on uniforms and others didn't. Some wielded guns and billy clubs and others didn't. Nancy had no idea how many cops there were. It seemed like an army.

Everybody was yelling and glasses were falling and breaking; then Nancy saw the cops go straight for David, all at once. There were plenty of people there to arrest, but it was David they grabbed.

The first one who got to him was in uniform and had a club but no gun that Nancy could see. It was like slow motion, watching David eject a huge wad of spit directly into the cop's face. And then the billy club came up over David's head and down in a blur and David was on the floor bleeding. They ignored her pleas to take him to a hospital but allowed her to sit next to him in the squad car on the way to the police station, his unconscious head bumping against her shoulder the whole way.

19

In May 1967, John Cline was convicted of armed robbery, kidnapping, and aggravated assault. A jury looked at him with disgust when Raymond and Pauline Welle told of their terror, their fear of death, and their continuing nightmares and said they would never forget the eyes of the man who had visited this hell upon them—the defendant, John Cline, whose eyes they still saw in their dreams.

Cline wept as the Honorable Roy L. Stephenson sentenced him to fifteen years in prison and remanded him to the custody of the U.S. marshals for transportation to Leavenworth.

On his attorney's advice, David pleaded guilty to one count of bank robbery, with sentencing left to the discretion of the judge. George did the same. Neither of The Boys' lawyers thought the judge would be too hard on them, given their ages and relative cooperation.

●

Virginia had confronted David about Nancy Lynch. It had been their worst fight to date, but she had at least gotten David to react. He'd screamed about something other than "the system." He'd screamed that she would not be able to handle his incarceration and that he was trying to prepare her for it.

Well, all right. She was mightily wounded that he could believe hurting her would help. But if he'd gone around with the Lynch girl for those reasons, she would forgive him. She loved him and she would not go away simply because the Lynch girl was obviously going to hang on, too.

Virginia had never been in a courthouse before and she searched her closet for what she imagined to be the right dress. Even though her mission required charm, she knew sexy was out. Something a little more formal, but how formal?

She finally settled on the gray dress she saved for job interviews. She smoothed her stockings carefully, checked her hair, and drove downtown.

The vastness of the place—the domed ceilings and the huge pillars reflected in the polished marble floors—overwhelmed her. She had a hard time locating the office she was looking for. It seemed to take hours. Even when she found it, she was plunged into deeper fright by the crisp, unfriendly-looking people sitting in the outer foyer: a secretary behind a shining wood desk and several men in uniform. They didn't look like police officers. She didn't know what they were. She took a breath and approached the woman.

"I'd like to see Judge Stephenson, please," she said.

The woman looked her over as if she'd just drifted up from some backwater sinkhole nobody wanted to know about. "Do you have an appointment?"

Virginia was not prepared for the question. She hadn't known judges made appointments. "No," she finally managed. "But I have something important to talk to him about."

The woman smiled as if this were the most idiotic statement she'd ever heard. "I'm afraid that is impossible." And she went back to her work.

Virginia felt panic rising. She *had* to talk to the judge. She had to explain David before he was sentenced. "It's important!" It came out as a shriek.

"Miss," one of the bailiffs had her arm, "will you please come with me and I'll escort you out." The grip on her arm was not friendly.

"I'm Virginia Fry and I know where the money is! I know where the Kellogg money is!"

The outburst stunned Virginia even more than Judge Stephenson's office staff, who now sat open-mouthed. Virginia tried to understand what she'd just done. It hadn't been planned, but for some reason, the staff's reaction gave her confidence. The grip on her arm relaxed. One bailiff slipped silently into the judge's inner sanctum, emerging within a minute to beckon her inside.

How to proceed? The judge watched her warily as she made her way toward his huge desk and took a seat in one of the chairs facing him. She was breathing hard and thought her hands might be trembling, but she didn't want to look down for fear that she would cry. The judge waited.

"Your Honor," she began. She thought that was right. Then the words tumbled out. "David is a good man. He is a fine person. He's been locked up all his life for silly things. He really is good to my children and he's not at all violent. He just doesn't see the world the same way because he went to—"

"Mrs. Fry, do you know where the money is or not?"

"I had to see you to tell you that—"

"You don't know where the money is."

Virginia shook her head, dropping it at the same time. Now the tears started. The judge sighed.

"I do not know how a person like you became involved with these criminals. But I will tell you that you have made a grave mistake. You now have a chance to correct that mistake. These influences will shortly be removed from your life. I suggest that you take the opportunity to rebuild. You are still young and attractive. You have your whole life ahead of you. These men have committed the most heinous kind of crime. Maybe when they are gone, you will see that."

When Virginia did not respond, Stephenson said, "That is all, ma'am. I'm sure you do not want the bailiffs to escort you out."

●

On June 30, 1967, Judge Stephenson took the bench in the matter of the sentencing of David Lee Grandstaff and Gerald George Weir, both of whom had pleaded guilty to one count of bank robbery.

Jerry Williams, the U.S. attorney for the Southern District of Iowa, appeared in person to present the state's assessment of David's character, which consisted of reading his record to the court. It had been agreed that the state would not get more inflammatory than that. Then it was Ballard's turn:

"I don't think my client is as hopeless a person as you might think from the record. He has never had what you would call a friend who had dignity and standing in the community. His entire background has been this way.

"He's an orphan of the storm, you would call him. Nobody has ever helped him before. I hope the court will help him today. I think there's lots more good in him than he knows himself. He trusts coming here before the court to . . . like you say . . . take your chances on what the judge will do. We ask you, Your Honor, to extend to us all the mercy that you can. Thank you."

Eventually Stephenson responded: "One comment I want to make and I think it is only fair and I should state for the record . . . I don't think it really requires any statement. I think all of the defendants would acknowledge it. We start with a vicious crime. There isn't any question but what in the case, people's lives were placed in jeopardy. I don't know what would have happened if someone had gotten a little nervous and pulled the trigger. . . .

"I have no malice in my heart. I regret that a young man like you, David Lee Grandstaff, who my record shows is in perfect health, would resort to this type of violence to make a living. I don't know. I regret it. I wish I could do what some counsel suggested: put you on probation or sentence you under the Youth Correction Act. I can't. I just can't do it. It's too vicious a crime. And society has to be protected."

David and George each received twenty years. David was sentenced to Leavenworth. George, because he had no record, was to be transported to the less terrifying penitentiary in Terre Haute, Indiana.

David Grandstaff's mother, Ava, with her second husband, Mike Damerville.

David, age three, with his sister, Sharon, in the Bottoms of Des Moines, Iowa. In his hand is a harbinger of what is to come.

David, age thirteen, and his best friend, George Weir, spent a few pennies to have their picture taken in an automatic photo booth. The boys were into their pigeon-raising venture at the time.

George at age twenty, looking like the Western outlaws The Boys admired so much.

David in a reflective moment at the Anamosa Reformatory, where he defended the calves he worked with from sexual onslaughts by other prisoners.

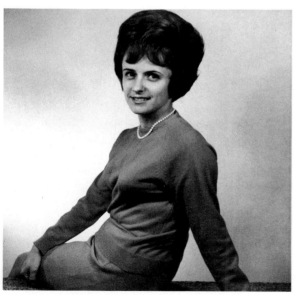

Virginia Fry (now Virginia Stevens), David's first love. David says she's the only girl he would have married, but his career ended that thought.

Doug Brown's sister, Lori, who hoped for a modeling career. David and Doug, a flamboyant career gambler turned bank robber, rescued her from an abusive boyfriend in Phoenix. David was instantly smitten by her, but refused her requests for marriage.

David's brother-in-law, John Oliver, a member of The Boys. John once ran to the wrong getaway car after a $1 million robbery, but David refused to leave the area until John was safely away.

The federal penitentiary at Leavenworth, Kansas. Despite its genteel exterior, it is one of the most feared prisons in the United States. Grandstaff spent eight years there altogether, but never saw a prison sentence for his biggest robbery.

David Grandstaff (top right), George Weir (bottom right), David's cousin Danny Davis (bottom left), and Jocko Ford, a soulmate, in Leavenworth around 1983. David and George, the original members of The Boys, had been robbing together since they were teenagers.

David, Nancy Lynch, Sharon Webb, and Ken Agee on a visit to Leavenworth. Despite David's demands that family and friends not concern themselves with him, they visited regularly.

David and Doug Brown leave Federal Court during the 1987 trial for the robbery of the First National Bank Depository in Tucson—which, at $3 million, still holds the record for the largest robbery of a standing bank. Doug carries a sign that says, "I am innocent."

Attorneys Bob Hirsh, who defended David Grandstaff, and Jeffrey Minker, who defended Doug Brown in the 1987 trial. They relied on the FBI's questionable procedures and on testimony from their clients' prison network in their defense.

David Grandstaff in retirement with his dog, Babs.

20

At first glance, the U.S. penitentiary at Leavenworth does not look like a prison. There aren't dank, grayish walls with slits for windows. The grounds in front haven't been razed and left to clouds of swirling teeth-coating dust.

At first glance, Leavenworth looks almost stately. Built in the late 1800s as a military prison, it was outfitted with a dome much like those on state capitol buildings. There are carved pillars and some interesting inlaid work, maybe because the army officers who would live there wanted to retain some illusion of genteel living. There are 113 regal stairs spanning the front of the building leading to the entryway. You can almost see trumpeters standing there to greet royalty instead of men who will be shackled at the feet, waist, and hands. There are gardens and landscaping, still kept up today. To complete the picture, a small herd of buffalo roams the grounds, drawing double takes from tourists passing by.

All in all, it is a queer joke of a setting for what is considered one of the roughest federal prisons in the country. The prisons in Atlanta and Marion, Illinois, have rivaled Leavenworth's reputation on occasion, but Leavenworth remains synonymous with images of violence and brutality, and that was even more true when David Grandstaff arrived there in late 1967 at the age of twenty-four.

David would end up spending seven years between Leavenworth and the U.S. penitentiary in Atlanta for the Kellogg robbery. He was shipped to Atlanta after orchestrating a prison strike against UNICOR, the federal factory that uses inmates to produce everything from light bulbs to shoes for cheap wages. That strike was settled quickly, but David and a handful of others refused to go back to work because certain living demands were not met in the settlement. The administration deemed him a leader and a threat and sent him someplace he didn't know anyone. There had been many Bottoms boys already in Leavenworth when David arrived.

For the most part, though, David was quiet in Leavenworth, staying mainly in his cell. He read everything he could from the sparse library. He was very fond of James Michener, believing he could become something of a historian from the books. He studied diet and health, and tried—in his job in the kitchen—to improve the food with what he'd learned. He exercised. He taught himself Spanish because the best handball players were Mexican. He studied politics and government and earned several educational certificates. He learned several trades, including welding.

He was not always a model prisoner. He ran the best poker games in the joint. David added little touches, a checkered oilcloth on the rough wood table, coffee, and sometimes even tidbits he'd smuggled from the kitchen. He dabbled in drug trafficking, although he, himself, was never affected by drug use. David had always done drugs, but never became dependent. He could go for months without thinking about them, then do them for a week. It was a trademark of his. Bob Mills would never forget how David gave up smoking in Anamosa because in prison cigarettes were currency. David couldn't see letting them go up in smoke, so he just stopped. Sometimes he'd smoke a cigarette, but the habit never returned for good.

He ran other gambling ventures and rarely had trouble collecting debts. For one thing, he allowed his debtors to pay him with whatever they had—shoes, jackets, shirts—even if it was something he didn't need or like. He would use the items he collected as barter for other things. Also, he gave people enough time to tap relatives for money. Not that anyone doubted there could be other consequences.

On January 26, 1970, after he'd spent almost two years in Leavenworth David got a letter from Leo Ballard informing him that the Cline family had retained J. R. McManus to try to get their hapless relative out of prison. In his letter, Ballard made it clear that McManus had been a kind of mentor and was still a close friend of his. Ballard assured David that McManus would do nothing to jeopardize David's interests and urged him to cooperate fully. The letter closed with a chatty paragraph about Des Moines and the hope that things were going well for David.

David had to smile. Ballard made it sound like David and he were friends and that David owed him a personal favor. Thank you for the twenty years, sir.

Attorney McManus had a nasty shock when he visited Leavenworth, asking David to sign an affidavit attesting to the fact that John Cline had not participated in the Kellogg bank robbery. After a soothing opening statement in which he appealed to David's own sense of being wronged and bemoaned the injustices of the system in general, McManus placed the affidavit on the crummy pocked table in the putrid green interview room. He placed an expensive pen beside the paper and folded his hands paternally.

David stared at the paper without comment.

"You must be joking," he said finally.

Stunned, McManus tried to evaluate the man before him. Surely he hated the system as much as all prisoners did. Surely he would leap at the chance to prove his persecutors wrong. McManus could not understand the cool, evil hatred in those eyes. He explained again that everyone knew that Cline hadn't committed the Kellogg robbery. That an innocent man was doing hard time over it and that surely David, with his background, could appreciate this opportunity to right an injustice.

"Why don't you take the fucking thing to the U.S. attorney and let him sign it, then?" David asked calmly. "I didn't send him to prison. They did."

"You won't have to give up any . . . uh . . . third parties in that robbery over this," McManus tried desperately. "I give you my word. . . . I've made a deal. . . . This would only help Cline. . . ."

"Fuck your deals," David said, deadpan. "I don't care if Cline ever gets out of prison. He was glad to send me here. He's a rat and I don't help rats."

David rapped on the door to be let out and was gone. McManus sat still, looking around the filthy walls of the interview room. He saw the grease streaks and cigarette burns only absently. He was struck by the similarity of the reactions—almost to the word—between George Weir and David Grandstaff. George had also refused to sign.

John Cline's appeal was denied.

●

George didn't last long in the "cushy" prison in Terre Haute.

A week after he arrived, he raised his fist to a guard who was threatening to hit him with a club for insubordination. That landed him in the hole. George did not know how long he was there, only that the toilet overflowed and somehow maintenance never got around to fixing it. He stopped asking after a while and slept on the floor in his own feces and urine.

When the guards did come to get him, he was woozy and sick. He was allowed to shower, but then was told to report immediately to his new job. He could barely walk. He felt as if he were moving around in a dream as the guards prodded him from behind, complaining that they were late.

One prod sent him sprawling. It was not a mean prod, it was just that he was so unsteady and ill, he couldn't keep up.

"Weir," one of the guards said sternly, "we don't care how sick you are. You better get your ass up and get out there."

"Fuck you," George said from the floor. "You can kill me right here. I ain't goin' out there to be killed like a dog."

After he got out of the infirmary, George found himself on a bus to Leavenworth to join the other incorrigibles. A couple of inmates applauded softly as they led him out of Terre Haute.

●

David and George were as respected as any two men could be in Leavenworth. Respect, George always thought, because you do not have friends in prison. It was like being in Vietnam. You couldn't make friends because they could be gone or dead at any moment. Still, they enjoyed the company of a number of other respected inmates. None of them liked unwarranted violence, but all of them were capable of it. Consequently, they were never asked to fight.

In prison, all kinds of events happen that determine your worth and standing—how many favors you can get and how many you can give. Sometimes it has to do with knocking somebody on their ass. You can't avoid that sometimes. But more often it has to do with just keeping your mouth shut.

David got thrown into the hole once for something he didn't do. Though he knew who had committed the infraction, he never told. This was considered a badge of honor. Though he had very little commissary money himself, George helped men who had no relatives on the outside to give them money. He did it without demanding interest. If a bit weird, this was also considered stand-up. It was well known there was no man George would not fight if necessary.

●

George was still having a hard time with the violence. David, he knew, had seen men killed in prison, though he had never talked about it on the outside. But in 1965, when David was in Anamosa, he'd seen a white guy kill a black guy over a cigarette debt. It had been a knife fight, prearranged, and the black guy had lost. The white guy was later acquitted at trial.

In Leavenworth a guy named Blacky Hays was stabbed to death two tables away from David in the chow hall. A guy named Hardaway was stabbed to death just as he was graduating from the prison college. He'd shorted some Mexicans on a heroin deal and a guy named Rhino practically died in David's arms after he was bludgeoned and stabbed in a hallway on suspicion of snitching to the guards. According to reports, the hallway was so thick with blood, guys were slipping all over in it, falling down and having difficulty getting up. They'd just slip back into the slime. David *said* he just happened to be there, but it was such a massive attack, George found it hard to imagine David not knowing where and how it was going to go down.

George was pretty sure David did not know about the murder the two of them ran into after a handball game. He never would have gone back inside if he'd known, despite the fact that he'd hurt his hand.

David and George had been in the yard playing hardball when David said his hand was too swollen to go on. They moved inside to C-Block where they lived in adjoining cells. It was recreation time, so the place was pretty well deserted. As they mounted the iron stairs, they saw two black guys from another block on the ramp outside the cells. It was Old Willie and a young guy, who'd been feuding over something to do with the laundry. They looked like they were just arguing until the young guy pulled out a knife and started plunging it into Old Willie's chest with a vicious frenzy George didn't think possible. The knife looked to be about twelve inches long, too. The young guy must have worked on it for weeks. Blood flew everywhere; some of it splashed George on the face and neck and he recoiled in horror and disgust. Old Willie was screaming—just this continuous banshee scream so loud George thought his eardrums would pop. When Old Willie stopped screaming, the young guy with the knife looked up at the two of them, breathing hard but otherwise not showing a thing on his face. Then he just turned and ran down the ramp. It was eerie.

Blood was dripping through the ramp grates and it was all over the walls. George suddenly remembered it was also on him. He felt David's hand on his arm, which was a shock, because David never touched anybody.

"Come on," David said quietly. "Get in your cell. Get cleaned up. Get out a book."

George thought they should maybe check to see if Old Willie was alive, but David shook his head at the unasked question, put his fingers to his lips, and motioned George into the cell. There really wasn't much doubt about Old Willie's condition anyway.

For a couple of weeks, the black contingent in Leavenworth circled George and David warily. The pair had to make a point of staying near reinforcements, in case they were jumped. The reinforcements would have been happy to oblige. Racial tensions, which usually lay quiet, if not dormant, were roused. White men had seen a black stabbing and they were expected to run to the administration. It was not part of prison protocol for whites to protect blacks and vice versa.

But after a few weeks, the looks thrown by the black inmates changed from challenge to a kind of amazement. It was clear George and David were not going to name the killer, even though they'd been hauled over the coals by the administration. After a while, the administration gave up and things got relatively back to normal.

Virginia was miserable. She'd tried hanging out with David's friends to ease the pain. Maybe she'd feel a little closer to him if she were around them more.

But one weekend they'd all gone to Las Vegas and she'd discovered their frequent gasoline station stops had nothing to do with getting gas or relieving oneself. They were hitting vending machines for money.

It plunged her into a worse depression. She could hardly get out of the car that weekend. She had no money and depended on her companions to get her back to Des Moines. Once they did, she never called them again.

But they, in turn, started spreading horrible rumors about her. They said she was cooperating with the FBI. Somehow, the story of how she'd gone to see Judge Stephenson had gotten out and now they all thought she actually had known where the money was and would have told.

It was ludicrous, of course. David would never tell her where the money was. She doubted that hardly anybody knew, although somebody must because David's family was doing well—even with minimal jobs. David himself was not hurting for commissary money.

Then there was the FBI agent. One of the ones who had come to her house after Kellogg. He had been plaguing her to go out with him and it was scaring her. One night she'd gone to a club with a girlfriend and he was sitting in her car when she came out. He only got out after she'd gone to the telephone booth in the parking lot to call a cab. It had been horrible. And maybe that's where the rumors were coming from. Maybe somebody had seen that and thought she was with the guy.

At first, she'd gone to see David in Leavenworth. The first time he walked out all pressed and combed, it took every ounce of her strength not to burst into tears. She knew he'd once ordered his mother—the only person he ever touched in public—out of a visiting room when she started crying. Leavenworth only allowed one opening embrace and one closing one. When she put her head to his neck each time she visited, she thought she would faint.

She'd thought they would discuss their future and how they would put all of this behind them when he got out. She still intended to wait, despite Nancy Lynch, Kellogg, gas stations, and supermarkets. But he didn't talk about that at all.

He talked about the weather. He asked about his dog. That damned dog. And he chatted about bland news from home. He wasn't unfriendly. It was just so *distant.* At first, she thought he just needed an adjustment period. But he did it the second visit and the third. And his letters were no better.

Finally, after the fourth visit Virginia cried all the way from the Leavenworth parking lot to her driveway—a seven-hour jag. After that, she didn't go back.

21

David did not receive a visit for five years after his transfer to Atlanta following the aborted UNICOR strike at Leavenworth. It didn't bother him. Seeing "free people" only made things harder and he didn't want his family wasting money on the trip.

Atlanta was a lot different from Leavenworth. It was filthy, crowded, and filled with unruly Latinos, whom he'd never encountered before, but David liked it better. The place was wide open. The guards did little, if anything, to stem the tide of drugs. Hell, some of them acted as couriers.

There were other benefits. The guards never got in your face. You had to do something pretty drastic to get a write-up or a trip to the hole. There was a better library, where David could check out three books at a time instead of one. On average, it was a better system.

And there was another bonus—maybe the best one. David was allowed to work in the prison dental clinic. Since he was a boy and his father had told his mother just to put clove oil on his aching teeth, David had envied the profession. Now he got to learn something about it. It was too late for him, of course, but he applied himself all the same. The dentist even fixed the overbite David was sure he had but no one else seemed to notice. In any event, the dental work made him feel great.

In Atlanta, David learned his brother Danny had signed up for another tour in Vietnam. David could only shake his head. Didn't Danny understand the war was being fought entirely for banks and industrialists? Money shouldn't have been that tight for Danny. He had other means. . . .

●

David was released from Atlanta in August of 1975, the summer that Patty Hearst was apprehended, President Gerald R. Ford escaped two assassination attempts in seventeen days, and Karen Ann Quinlin's family raised the right-to-die issue by asking that her life-support system be shut down. It was a new world.

He left the prison as most prisoners do, with a cardboard box filled with papers, letters, and accumulated keepsakes, a few clothes, and a little money from UNICOR. All of the clothes fit in a paper sack. One of the letters was from a friend who'd been released a few months before. It contained an address and it promised David a nice lay for that evening. But when he got to his friend's house, the girl had been called into her job as a waitress and was not expected to get off until late. David decided it wasn't worth it and changed a plane ticket bought by his family so that he could fly out of Atlanta and into Des Moines that night.

Virginia met him at the airport. She was nervous; during David's incarceration she'd married and divorced, and she'd given birth to two Down's syndrome sons. Although she knew David would never say a word about it, she was well aware of his aversion to illness of any kind. He hated to be reminded of mortality.

She was taken aback to see that he didn't look any different as he walked off the plane. She wasn't sure what she'd been expecting, but she'd expected *something* unusual to happen to a person's appearance in prison. She knew the stories as well as the next person. But there he was, cleaned and combed as always. He looked healthy and fit and not a bit broken. He walked with the same offhand confidence he'd always had. Not cocky, but serene and unself-conscious, like a well-bred animal. Women and men alike gave him sidelong glances as he crossed the tarmac with a cardboard box held almost loosely against the crook of his elbow, yet she knew that box would never drop. It reminded her of the way he'd held her daughters. It had always looked like they might slip, but she knew it wouldn't happen as long as David had them.

It gave her heart a jolt she hadn't felt in years, not even with Steve, the new guy she was casually dating now. Suddenly she wanted to race over and hurl herself at him as if nothing had happened. All was forgiven. All could be normal after all. She felt hot tears as she ran for him and saw him smile as he caught sight of her. She wrapped her arms around his neck and he placed his around her waist, but he did not put the box down. She pulled back to look into his eyes and they were smiling, but his hard shoulder muscles had not relaxed and there were mirrors behind the happy eyes.

"Good to see you" was all he said and then he disentangled himself, saying, "Let's get out of here."

Give it time, Virginia thought. He needs time. But in her heart of hearts, she knew it wasn't true. He was the same. He would always be the same. He was like a constant in the universe. She drove him to his mother's house to get clothes and watched him make small talk with the relatives there waiting to greet him. He met all of this with detached emotion—except for his mother, whom he embraced at length. But his brother Danny seemed downright intimidated and Kelly seemed just bewildered. Sharon was adoring as always. Sharon had always been the one who said there was a deepness to David that simply had to be accepted if you couldn't bring it out, and right then Virginia knew she couldn't. Twenty years later, she would say, "After realizing it, it wasn't hard to lean the other way." She dated David sporadically for a month and then married Steve Becks. There would always be a part of her that regretted the inevitability of it all.

●

For his part, David was happy to see Virginia, but there was a dead zone. For one thing, she'd put on too much weight. David disliked that. It showed a lack of discipline. In addition, she'd married while he was in prison and without informing him. He knew it wasn't rational for him to feel betrayed. He had, after all, chased her away. But there was a twinge, however deep he shoved it down.

Then there was the problem of the two Down's syndrome boys. Illness made David uncomfortable. He avoided his own family members when they were ill, opting instead to send flowers or cards, reappearing only after they'd recovered. It was a source of hurt for his family, but they understood he saw illness as a reminder of death. They'd given up reminding him that his constant workouts and his obsession with nutritious food would not spare him the ultimate conclusion. It seemed he didn't—or wouldn't—believe it.

Illness was bad enough, but genetic disorders unnerved him. Maybe he had seen too much of it in prison, but the first time he saw Virginia's boys, he felt like he couldn't breathe. He felt the walls closing in around him. He felt ill—the ultimate horror—and after controlling himself for what he hoped was an acceptable period of time, he excused himself and drove over to Nancy's. He knew that was the end. He admired Virginia for caring for the children herself, but he wanted no part of it.

At the airport, however, he put the boys out of his mind. Virginia offered to take his box, but he declined. On the way to his mother's house, he spoke of the wet Iowa heat and inquired about mutual friends. Virginia thought he did so without hearing her answers, although she had no proof. He never asked the same question twice.

He was glad to see his family, but again, there was a strangeness to it. His father merely shook hands and moved off to a corner. They didn't speak for the hour he was there. He enjoyed his mother, but the conversations with his brothers and sisters were stiff. Or at least he thought they were stiff. Everyone else seemed perfectly happy.

Rather than hitting the bar where his friends had planned a gathering, he took Virginia to a motel room. Maybe making love to her would bring it all back. It didn't, though. He went through the motions with some difficulty, but after it was all over he didn't remember much about it.

He didn't remember much about the rest of the evening, either. He drank and did his best to whoop it up, but it all seemed rather forced. Even stupid. It wasn't like he was returning from a glorious war. George had gotten out of Leavenworth months earlier and every so often, David would catch him looking at him, George's light blue eyes seeming to mirror David's own emotions. David did not talk to him much that night. There would be other nights.

When it was all over, David drove Virginia home without once considering the possibility of her staying at the apartment his family had rented for him. When he got "home," he pulled the drapes, sat down, and listened to the silence. Such silence seemed impossible, but he had no trouble adjusting to it. He sat and sat and listened to it until morning, never moving, never touching the television or the radio. In the years to come, friends and family would learn never to knock or call when David's curtains were drawn in the daylight. He would spend up to three days in his house, alone and silent. The penalty for disturbing him was a vicious tongue-lashing and a period of ostracism.

●

Everything was so different. Everything was so new. As he drove around his hometown streets, David fought down feelings of alienation.

There were buildings he didn't recognize. Streets he'd never negotiated. There was long hair on the young men walking around. David shared none of the political ideologies associated with long hair. He realized long hair was associated with "hippies" or people who were against the Vietnam War. Lately, since the war had ended, the hair was just considered to be the sign of malcontents. He himself had no problem with malcontents. When Danny had gotten home from Vietnam, he'd had to fight like a badger to get the benefits they'd promised him when he'd enlisted. It had taken a crusade by the *Des Moines Register* to finally shame the government into giving Danny the housing and education loans he'd expected. David didn't know the details of it, but the government's actions hadn't surprised him at all. He expected them to take things and then kick you in the ass. Especially if you were from the Bottoms. Hair or no hair, it was all the same to him. David just didn't think long hair was attractive on men.

Still, it made him painfully aware of his own prison crew cut, prickly and stiff on his scalp. His short hair reminded him of the anal cavity searches and the reek of disinfectant poured over him when he entered new facilities. His hair felt like a brand.

Music also had changed. He'd prided himself on keeping abreast of current events when he was inside but realized now the limitations of the prison library. There were groups around he'd never read about, much less heard. The odd thing was, this was one of the hardest adjustments. He was thirty-one years old now. But most of the places he revisited were populated by people eight years younger. It was like a time warp. They talked about music he knew nothing about. Danced steps he'd never seen. Young girls smiled condescendingly at him when he approached. Yet, he felt he *should* have belonged with them. He was one of them before Leavenworth and Atlanta. Why did they look at him queerly when he entered what was rightfully his domain? Time had not stood still for him and it made him bitter.

Usually, he went out alone trying to get his bearings. He drove past the bridges where he and George had captured pigeons. Past the parks where he and Virginia had picnicked. He spent time at his cousin Ken's, who was rising steadily in the world of paint contracting. He took long walks. He worked for Ken a little, mainly to appease his parole officer. His hair grew out to suit him. He called Cheryl Rivera.

There was a Peter Frampton concert in downton Des Moines. Frampton was a musician he'd at least read about and he wanted to attend. Cheryl, a new friend, was happy to go with him.

He felt uncomfortable in the parking lot, watching the hordes of people heading for the gates. But it was a mixture of alienation and excitement he'd been unable to pinpoint until that point. It was all different, but it was *interesting*. He really wasn't upset that the old things were gone. Their disappearance made the world new. He could meld into it. The Bottoms was still the same. He could always go back and look there, as he had dozens of times since he'd come home.

He glanced at Cheryl, radiantly younger than he was and happy to be among her peers instead of—he supposed—The Boys and their wives. That group had now closed ranks, keeping mainly with one another and going out to bars owned by a gregarious, stocky man with curly, sand-colored hair and blue eyes. Odd, David thought, that a man with an Italian name like Gabriel would have blue eyes and light hair. He'd read somewhere that northern Italians had that coloring. David wondered if Mike Gabriel's family had originally come from that part of the world but thought it boorish to ask. He sincerely enjoyed Mike, who seemed to have a dangerous side under the jokes and the gaiety. He enjoyed the evenings at The Gaslight where he could be perfectly comfortable, talking about the old days and drawing the admiring—if apprehensive—looks of the "straight" clientele. Cheryl, however, seemed happier in this parking lot, moving with the herd into the stadium.

It occurred to him that the people here *were* acting like a herd. He hadn't noticed it before out of his own nervousness. But now it seemed perfectly clear. He'd seen it before in the chow lines and the churches and the checkout lanes. If somebody had screamed "fire," people would have stampeded all over one another to get out of the way. People would be crushed. Nobody would stop to evaluate whether there really was a fire. Nobody would take charge.

Now he perceived that many of the folks in the parking lot were walking unsteadily. They'd stumble into their boyfriends or girlfriends and laugh, as if it were something hilarious to be half-conscious. As if it were a badge of honor to prove that you could take enough drugs to fall down. David thought of Atlanta and how quickly these people would have discovered what this kind of stupidity would earn them. Even in the Bottoms they would be open prey. He glanced at Cheryl, jubilant in the scene. They really didn't know, he thought as his throat tightened. They had really never had a taste of it. It occurred to him that maybe he didn't belong. Maybe he had never belonged. Trying to belong may have caused him a hell of a lot of unnecessary heartache.

He went to a few more concerts and then quit. It was the Stevie Nicks concert that did it. He looked around at the glazed crowd and then at the clothes he wore—purchased to fit in with the crowd. Now, they looked simply idiotic. He left early, drove home, and threw them away. Then he donned pressed Levis and a simple crewneck sweater and drove to The Gaslight, where he knew he would find at least some of The Boys.

●

George had been out for months before David was. The first thing he did was move Patti and the kids outside the city limits. Not that you had to go far to get into a rural area. But George thought the country life would be better than what he saw as the dangerous metropolis of Des Moines. He did not want the kids to be tempted by the same circumstances that had earned him six years behind bars.

Even now, his oldest, Joe, was showing dangerous signs of delinquency. He was hanging out with Danny Davis's boy, and it was rumored that the boy was testing his wings with petty criminality. George did not worry about his twins. They were model students, popular with their teachers and peers and earning good grades. Patti's girl was also well behaved. But George did worry about Joe.

Nonetheless, George ended up setting a poor example. Like David, he'd been affected by the passage of time. When he got out of Leavenworth, he felt lost and stupid—a relic in the eyes of an age group he still felt was his. He grew his hair long. He wore beads, even though he thought they were silly. Then, thinking he could make some money on the weird social changes, he opened a head shop. He sold pipes, incense, trinkets—all the things he saw people around him coveting. He even had a small pornography section, although he never was certain why he included it. George himself was not interested in pornography. He had no idea why he thought his clientele might be.

The shop attracted a group the rural Iowa famers had not known existed in their parts. Until now, the leather-clad, filthy bikers had been part of the evening news. Something that gave the locals reason to clack tongues and thank the Lord that California seemed a continent away. The bikers were worse than the stringy-haired youngsters in their ripped clothing who now idled around the streets with no apparent purpose. But it was all bad. And it got worse when George started having big, all-night parties at his home with his customers.

George did not think anything was wrong. He was an honest businessman, making an honest buck. He knew everyone in the tiny community and they knew who he was, but he thought he was changing their minds about his character. He didn't notice that Patti was becoming more and more listless, spending more and more time with her pipes and her tiny silver spoons. He didn't notice that the twins had become quiet, often going straight to their room after school. George maintained his rented property with the concern of any home owner, but he didn't see that anytime he was working in the yard, his neighbors gave him black looks and hurried inside their homes until he was gone.

Then his two dogs were poisoned. George was working at the time. The twins came home from school and found the German shepherd in its death throes. The dachshund was already dead, blood trickling from her mouth. It would have been bad enough for the two nine-year-olds to find their pets simply dead, but to find one of them frothing, screaming, and biting chunks from its own body was so enraging to George, he almost took his gun out of storage. Patti described how she'd been awakened by the children's screams for help and rushed outside to find them racing madly around the dying animal—afraid to touch her, but unable to leave the grisly scene.

George did not suspect poison at first. He thought the dogs might have been bitten by a rabid animal, although that seemed unlikely. There should have been signs. He had fed them that morning and they'd seemed perfectly healthy. Standing over them, he knew. He'd seen poisoned animals before in the Bottoms. He walked calmly back to the house, the black anger beginning to cloud his vision. He instructed Patti to send the children to their rooms and call animal control to remove the carcasses before they could see them again. He then combed his shoulder-length hair, put on a clean jacket, and drove to the sheriff's office.

No proof, the deputies told him. They didn't seem concerned to George and it was taking everything in his power to control the anger. "It's obvious," he insisted. He demanded that they come out and investigate. His children had been emotionally scarred.

"Mr. Weir," he remembers one of them saying, "you might think you are a pretty tough man, but we just can't go runnin' around the county every time somebody's dogs have a mishap. You get us the proof, then we'll come."

The blackness descended and George banged the man's desk with force enough to lift it off the floor. The deputies watched goggle-eyed as George left the office, upending a chair on his way out.

●

Iowa winters are cruel. Even the state's most ardent defenders dread the cutting winds and bitter, subzero temperatures. When humidity is added to the equation, no amount of clothing can keep the cold from sinking deep into your bones.

So George was surprised when he saw his children standing on a street corner in February—the coldest month of the year— waiting for their school bus. There was a pharmacy on the bus stop corner and the owner always let the schoolchildren wait in the warmth of the store for their rides. George had overslept that day and was driving to work late, or he never would have seen them. He was puzzled. Stopping the car, he leaned over and rolled down the passenger window.

"What are you boneheads doin' out here? Why don't you go and wait in the pharmacy with the other kids?"

It hit him that the kids must have been outside for quite a while. There were globs of ice on Shana's mittens. All of their hair and eyebrows were dusted with blowing snow. One of the twins, who appeared close to tears, was huddled into himself so tightly, George was afraid he'd frozen in the position. The children said nothing, but now they didn't have to. How long had the pharmacist refused to allow the Weir children refuge from the cold?

"Get in," George ordered huskily. He opened the door. He thought his voice would crack. The children piled in and George took them to school. He then returned to the pharmacy, banging the door like a shotgun as he stood before the shopkeeper, who had taken several steps backward.

"I don't care what you think of me," George told him, "but you leave my kids out of it."

"I can't take the chance," the clerk stammered, "that they might steal somethin'," It was the wrong thing to say.

"My kids ain't thieves!" George bellowed. "They're good kids growin' up right!"

Thinking better of a frontal assault, George turned instead to the racks containing everything from magazines to candy bars. The merchandise was soon on the floor with the upturned racks. When he got home, he informed Patti they would be returning to Des Moines. The country was not so hot after all. Patti took the news without comment, and went upstairs to get the suitcases out.

22

David, George, and Mike See were killing an afternoon in the Plaza
Bar. David felt comfortable in the bar, with its scarred chairs and pool
tables. It reminded him of the Brewhaus days. A little raunchy, but not
a dive, even though some of the men hanging around in there looked
like they'd be at home in one. David's group was certainly the best
dressed in the place. David sat in his pressed jeans, shined cowboy
boots, a gray cashmere turtleneck, and an off-white seersucker jacket. Of the magazine fashion advertisements he'd studied in prison,
David had always liked this casual elegant look the best. Mike always
favored a more preppy look. Loafers, yellow socks, and tweed. The
ensemble might have earned him jeers if the bar patrons hadn't been
aware of the group's identity.

"I have got to make some money, man," George complained.

"If you didn't give it all away, you might have some," David answered dryly.

George looked at David sourly. "Ain't no crime in giving people in
need a few bucks here and there. You do it."

"Last month you gave me five hundred dollars more than you owed
me on that debt. If I were a pig, you'd just be out the five hundred
dollars."

"That was an honest mistake," George said petulantly. "I just got
two rolls mixed together somehow. It could happen to anybody."

David sighed inaudibly and looked off. It was pointless to lecture
George on the importance of finances and the future. This was a man
who drank Pepsi like water, despite the fact that he had high blood sug-
ar. David had always made it a point not to live too high or let anyone
see what he had. It was important for the future. He would never have

a pension or Social Security. And whereas he'd managed a little to convince the others not to walk around like Diamond Jim Brady, he'd never been able to make them believe that someday the scores would end. It seemed like anybody could walk up to George's front door with a hard-luck story and get cash they never should have seen. When George had it, it didn't matter. When he didn't, he acted irrationally.

Though he didn't preach, David was aware of several nearly disastrous grocery store robberies George had committed with Mike and that punk Bruce Fennimore. They were so ill-planned and Fennimore was so untested that any false move could have caused a bloodbath. It made David's skin crawl.

David hadn't even raised the Fennimore issue yet. He didn't want to raise his blood pressure. The Dahl's Market robbery on Merle Hay Road had really been the limit. They had mistimed the arrival of the armored cars and never bothered to figure out that the manager's office was in the back of the store. They came late with not enough men to be able to post one at the store entrance to intercept new customers. The goddamn thing turned into guerrilla warfare, with George having to scour the aisles like he was in a television program, looking for hapless shoppers. The newcomers no doubt wondered where all the checkout people were before George gave them heart attacks with his drawn gun and dragged them to the back with the others.

George and Mike had about thirty people hostage, lying on the floor like stacked logs while The Boys waited for the armored car. It gave David a headache. Fennimore had apparently been so jumpy it was a wonder he didn't just start shooting like that Lieutenant Calley at Mylai. The goddamn guy was a car thief, for Christ's sake. And not a very sophisticated one at that. You didn't put a gun in his hand. And they'd only gotten $12,000. It was lunacy. David did not think he wanted to work with George anymore. Or with Mike either, for that matter. Mike had a gambling jones that drove him.

As if reading his mind, George said, "None of that insanity would have happened if you had planned the thing. You know I'm not good at planning." When David didn't answer, George added, "If you just took a look around town, I'm sure you could come up with a nice little score."

George was still salivating over the Hy Vee supermarket robbery on Fleur Drive, the only one David had participated in since getting out. It had been a nice, quick haul with good results—about $50,000. But, of course, David had watched the place for weeks. He knew exactly when the check-cashing proceeds went into the armored car. He knew the driver was lax—almost careless. One time he'd left the car open when he went inside the store. It hadn't been any trouble at all to overpower the guard and snatch the bags. The whole thing had taken thirty seconds and they never had to go into the store at all.

"I know a pretty easy score," Mike said slyly. George, who had been watching David anxiously, looked up with hope. David scratched his forehead lackadaisically. Mike thought all scores were easy—just as he thought he'd someday become a millionaire at the racetrack. For a guy who spent half his life gambling, Mike was one of the worst poker players David had ever seen. The only reason he didn't lose everything in Las Vegas was because the women he saw had the good sense not to give him any money when he ran dry. The only reason he'd managed to avoid a life sentence at Leavenworth was because he didn't rob on a regular basis. Mike could go for years without doing a robbery. He didn't mind being broke and usually he could find some woman to take care of his basic needs. That incensed George, but David figured it was the woman's problem.

"No, really," Mike insisted. "Big money. At least forty thousand dollars. And it's not a straight establishment. Hell, they're not even hard-asses. They're gamblers."

Mike waited for questions, but the questions didn't come. David was remembering the high-stakes, private poker games he and Mike had robbed years ago. Put on the masks, burst into the expensive, rented hotel suites, and clean out the bank. The hauls hadn't been bad, but you really never could tell who was playing in those games. Mike's assumption that gamblers were not hard-asses was half-baked, as usual. The gamblers Mike played with might not be. But it was likely they would be the only ones he could successfully cheat. David had played with men who would cut your nuts off—if not on the spot then next week, next month, next year.

"Well?" George demanded impatiently. "Where is it?"

"The Locust Room. Doug Brown's famous pool hall," Mike said.

"I don't like that kind of action," David said flatly.

"Why not?" George asked, astonished.

"Man's trying to make a living," David said.

Mike exploded. "What are you talking about? That punk has been taking people's money all over this damned city for years. Him and his scum of a father, Clyde. Those sons of bitches deserve to get taken down once. Hell, they've probably made hundreds of thousands of dollars. . . ." Mike stopped, seeing David's smile.

"Strange words comin' from an armed robber and fellow card cheat, Mike. Don't ya think? And by the way, this good anger wouldn't have nothin' to do with the fact that you've got the hots for Clyde's old lady, would it?"

●

For years, The Boys were only dimly aware of Doug Brown and Bruce Fennimore, who was eight years younger than David and only known by reputation as a pretty good car thief who had learned his trade from a crooked cop who had gone to prison over the whole thing. But Fennimore was indiscreet. He liked the attention of bar fights, wore dirty clothes, and didn't comb his hair. He swaggered. All this when his alleged real father was some franchise owner who should have done better by him. It left a bad taste in David's mouth.

Doug Brown he remembered dimly from the days when Brown, about four years younger, used to throw rocks at The Boys when they were eating lunch in taverns in an attempt to make them chase him. They never did and David always wondered what was wrong with the kid.

Brown had become mildly interesting, though. His father, Clyde, had been known around Des Moines for years as an enterprising small-business man who owned several rowdy bars, but Doug, even as the teenager he was, seemed to be putting a more classy spin on his father's profession and was turning out to be quite a good pool player and card player. This was surprising because it was said Clyde beat the tar out of the kid regularly and had been doing so since he was a child, when Clyde started taking the boy along on business trips in a three-state area. Doug had become accustomed to spending hours alone in the locked car without food. He became a surprisingly good hot plate cook because Clyde never thought to bring supper back to the hotel rooms.

From Clyde's perspective, the roughness had been a necessity. At age four, Doug had taken every butcher knife in the kitchen and placed them in a circle around his sleeping grandmother. The woman had awakened with a start to see her grandson rocking on his haunches before her with several additional knives stuck in his pants. He was grinning. She'd administered the usual treatment, taking the boy upstairs and wiping his anus with a piping hot towel.

Clyde administered his own punishment when told of the incident, but the events didn't stop. When Doug was eight, Clyde was called to collect his son from the top of the thirty-foot-tall, revolving Katz Drugstore sign. He'd skipped school—not unusual—and climbed to the top of the sign where he'd been revolving around for hours with no apparent intent. Calls from bystanders below had gone unheeded by Doug, as if he were in a different universe. Somebody finally recognized him.

Doug's ambition from an early age was the priesthood, and he would remain a devout Catholic his entire life. Despite that, by age fourteen he'd dangled a girl who had offended him out of a third-story window, used his beautiful sister as a reward for friends who did him favors, and set up card games he always seemed to win.

Before his arrest in the late seventies, he had set up one of the largest bookmaking operations in the Midwest, owned two pool halls, and made tens of thousands of dollars himself, including, it was said, once winning the Jerry Buckland showroom—completely stocked with new cars.

At the time of David and George's first robbery, though, The Boys regarded him as an individual showing potential, but with serious personality flaws that would in all probability hamper his success. Doug Brown stories had been circulating for a while and, frankly, he was deemed a bit irrational.

By that day in the bar, though, David had come to have a certain respect for the Brown family. Doug Brown had turned the Locust Room into a profitable enterprise. He was good at what he did and dressed well to boot. David didn't know Doug Brown, but he didn't feel like robbing him.

Mike's face was red with anger, but before he could retort, a form lumbered up behind him. The man had curly, black hair, rather nice blue eyes, but no chin or jawline—a genetic deficiency David detested in men. There wasn't enough ass to hold up the jeans and a slight paunch pressed his belt down even further. David hated the condition of the jeans, which he imagined were just dirty enough to smell. The T-shirt was not clean either and the jacket was worn sloppily, as if the man had no self-confidence. David leaned back in his chair, glancing at George, who looked away quickly. George knew David's opinion of Bruce Fennimore.

"Well, lookee who's all here," Fennimore said, much too loudly. He looked around the bar to see if the other patrons had noticed who he knew.

No chair was offered and with David and George silent, Mike was left to do the chitchat portion of the chance meeting, but Bruce eventually became impatient.

"You're David Grandstaff, aren't you?" he asked, extending a hand over the table. "I've heard a lot about you. Guys say you're pretty tough."

The remark wearied David. It was just like a moron car thief/bar brawler to think fighting was the measure of a man. He considered for a moment, then rose, scraping his chair back.

"Well, I got things to do," he said quietly. Bruce withdrew his hand awkwardly.

"I'll walk you out," Mike said quickly, as David fixed his collar for the wind outside.

By David's new car at the curb, Mike said, "Fennimore really is a good car man, David. The best I've ever seen. It's a gift. I mean, he can pick 'em and get 'em out of the parking spaces in twenty seconds. He can fix anything that moves. And he's a hell of a driver. He could outrun anything on the road. He's—"

"He's a hog and a loser," David cut in. "And you and George are playing with your lives messing around with him. You mark what I'm saying. You're gonna regret this and I don't want nothin' to do with it."

Mike shoved his hands into his jacket pockets and looked away toward the Gold Dome.

"I'll take a look at the Doug Brown thing," David relented. "Just to look. I ain't sayin' I've changed my mind on it."

"Okay," Mike said without emotion. But David could tell he'd made him happy.

●

Doug Brown had noticed Mike See coming into his pool hall off and on for several weeks. Doug knew he wasn't there for the pool. See didn't play pool. He played some poker, but Doug would never have admitted him to the private high-stakes poker games he hosted in the back of his establishment. It wasn't just that See cheated. That would be his problem. It was that he was a deadbeat. He never had any money and even when he did, he didn't pay off debts. Doug could not afford for his place to get a reputation like that.

"You want me to get rid of him?" an employee asked Doug during one of Mike's forays.

"Nah," Doug said languidly. "Let's see what he's up to. No doubt it has something to do with the other baby-fuckers in their tired little group."

Doug watched David Grandstaff enter the Locust Room, move casually over to a pool table, and rack the balls. Doug knew David by reputation and sight—enough to nod on the street—but had never had a lengthy conversation with him. And although David had never been in the hall before, Doug was not surprised at his presence. It explained Mike See.

David shot ponderously and not particularly well. Doug didn't know what kind of a pool player David was, but it was hard to be that mediocre on purpose, given the man's reputation. Still, Doug could not actually see David Grandstaff casing his hall.

Finally, Doug meandered across the room, chatting with customers as he went. He arrived at David's table, knowing the man had seen him coming even though his back was turned.

"How ya doin'," Doug asked.

"Not bad," David answered without looking up.

"You're hooking to the right."

"Know it. It's a bad habit I'm trying to correct."

"That why you're in here? Correcting habits? Because I know some people who might like a little profit off it."

David straightened, standing the cue straight up. "No," he said, looking at Doug. "That ain't the reason."

"Yeah, well." Doug ran his hand through his dark hair. He looked off at nothing in particular. "If there were another reason, it would be a real bad idea."

David returned to his game. "Sounds kinda like a threat," he said without interest. He missed another ball. "Damn!"

"Now why would I threaten you?" Doug was starting to enjoy himself. He spoke without inflection. "You're buying beers and making me money."

"If it makes you feel any better," David said, taking another shot, "I wasn't interested to begin with. I wouldn't have done it even if I hadn't noticed that you move your receipts out in small numbers several times a day. What do you have back there? A couple grand at a time?" Another ball clacked into a pocket. David stood but did not look at Doug. "Not hardly worth the trouble, I'd say."

Doug smiled. "Well, that's very comforting."

23

David bought a house on Palomino Parkway. It was the beginning of his interest in real estate as an investment. He put a few thousand down and made the mortgage payments religiously. He knocked out a few walls and installed an iron spiral staircase in place of the normal steps. It was an elegant touch, he thought. It pleased him every time he looked at that staircase. He meticulously selected the paint mixture himself—a kind of light lavender. The drab tans and greens

of prison had left him with a taste for cheery pastels. He liked startlingly bright colors, too, but didn't think they would be appropriate
as a wall color.

He went to great pains to furnish the house, and refinished the
basement, putting in a pool table for relaxation. He was outraged to
discover the previous owners had lied about the plumbing—never
thinking that he should have hired someone to check it himself. Within a month of owning the house, the basement flooded routinely because the pipes backed up. The Roto-Rooter man could not fix the
problem, so he spent thousands to yank up all the pipes and re-lay
them. It was the principle of the thing that enraged him.

Meanwhile, George continued to badger David about heading up a
decent robbery crew. Working with Mike See was a drag, George insisted. He'd disappear for days at a time. He was skittish to the point
of distraction before going in. Once inside, he was okay, but it was unnerving watching him jump around prior to the throw down.

David placated George by evaluating some of the possible jobs
George selected, with the understanding that he would not be going
on them. George took it as a first step, but he was dead wrong.

David's tutoring seemed to fall on deaf ears and David wondered
how they'd ever worked together to begin with. George had the heart
of a lion, David thought, but the emotional restraint of a rambunctious
puppy.

Then came a series of disasters, which—if they hadn't been so dangerous—would have been comical.

George had mentioned the Brenton Bank at 42nd and University in
Des Moines. David took a look, concluding that it was a lousy score.
Based on the armored car activity and the marginal neighborhood,
there probably wasn't very much money in the vaults and it would
take at least four men to control the situation. The bank was small,
but had several entrances, and there was a lot of foot traffic on the
sidewalk that bumped the front door. The proceeds would not make
up for the risk.

George remained stubborn about his decision, though, so David
simply advised that—if he absolutely had to have that bank—he
should be certain to arrive just as the manager opened up. Banks that
size rarely left their vaults open all day. David guessed they'd close

them by 11 A.M., after the pathetic small businesses in the area had dropped off their receipts from the day before.

George had Bruce Fennimore on line to get the cars and Mike See to go in with him, but he agreed with David that a fourth man was needed. The problem was, nobody wanted to go. At least nobody reliable. George had been working on Mike Gabriel, The Gaslight owner, but Gabriel still seemed unwilling to cross the line between vicarious association with the outlaws and induction by fire.

George turned to Larry Blackstone, who had done time with David in Atlanta and been promptly busted for bad checks in California after his parole. He'd jumped bond and come to Des Moines where The Boys got him a fake ID, a job, and an apartment. Lately though, he'd been grousing about his grim life-style and George thought he might be ready for a change.

"I don't like guns, George," Larry said peevishly after hearing George's proposition. "You know I don't like guns. I've never even owned a gun. I wouldn't be able to do it."

"Course you could," George urged. "There's nothin' to it. And it isn't violent. The guns are there to *prevent* violence."

David felt Blackstone was probably shamed into going, but that was his problem if he didn't have the guts to say no. David heard about the whole mess later.

First of all, George arrived at the bank at 2 P.M., not 7 A.M., as David had instructed. The vaults *were* closed. The place *was* crowded and Blackstone, frightened and sick at heart, allowed an elderly woman to run by him and escape the building to the sidewalk where she screamed bloody murder.

"It's a rout! Let's go!" Mike See yelled desperately. George was still trying to make the manager open the vaults, which was impossible because they were on a time lock system.

George looked around in exasperation but saw the wisdom of Mike's words. He grabbed at a cash drawer on his way out, his long coat flapping as he vaulted the tellers' bar. Blackstone stood rooted by the door, as if he were only watching the events, not participating in them. George spun him around roughly and shoved him through the door so hard, Blackstone nearly toppled to the pavement.

They piled into the waiting car and Fennimore floored it. George screamed for him to slow down and not run any lights. It would only attract attention. But they already had.

A Camaro full of young men was giving pursuit. Fennimore surged through the intersection on the red light, but he couldn't lose them. "They're good," he muttered fiercely, fishtailing into an alley.

"Just stop," George instructed. Bewildered, Fennimore did as he was told. George calmly exited the car and stood with his .45 resting on the roof. When the Camaro turned in, he took a few shots at the hood. The guys in the Camaro burned rubber backing out of the alley. The incident was never reported.

Next came a Weir/See/Fennimore robbery of a suburban bank none of them had cased. As in many of their jobs, Fennimore really just acquired the cars. After the throw down, Mike See let a lady rush past him screaming at the top of her lungs. He was so startled, he didn't think to put an arm or a foot out to stop or trip her. She made it onto the street with her message. George and Mike had been lucky there was a back door.

●

David was really starting to like Mike Gabriel. The sandy-haired, blue-eyed son of first-generation Italians was too self-confident to rise to cheap ethnic insults—which were common at the time. At first, David thought Gabriel's lack of concern about the slurs he could clearly overhear might be rooted in mental cowardice. It couldn't be physical because, although Gabriel was short, he was built like a fireplug and clearly worked out regularly—another plus. And it wasn't that David expected Gabriel to get physical at every slight. David himself didn't care what people thought or said about him and he saw brawling as a distasteful last resort. But it was, after all, Gabriel's bar. The rules were different when you were in your own domain.

But David's speculations about Gabriel's heart were laid to rest when he pulverized one particularly obnoxious patron who had started bothering the women customers as well as making "dago" jokes. David liked the way he did it. It would have been how he would have handled it.

Gabriel had been sitting at The Boys' table, yukking it up. The offender was at the bar. After the last "Come sit on Papa's face" remark, Gabriel set his beer down, looking into it sorrowfully, as if he were pained by the state of Western civilization.

"Excuse me, gentlemen," he said, pushing his chair back.

The Gaslight employed bouncers, but Gabriel waved them off as he walked directly to his customer. He did not say a word, but slammed his fist directly into the man's face with a force that dropped him to his knees.

David did not consider it a sucker punch. The idiot had seen Gabriel coming. He'd seen the steady walk and the braced arms. He'd just been too cocky to think anything would happen. And besides, David believed that enemies deserved no warning. There was no real fair play in these matters and Gabriel had been as honorable as he needed to be. More, in fact. What did that bozo think was going to happen, for Christ's sake?

"I hate assholes," Gabriel said, after the customer had been ejected onto the pavement. That was the extent of the explanation and it was all that was required. David liked the absence of embellishment, and lit a cigar.

"You do a good business here," David observed through the blue smoke. Gabriel shrugged.

"Decent."

David had always admired successful restaurateurs. Between stints in Anamosa, he'd worked as a busboy for Johnny and Kay's Restaurant in Des Moines. The couple who ran the place had thought he had great potential, and tried to teach him the business. Eventually, they'd allowed him to inventory stock and generally eased him into the financial end of a successful restaurant. Unfortunately, the stock had also included liquor and in those days, David's fondness for liquor and waitresses had outweighed his commitment to the education.

Nonetheless, he'd never lost interest in the industry, although he had to admit he preferred the social end of it. Getting a good crowd, he thought. The right people drew in other right people. And what better way to make a living than spending your work time around people you enjoyed? He felt he could handle that end.

Gabriel seemed to be able to handle the other. And David had more money than he knew what to do with.

"I don't know," Gabriel was saying. He was smiling like a boy, shaking his head ruefully as if he knew he'd been a bad one. "I just love women. I love the way they look. I love the way they smell. They're just great."

"Yeah," one of the men at the table said. "Well, that doesn't mean that you have to buy them a house, new furniture, and a car. Christ, she only let's you over there a couple times a week. I think you've lost your mind."

David had come to have an unkind opinion of women—except the ones in his family and, of course, Virginia, whom he hadn't seen in a couple of years. It seemed to him that women were transparent when it came to money. Their eyes lit up, their legs spread, and then their hands opened. David did not share the hormonal cravings he saw in Gabriel, but he understood them. And now, he did not suggest what he thought Gabriel's dream girl was doing during the days that he wasn't there.

The little conversation had been enlightening. Gabriel had a financial Achilles' heel that translated into rich, dark hair, long legs, and blue eyes. David became a silent partner in both of Gabriel's bars and under his stern supervision, they both prospered.

24

Later that year David found out that Gabriel had finally been seduced. His wedding bed was a score David would later refer to in his scribblings in the margins of court documents as "the joke of the century."

Having been ever so slightly humbled by the Brenton Bank disaster and the one following it, George, Mike, and Bruce Fennimore had taken to easier robberies—namely grocery stores. George had mastered that technique and even though the takes were small by David's standards—between $20,000 and $30,000 split three to four ways—he still thought George should have money under the mattress.

George didn't, though. And David knew why. David still refused to associate with Bruce Fennimore, so he didn't know what that man's excuse was. Mike See and his horse tracks annoyed David, but at least Mike didn't have a family to support. George, on the other hand, needed the counsel of friends.

David and a new girlfriend, Sandy Wood, were frequent guests at the Weir house and he saw the way George doled out money. His kids got anything they wanted. His friends got help anytime they felt like dropping by. David tried and tried to show George that the friendly visits stopped as soon as George ran out of money. David would have drawn him a chart if he could have. But George would not believe it. David's recriminations were all a lost cause. George defended his family like a tiger. His kids deserved good things. Had David forgotten the Bottoms? To David, it was a blind rationalization. But even today he would still say that, of all the men he crewed with, George Weir was the only one he would have banked his life on.

In his heart—from the pigeon days—David knew that in 1977. But he still couldn't believe the Lewis System armored car robbery that had popped Mike Gabriel's cherry.

George, Mike See, Gabriel, and Fennimore acted on the worst kind of information. David never knew who had received it, but it was reminiscent of the information Mike See received in 1967 from a freind of a teller at the Kellogg bank. A checkout girl swore the Lewis service picked up at least $185,000 in cashable checks every Thursday. The information was not checked. The Boys just got ready to go.

They waylaid the armored car, dragged out one courier, and held another at gunpoint, forcing him into the stolen getaway van after the bags had been transferred. George did not like the hostage idea. It wasn't manly.

"Slow down!" he yelled to Fennimore.

"Are you crazy?"

"Slow down!"

Fennimore did as he was told and George kicked open the back doors of the van. He held the courier by the shirt, holding him from falling from the moving vehicle.

"I'm gonna set you down," George said. "Don't lose your balance and don't look back. When you hit the ground, just run. Do you understand?"

The terrified man nodded, his eyes focused on the moving pavement beneath his feet. George let go and he dropped. The courier did lose his balance and fell, but he was up quickly, running hard in the opposite direction of the van. (Fennimore would later testify that the courier was thrown out at a high rate of speed. The courier denied this. He sustained minor scratches to his legs, but was not hospitalized.)

Gabriel was leaning easily against the wall of the van, leafing through the checks. He had a smirk on his face that made George uncomfortable. It was one of those teacher smiles. The kind that says they have the answers and you don't.

"Worthless," Gabriel said, almost good-naturedly. "Totally, totally worthless."

"What are you talking about!" yelled Mike See.

"They are all canceled checks. Geez. I wonder if our little informant was setting us up. Or are we just stupid?" Gabriel turned away in disgust. "The big time," he muttered. "I was promised the big time and I get Big Bird."

There were $185,000 in worthless checks. Once in the "clean units," the crew dumped them into the Des Moines River. It was one of dozens of robberies they were not charged for. There was no proof.

●

George ended his tenuous winning streak by robbing a bank in Pleasantville. The bank had not been his first choice. He and Danny Davis, David's cousin, had selected one in Des Moines that turned out to have much more security the day they arrived than what they'd seen in casing it. George, however, was ready to go and he was sick of the planning stuff anyway. What good was it? Nothing ever turned out the way you thought it was. He and Danny drove the thirty miles to Pleasantville, entered a bank they'd never even seen, much less cased, and robbed it. George made the mistake of cradling his shotgun over his left arm, something David had repeatedly warned against. George was one of the few left-handed bank robbers in the country. It was an easy identification.

The FBI arrived at David's house on Palomino Parkway with a warrant. Uncharacteristically, he let them in without making a time-consuming, painful examination of the paperwork. He'd heard about the robbery on the radio. This time, George had really done it.

David had stayed clear of the bank robberies. The agents had to know that. They were fishing. Fine.

What David had forgotten about were the photographs of the female federal parole officer he and Doug Brown had taken. David and Doug had picked her up at the "outlaw" bar she'd chosen to frequent to better understand her clients. Except that she'd started to see her potential clients as a more interesting breed than her colleagues. David and Doug had presented a good challenge and she'd discharged her date to go with them to Palomino Parkway, where she was photographed in various positions, sometimes handcuffed, that left nothing to the imagination. David had gotten some pleasure out of it, because of who she was. She was subsequently fired. It was clear from the confiscated photos she had not been forced.

●

George and Danny were eventually caught through an informant. The informant, needing a way out of his own problems, told the authorities that George had shown up directly after the Pleasantville robbery with cash. The informant was later driven out to a weed-choked dumping ground and shot. Though he survived by belly-crawling through the weeds as his kidnappers tracked him, he never did say who had abducted him. He only testified as to his knowledge of the bank robbery. George and Danny were sent to Leavenworth, but not before Bruce Fennimore appeared before a grand jury and lied on George's behalf, providing alibis and generally saying that George could never have had anything to do with the series of robberies that had ripped through Des Moines.

The grand jury incident impressed David. He started to think Mike See might have been right about Fennimore after all.

25

David tried not to think about George. He knew George would be okay in Leavenworth, but he tried not to think of the clanging bars and the tiny bunks. He tried not to think about what was going to happen to Patti and the kids. David would watch out for them as best he could, of course. But Patti was not in a good way. David did not know what he could do about that.

He spent his time visiting relatives and friends, trolling the malls. Buying shoes and jackets.

David insisted on American cars. He did not approve of the Japanese economic invasion and did not believe they made better cars, anyway. He favored strict trade embargos but since the politicians didn't have enough guts to enact them, he made it his personal quest to buy American on every level, but particularly cars. He sometimes gave dirty looks to people driving Mitsubishis or Hondas, even though he realized the drivers would not understand why.

●

Driving around alone one golden afternoon, David started when he passed the Wakonda Country Club. The club did not conjure any particularly bad memories for him, he'd just been surprised to see it and realized that he'd probably intended to visit Gray Park nearby, where he used to picnic with Virginia and her kids. His mind had just gotten away from him.

He was deciding whether to turn around or not when he noticed the Coca-Cola plant across the street—the one where he'd found the vending machine keys in the basement a lifetime ago. What caught him wasn't the plant itself, though. What caught him was the armored cars unloading sizable money bags and the lax attention of their crews, who stood chatting and drinking coffee.

From a professional standpoint, David had watched armored cars over the past years. Experience had taught him what grocery stores or banks could reasonably be expected to hold what sums of money. He'd noticed that the size of the bags carried by the armored car drivers varied according to the establishment's proceeds, and the ones being unloaded into the Coke plant were larger than average. Not the largest he'd ever seen, but large enough to be worth a serious risk.

The aimless drives became focused as he timed his drive-bys for different hours, watching to see when deliveries and pickups were made. He followed the cars. He borrowed other cars, on the extremely thin possibility that some employee or guard might notice his on the busy street. He munched potato sandwiches in the parking lot across the street, careful not to sit too long to attract attention. After a few weeks, he thought it could be done. He was getting bored anyway and the money would not hold out forever. He hadn't been doing well in Vegas.

●

Mike See had been watching David's leisurely life-style with increasing impatience. When was the man going to get back to business? With George and Danny Davis gone, Mike didn't have a good way to make money. There were other people he could crew with, but they were punks. Untrustworthy and unstable and worse than unprofessional. He didn't dare pressure David about it. David would have cut him off immediately. But he felt certain the time was near. David's money couldn't last forever, even if he had the uncanny ability to stop gambling in Vegas when he was losing. Mike never could stop. He had no idea how much money he owed David for getting him out of that town after losing streaks, but it was enough that Mike knew he needed a big hit to make it good. And this was one debt he would have to make good.

When he walked into The Gaslight one evening, Mike saw David in a quiet conversation with Mike Gabriel. This was it, he thought, and took a seat near the door to wait.

●

Before David left The Gaslight, he stopped by Mike's table. He was still alone, having chased off a half dozen people in anticipation of the moment. David looked him over, considering whether to include him. Mike made a case for using Fennimore as the driver. Because he'd lied for George, David relented and agreed.

"Stay off the booze," he ordered Mike after including him as well.

●

The armed robbery of a Lewis System armored car at the Coca-Cola plant was nearly a disaster because Bruce Fennimore left his post. Bruce had done a good job of stealing the proper cars for the drive-up, and a U-Haul van had been hiked for the getaway. The "clean units" were parked some blocks away.

The plan had been for Mike, Gabriel, and David to pull into the lot just after the money bags had been loaded into a freight elevator that would take them to the offices two floors above—as the inside man had described. Armed with assault rifles, Mike See would jump onto the hood of the truck to hold the driver—who would be remaining inside—at bay. The truck's windows were allegedly bulletproof, but David did not think they could withstand an onslaught from an assault rifle. In any event, Mike See was to make certain that the driver believed they couldn't, and that his face would be blown to smithereens if he tried anything.

As a backup, Bruce was to pull the U-Haul into the loading area behind the armored car, blocking the truck's exit path should the driver decide to put faith in his company's reassurances about security. David and Gabriel would follow the other guard inside, disarm him, grab the bags, and be out before the freight elevator arrived to transport him. Afterward, they'd force the captive guard and his driver to open the truck and get the rest of the money inside.

Their luck wasn't real good. The guard was disarmed properly. In the usual way, he wasn't paying excellent attention to his chore and was surprised. Then, he thought the two muscular masked men in front of him were playing a joke. He laughed heartily until he was hurled to the floor and bound with duct tape.

David noticed Gabriel was shaking some, but it didn't look like anything to worry about until the freight elevator door opened without warning, revealing a mousy-looking secretary-type who fell back in confusion when she surveyed the scene. Then a whistling janitor appeared from nowhere, tugging a mop and bucket on wheels behind him.

"Jesus," Gabriel hissed.

"Get the fucking janitor," David yelled, hoping to startle Gabriel out of whatever shock he might be in. But as it turned out, it wasn't necessary. Gabriel had already started toward the janitor, who put up his hands gravely and without noise.

"Don't worry about it, pal," Gabriel said. "It don't mean nothin'."

"I know that," the janitor murmured, allowing his hands to be tied. "Just stay cool."

"I'm cool, man. I'm cool," Gabriel assured.

"Just come out here," David told the secretary quietly. "Nobody is gonna get hurt." He disabled the elevator and whirled.

"Forget them," David said. "Let's get the rest of the truck and get the fuck outta here. We still have a few minutes."

They picked up the bags the prone guard had carried and headed to the loading bay. Mike See was perched on the truck's hood, but there was no U-Haul in sight.

David did not have time to ask questions. "Let's go," he said, motioning toward the stolen car. "Just keep the guns on the driver as we back out."

"Shit," Gabriel said. "A getaway in a stolen car. Perfect."

"The clean ones are close."

Bruce was sitting in one of the clean cars, waiting for them. When Mike See got in, throwing money bags before him, he tried to strangle Bruce.

"You miserable son of a bitch! I should kill you! You nearly got us all killed! Where the fuck were you!"

"Knock it off!" David yelled. Gabriel pulled Mike See's hands from Bruce's neck.

"He can't hardly drive while he's being choked to death," Gabriel told Mike. "Why don't we wait until later?" The humor gave David a lot of respect for Gabriel.

●

Bruce's sullen and insistent explanation was that a roving traffic cop had ordered him to move the U-Haul van just before it had been time for him to pull into the loading area. He drove around the block, but when he got back, the deed had been over. He parked the van on a side street and went to the clean cars to wait.

"The fucker is lying," Gabriel said, after Bruce had been dismissed from the room. "He just got scared. He's unreliable and I say we give him his cut and let him go."

Mike See looked at the floor. His responsibility for introducing Bruce to the group had stripped him of any right to comment. David glanced over at Mike, then looked at Gabriel.

"It could have happened the way he said," David said. "He did everything else right. If he's not lying, it would have been stupid to start arguing with a traffic cop who was telling him to leave. The van was stolen."

Gabriel chewed it over. "I still think he's lying," he concluded. "But it's your ball game. Call it the way you see it."

The take was $300,000. David was reassured to see the morning papers reporting the take at $500,000. More insurance fraud. It made him feel all right about being an armed robber. At least he was honest about it.

26

The year of 1979 went by without much activity, except for the fact that Doug Brown was released from the Leavenworth camp in late 1978 and met up with David shortly after New Year's.

"Hi," Doug said, slumping down at the barroom table. David had been contemplating a pool game, but now looked at Doug as if this might be more interesting. "Remember me?"

"Naturally. How was it?"

"Not bad," Doug said nonchalantly. "I had to kill a few newborn babies and leave their guts smeared on the walls, but it wasn't bad."

David nodded thoughtfully. "Well, it's good they were able to get the babies to you. There's often a shortage of newborn babies in Leavenworth."

"I know what you mean," Doug said. "Any action in here tonight? I'm a little short of cash."

"Chump change." David looked at Doug. The man's expression was calm—even peaceful. But there was an implied danger in the way he held his body. "I wonder why you're short of cash," David said. "I thought a high-powered businessman like you could just pick up where he left off."

In fact, David knew what had happened. Doug's partners and friends with whom he'd entrusted the Locust Room and several other interests had taken them over and run them into the ground.

"You live in this town, don't you?" Doug did not wait for an answer. "So you know what happened."

After a while he said, "I am looking for another line of work."

"What's wrong with the old one?" David asked.

"Heat. Too much heat."

David nodded. The Las Vegas bookies would have to steer clear of Doug Brown for years. "You've never worked with a gun," David stated. "It's different. I don't like introducing people to it. It makes me more nervous than they are."

Doug turned to him sourly. "Suit yourself. But you're making the same mistake about this you did the first time. You want to hang out with drunks, it's okay by me."

David stopped him before Doug could get out the door. "Hold up," he said. "I don't think I want to play pool today anyway."

●

David was impressed by Doug's mother's home. Norma Brown and Clyde had been divorced for years—Clyde having taken up with a young barmaid named Susan Smith, who would later become Mike See's girlfriend. But Norma had maintained a very nice environment, despite Clyde's lack of attention. The furniture was clean and modern, the carpet thick. Artwork adorned the walls and Norma kept pictures of her children all over the house. Doug and Norma left David alone with the photographs as they went into the kitchen for a private talk.

David's eye fell on a photograph of a young woman, her black hair swept back as if it were taking on a sea breeze, her dark brown eyes glittering with elfish mystery and promise. She was beautiful. David could not put the picture down.

"My sister," Doug said, coming up behind him.

"Very nice," David said, trying to keep inflection from his voice. He was a little embarrassed at having been caught.

"Like to meet her?"

David had the feeling Doug was toying with him, but he answered, "I wouldn't mind."

"Good," Doug said. David noticed that he had a suitcase in his hand. "Then you can come with me to Phoenix."

●

Lori Brown had called Des Moines from a pay phone in Phoenix. She had a black eye and had had to bum the quarter it took to make the collect call to Clyde. Her boyfriend had been beating her for weeks. He'd forced her to quit her job, denied her money or transportation, disconnected the phones, and kept her a captive. The only reason she'd been able to get out to make the call at all was that he'd passed out drunk. The clothes she wore were tattered and people stared at her as she sobbed into the receiver. Despite their past differences, Clyde knew his son Doug was the one to handle the situation. He had called his ex-wife, who had imparted the information to Doug. Telling Lori to call the police was, of course, laughable. The police wouldn't do anything but look bored by another domestic dispute.

●

Doug and David borrowed Susan Smith's car and took off. Doug was calm as his eyes hugged the road. His hands on the wheel were relaxed and dry, but he said strange things. Designed to shock, David thought, but only those people too inept to see through it. It made David think Doug might be right for a crew. Being a good armed robber was no different from being a good Avon saleslady, David always thought. You had to make people believe. Watching Doug's demeanor, David believed he had the gift. Maybe more of it than he needed.

They took turns driving. It was understood there would be no stopping. The situation was never discussed, but it was understood that it was urgent. Doug's physical stamina under the circumstances added to David's estimation. The man had to be under a strain, yet the lack of sleep or food seemed to have no effect on him.

Pulling into Phoenix after forty-eight hours, Doug stopped abruptly at a gas station. He wanted to freshen up, he explained. Wanted to comb his hair out, take a shave, and wash his face. David understood that Doug was orchestrating his attack. Confronting a composed enemy was far more terrifying for the object than seeing a bedraggled, bloodshot-eyed figure. David had separate reasons for following Doug into the restroom and washing up. He wanted Lori Brown's first impression of him to be a good one.

As it turned out, Lori was not in any condition to gather impressions after her boyfriend opened the door. David first saw him, bleary-eyed from drink, and looked quickly past him for other adversaries. What he saw was Lori, head bent in her hands as she slumped over her knees on the couch. Her hair, David noticed with distaste, was greasy and limp and her skin was white. Not the creamy, milky white of the photograph but a sickly white that reminded him of disease. She looked up briefly, displaying dark-pocketed eyes that had nothing in common with the glint of her pictures. She seemed to recognize that Doug stood in the doorway, but made no mention of it before dropping her head again.

Doug didn't look at his sister. He was fixated on her boyfriend's face.

"How are ya doin', bro?" Doug asked casually. "Nice to see you again."

"Get outta here, you convict," he said, not very steadily. "This is between me and her. You got no right comin' here and stinking up my house."

Doug looked at David and sighed happily, as if these kids today really had themselves some wild and wacky life-styles. Wasn't it a kick? Then Doug punched the man full in the solar plexus, sending him sprawling.

David admired the force and assessed that Doug needed no assistance. He went instead to Lori, lifting her chin to force her to look. She wanted to know who he was. Her voice was not good. David told her he was a friend of her brother's. She seemed to understand, and began sobbing hysterically.

●

Lori wanted to wait in the car. David agreed, led her to the automobile, and then asked her where her stuff was. He would pack it. Lori said her boyfriend had destroyed most of it. She thought there might be clothes left in the closet and drawers, though.

When David returned to the apartment after locking Lori in the car for safety reasons, he found Doug had already been getting her things into a suitcase. Doug wasn't packing at the moment, though. Right now, he had her boyfriend spread-eagled on the bed, straddling him and holding a knife to his neck. The skin was dangerously compressed where the metal met it.

"If you ever come near my sister again—or even think about contacting her—I will kill you. Do you believe me?"

The man gagged as he nodded.

"I wish you wouldn't do it here," David said, folding some of the clothes Doug had just thrown into the bag. "Throat wounds leave a lot of blood. It will get all over you and you'll have ruined a perfectly good set of clothes."

Doug removed the knife and stood. He was not breathing hard. Lori's boyfriend did not move. He never attempted to contact Lori Brown again.

●

The trio decided to detour through Las Vegas on their way back to Des Moines. Perhaps the bright lights and nightlife would make Lori feel better. Doug said nothing about the way David coddled Lori. Coddled in David's way, that is. Offering to get her a Coke or asking if she was hungry. Doug saw Lori beginning to rise under the attention. It made no difference to him one way or the other. He only asked that she not be abused.

In Las Vegas, Lori showered and washed her hair thoroughly, then examined her face carefully. It was a mess. She knew she had the looks to be a model, but you couldn't tell it now. She didn't want to be seen in public and was relieved when Doug came to her room, announcing that he and David were going gambling for the evening. She slept very well, and mid-morning the next day David gave her two $100 bills, telling her to go and buy some nice things for herself while he and Doug finished their games. Despite her brother's and father's occupations, Lori had never seen a $100 bill before. She felt like a princess, walking into the finer shops knowing she could flaunt her stuff. But she ended up buying only a white silk blouse and a little makeup. She couldn't bring herself to spend all the money at once. When she proudly showed David her purchases, he looked perplexed.

"Did that blouse cost two hundred dollars?" he asked. It wasn't accusatory, yet Lori sensed she'd done something wrong.

"Of course not," she said, feeling the tears coming. "I've got the rest of the money right here." She offered some crumpled bills in her hand, along with a neatly folded $100 bill.

"Well, dear . . ." David seemed at a loss. "That's not what I meant. Why didn't you buy some clothes? That's what it was for. I mean, the things you have are . . ."

David stopped, feeling like he was about to make a social blunder. Lori was affecting him like no other woman had, not even Virginia. One night's sleep and a shower had restored a radiance that hadn't even come through in the photographs. He felt like a fool. "Go ahead and get some clothes," he said gruffly. "My poker game is still going."

When he quit the room, Lori felt like she would have done anything for him.

27

WALNUT CREEK AND THE OTHERS

"Who is John Oliver?" Gabriel asked skeptically. "I hope I'm not being too forward by asking, since it's only my life that depends upon it."

"My ex-brother-in-law," David said, refusing to rise to Gabriel's tone. "He's all right. I'll vouch for him."

"I'm not wild about Bruce, either," Gabriel persisted. "You know how I feel about that little fuck."

"All you have to do is work with him," David said, exasperated. "Nobody's asking you to take him to a dance."

"Yeah, well, you just better hope he doesn't take us to one."

"Gold has gone to eight hundred and two dollars an ounce," David said, knowing that Gabriel had acquiesced. "Maybe we should get some gold."

●

On February 28, 1980, three men walked into the Davidson and Licht jewelry store at 1258 Broadway Plaza in Walnut Creek, California, the hometown of Jimmy Smith. They walked in one at a time and examined the glass cases with the interest of prospective husbands looking for engagement rings. They had their hair combed back and one of them wore thick glasses with clear frames. They'd dyed their facial and head hair. When everyone was in place, the guns came out.

John Oliver waved at an elderly couple who'd stopped to admire some jewelry. They were puzzled when he motioned for them to enter the store, but did so and were seized from both sides at the door. Mrs. H. Isobel Oldfather told police she was unnerved when the smiling young man said, "You rich broad, I'll blow your fucking head off."

David watched John's performance with distaste. "Be cool," he snarled. Gabriel looked jumpy as well. He'd had a fistfight with Bruce the night before, as they were finalizing their plans.

"You don't tell me what to do," Bruce had told Gabriel, jutting his chin out and strutting. It had been too much for Gabriel. He'd jumped up and punched Bruce full in the face. David had made a mental note of the fact that Bruce had cowered under the assault. It was Gabriel David had had to throw backward against the wall. For a moment, he'd thought Gabriel might take him on, too.

"I can't believe you assholes," David had said. "The night before what might be the last day of our lives and you want to act like idiots."

The robbers at Davidson and Licht Jewelers left with $500,000 in merchandise. They used their normal fence in Madison, Wisconsin, and took 17 percent. Split four ways, it didn't last long.

PHOENIX, ARIZONA, MAY 22, 1980

David and Lori ate at her favorite Phoenix restaurant—the Velvet Turtle—as he finalized the plans in his own mind. Lori was under the influence and was being far too loud for David's taste. He didn't want anyone to be able to remember them. On the other hand, he recognized the futility of trying to silence her. Lori could be pretty crabby when she didn't get the attention she felt she deserved.

He left his food untouched. Several courses had been pushed aside as nervous waiters tried to decide whether to remove them or not. David did not bother to solve their dilemma. He waited for Lori to spend herself, then threw a couple of $100 bills on the table, and helped her out. Back at the hotel, he called Doug.

"Everything set?"

"What do you think?"

"I think I'll recheck the guns."

"Suit yourself, secret agent man," Doug said and hung up.

●

Doug entered Jewels by G. Olsen at 2047 E. Camelback Road in tandem with Gabriel, who had driven to Phoenix from Flagstaff after renting a car using his MasterCard.

Doug watched Gabriel engage a salesclerk in viewing rings while Doug got Neal Yukolis, another employee, to open the cases that contained the porcelain.

"What pieces do you already own," Yukolis asked pleasantly.

"I already have a Boehn and Cybis piece," Doug said. He glanced at the pieces on display and decided they would not be taken for his collection. They were of inferior quality.

Doug watched John Oliver place the black briefcase containing the police scanner on a counter and saw David move to the back of the store. As always, Bruce entered last, hanging by the door. John pulled his gun out first. The rest came out immediately. A half dozen employees were herded to the back of the store as the jewelry came out of the cases.

The men spent twenty minutes in the store, then sashayed out the front door carrying shopping bags like any other customers. They split up. David and Gabriel walked to the blue Ford Torino, got in, and started the motor.

"Where the hell is he?" Gabriel groused over John Oliver's tardiness. They needed to get the hell out of there.

"He went out the wrong exit," David said quietly, watching John stumble around the parking lot, peering at every blue Ford in sight.

Gabriel followed David's gaze, noting a couple looking at them with irritation because they were blocking a handicapped entrance to the shopping center. "Jesus," Gabriel said. "Let's get out of here."

"We're not leaving John," David said firmly. "He'll never get out of here if we do."

Angry, Gabriel leaned over and honked the horn.

"That should attract enough attention to put us away for twenty years," David said mildly.

"He sees us, doesn't he?" Gabriel said irritably. "It's better than sitting here waiting for the cops to show up and cuff us to the back of their bumpers."

●

The take was $1.5 million retail, and David wanted to fence the jewels in Las Vegas. The percentage, he argued, would be higher there and they could use Doug's connections.

They stayed at The Dunes, where Lori was now working as a hostess and Doug's brother, Dale, was working as a card dealer to put himself through college.

They paid an appraiser $1,000 to evaluate the gems—just so they could be sure they wouldn't be taken by a fence they'd never met. It took eight hours for the man to appraise the merchandise and The Boys amused themselves by drinking and entertaining hookers as he went over each piece. David felt he'd done such a good job, they gave him a diamond ring as a bonus.

But the deal went bad when the anticipated fence was blown away in a high-speed chase and rumors in The Dunes had it that the movers in town were unimpressed by The Boys' reputations. You didn't move into Las Vegas with a haul that big without offering a cut to the locals. David decided it was time to leave, discretion being the better part of valor.

●

Back in Des Moines, David advised everyone to sit on their shares until things cooled down. Everyone should go back to work, picnics, and kids. The problem arose because Mike Gabriel had a new wife and he'd run out of money treating her well.

On August 17, 1980, Robert H. Horton of Horton-Methlie Jewelers contacted the FBI. Michael Gabriel, whom he'd done business with for years, had come into his shop with a bag of pretty impressive jewelry. Horton was goosey. Was the FBI using Gabriel to set him up? No, the agency responded. But Horton now needed to set Gabriel up to stay out of trouble himself.

Gabriel wanted $17,000 for the first batch of jewels. Horton didn't have the cash. Roxanne Conlin would later say it was the buy for which Agent Dave Oxler dug into his own pockets to provide the cash. The FBI bugged the shop.

Gabriel and his wife, Deborah, returned to Horton's shop at around 3:30 that afternoon. Horton explained that his contact was in town for only a short time and there was no time to dicker about price. Gabriel thought it over. He'd been trying to up the price to $18,000, but now changed his mind.

"Can I use your phone?" he asked Horton.

"Sure. Please," Horton said.

Gabriel dialed, then said, "Hey, is D around? Sit tight. I'll be right over." He turned to Horton, saying, "I'll give you a phone call in about thirty to forty-five minutes."

When Gabriel returned, the FBI was waiting.

●

David was lying on his couch, trying to decide what to do with the rest of the day. There was still enough light to do a quick round of golf. He checked himself. Cutoff sweatshirt and not-too-clean blue jean shorts. Not exactly presentable, but for the public golf course down the street, it would be okay.

Suddenly, Bruce rapped at his screen door. "Let's go for a drive, David," he said.

David was actually glad for the company. He'd spent the last few days chasing people away and was ready for companionship. "Let's play a few holes," he said. He said it as a statement, not a suggestion, and Bruce readily agreed, as David knew he would.

David gathered his golf bag and slung it into the backseat. As Bruce backed out of the driveway, David saw a black sedan up the block.

"I've never seen that car around here before," he mused. He got alarmed when he noticed two other cars like the sedan parked along the street. "Those aren't neighborhood cars," he said slowly. "Those are heat cars. . . ."

"Oh, David, you're just so paranoid," Bruce said cheerfully. "Always seein' the worst in things."

"Drive slow," David commanded. "Drive very slowly to the golf course parking lot and pull up by the pay phone in front. We're gonna need lawyers and you better have done like I told you and put some money away for it."

David did not have to turn around to know the black cars were following. He didn't get a chance to drop his quarter in the phone box before a half dozen guns were leveled at him, accompanied by shouts of "Freeze!" He turned slowly, his hands in plain view. He'd told that idiot Gabriel not to fence his cut in town. He felt like he'd come full circle. Golf courses seemed to be the places to make arrests.

28

"Well," Larry Scalise, David's attorney, was saying, "our friend Mr. Oxler gave himself enough rope to hang with this time." He chuckled. "There was no positive ID on any of the lineups for either jewelry store robbery. Of course, two of them were a little ridiculous to begin with."

The two Scalise referred to were lineups for Mike See, who had been arrested along with everyone else after Gabriel's fencing exhibition. Of course, Mike had been nowhere near either Walnut Creek or Phoenix during the jewel robberies. In point of fact, he'd been playing cards with a municipal judge during one and in full view of his bookies at the racetrack during the other. The FBI had eventually confirmed the alibis, but not before Mike had spent some time in jail. David's mind had flitted momentarily to John Cline.

"I spend more time in jail for talking to you than I do for any insanity I've ever committed," Mike had complained, after David posted his bond. "You could have at least included me if you're going to get me arrested."

David turned to Scalise. They were sitting in the basement cafeteria of the Des Moines federal courthouse. David had an untouched tuna salad sandwich in front of him and Lori sat next to him, fidgeting. David had been trying to assure her he would not go to prison over the charges. She didn't seem to believe it.

"Of course," Scalise said, "I'm sure that guy in your lineup was merely coincidental." The attorney winked. David hated it when Scalise played at being a bad guy. Wasn't it enough that David paid him a fortune? Did he have to pretend he actually liked David?

"I don't know what you're talking about," David said wearily.

But he did. After the search warrants had been executed and some of the Phoenix jewels had been discovered in David's, Doug's and Bruce's homes, the FBI had been so confident of conviction that it had allowed the charged defendants to select their own subjects to stand in the lineups. David had promptly found an aging hippie of his size and build, paid him to cut his hair, and dressed him in the same disguise David had worn at the Phoenix robbery. The hippie was identified as the culprit by witnesses. He was not charged because both Conlin and Oxler knew who he was. It had been a hoot.

"Of course," Scalise continued, checking his watch, "the lack of witness identification does not take away from the evidence seized during the searches. The jewelers in question have positively identified the property. Not to mention Mike Gabriel being caught redhanded. And although Mr. Gabriel has not given a statement, I understand he will be charged out of state court in Arizona as well. They have him, as they say, by the short hairs. They could put him away for life by stacking the federal and state charges. That is powerful incentive to talk."

"I don't know nothin' about any jewelry robberies," David said tonelessly.

"Of course not," Scalise said impatiently. "But a man of your . . . experience might want to consider a quick plea. In and out. Plead to possession of stolen property—even interstate transportation. I could get you a deal for ten years. You'd only have to do five. It might save you a lot of time in case they come up with more evidence."

Lori sat upright, but didn't look at David. She didn't look all there, he thought.

"I'll let you know," David said.

●

On October 16, 1980, Sandy Wood was putting the finishing touches on the decorations for David's surprise birthday party. She'd been pretty pleased with herself, getting the huge bash ready all on her own. She'd shopped for food for fifty people and cooked, scrubbed, and cleaned without David's even finding the frozen cakes and baked hams. All of his friends and relatives had accepted her invitation enthusiastically. That made her feel good, too. They were all prosperous now and she felt like she might finally be accepted as David's future wife. Of course, she had not invited the Browns. Not that David had anything to do with Lori, naturally. She just felt they were from a different part of town.

The party had been scheduled to begin at 7 P.M. and at around 10 P.M. she called David's cousin, Ken. No guests had arrived. The phone hadn't rung. The candles had burned down to their holders.

"Sandy," Ken said gently, "don't you know David is gone? He jumped bond this afternoon. Didn't anybody tell you?"

There were no words to describe her agony as Sandy replaced the receiver, sank against the wall, and stared dry-eyed at her crepe paper decorations until the sun rose. He would, she knew then, call her from South America or some other exotic place and send her a plane ticket. She just knew it.

●

David called Lori to let her know, then began packing. They'd set a firm trial date for him. There would be no deal and he wasn't interested in one anyway. He had no intention of returning to Leavenworth.

Bruce had shown up and become hysterical when he'd realized David's intentions. "You're just going to leave?" he shrieked. "You're just going to leave me here?" He was crying, David thought, like a girl. "I can't go to prison alone," he wailed. "I've never been to prison."

"Then come along, if you want," David said. The offer was made as much from practicality as sympathy. A good mechanic would be useful on the lam.

Doug had also decided to go. The offer had not been extended to Gabriel, who—David thought—would not fare well as a fugitive. Gabriel's background was too different. He would miss things David had never had. His feelings would be hurt, but David did not think they would squeeze him on the charges in the way Scalise thought. He would do a few years and get out. David was wrong about that, too.

●

"We need some traveling money," Doug said matter-of-factly. "I figure the Dahl's supermarket on the west side is good for at least twenty thousand. And the manager's office is in front. They must not be reading the papers real well. Or else their management seminars leave something to be desired on the issue of the criminal element."

"Well," David said dryly, "if people won't educate themselves, I guess they'll have to have it done for them."

Bruce looked around nervously. "What is the plan here? I mean, maybe it isn't a good idea. We might get caught and we've got charges. . . ."

"Shut the fuck up," Doug said. "Geez, you are a whiny son of a bitch. How do you think we're gonna put gas in the car?" To David, Doug said, "I hate this fucker. Why are we taking him?"

David didn't answer.

●

David and Doug left Bruce in the car when they walked through the electronic doors at Dahl's at 8 A.M., just after the armored truck left and the money bags sat on the front checkout counter. Shotguns swung unobscured against their sides and women pushing carts full of new-ly squeezed grapefruits and pinched apples stared curiously at the ski-masked faces. What pranksters, these kids today were, their expressions said, as they clucked their disapproval and moved to their cars.

Doug hoped to discourage the notion that the situation was funny when he rammed his shotgun into the chest of the first man he en-countered, knocking him to the floor. Doug knew the man was too stunned to present any more trouble, and wheeled the gun in an arc, looking for sudden movements.

From the corner of his eye, he saw David leap the counter and land flat-footed in front of the terrified store manager.

"If you don't mind," David said softly. He indicated the money bags with his shotgun.

Puzzled shoppers watched as two men in ski masks carrying shot-guns walked calmly from the store, got in a car, and drove away. The whole episode took thirty seconds. The take was $15,000.

●

They meandered around the country, sometimes splitting up, some-times traveling together. David once threw his $1,800 watch at Bruce's head, shattering it against the car windshield because Bruce would not stop needling Doug. Bruce had been calling Doug a pansy just be-cause he liked fancy foods and understood art. In fact, Doug had al-ready told David he'd nearly killed Bruce some weeks before, after Bruce had made a spectacle of himself on an airplane. It was sheer luck that the pilots had not radioed ahead to have them arrested. If fewer people had been on the tarmac, Doug would have pulled the knife he always carried and taken care of the situation. David did not know the truth, but he'd understood the gravity in Doug's eyes.

●

In Februrary of 1981, the Mid-States' Bank in Denver, Colorado, was relieved of $98,000. One of the six tellers taken hostage that morning told police a robber apologized for making her bonds too tight, and released her. An off-duty policeman moonlighting as a security guard had his .45 returned to him after he told the robbers the weapon had sentimental value from World War II.

"I'm gonna have to unload it," David had said mischievously as he placed it on a counter, "so you don't shoot us on our way out."

The robbery was not associated with David, Doug, or Bruce until April 22, 1981, when the First National Bank cash depository was robbed in Tucson, Arizona.

PART FOUR

A MERRY CHASE

29

On April 25, 1981, two days after TUCROB, Bert Williams called the FBI.

David was leaving Cheyenne, after having seen his photograph in the paper. He'd gotten a perm, and was on his way to Denver, after making arrangements to have the yellow Ford cut up and scattered to the four winds.

Bruce—not yet arrested—was in Des Moines, depositing $450,000 with his mother with instructions that she bury it in the backyard. Another $400,000 went to his father, Harry Flowers. The rest was in a suitcase, which he would take with him to Miami and his ill-fated encounter with David.

Doug was in California with Linda and would soon join David in Miami for what he thought would be a private parting of the ways.

None of them could have imagined what the Williams call would mean. The cops couldn't even believe it, though it would take some time to sort it all out. A true fluke.

A free-lance advertising man, Williams had a built-in flair for the dramatic. On April 10 of 1981—twelve days before TUCROB—he was working on a proposed account that could mean lots of money for him. It was a big deal. Lots of potential and he wanted to do it right. He had a 9 A.M. appointment at the Safari Club to discuss it.

Williams had a pristine, restored 1962 Corvette, which he'd been unable to drive for a while due to a skiing accident. He'd broken his leg and couldn't manipulate the clutch. April 8 was one of the first days he'd been able to drive the cherished car to work.

He told the FBI he left his office at 8:45 for the meeting but felt goosey as soon as he'd shut the door. Worse than goosey. He was downright terrified. He couldn't understand why. He began looking around, thinking there might be somebody lurking nearby waiting to crack him one on the head. There was nobody. So he started to the car.

He hadn't gotten there when he noticed a large American-made sedan driving very slowly through the parking lot. There were three men inside. His first thought was that they were after his car. He made his way to the car, hoping to get there first. The sedan passed just as he arrived at his Corvette and he had eye contact with the driver. Williams later said the driver had the most "scary" eyes he'd ever seen.

At the same time, he realized the men in the car weren't looking at his Corvette at all. They were looking up the street, toward the First National Bank branch Williams usually frequented. They seemed to be gesticulating in that direction as they passed him and headed out into traffic.

Something told Williams to follow the car. He took the license plate down on a file folder lying in his passenger seat. It was the folder for his appointment at the Safari Club.

Williams didn't think much more about the incident until the twenty-fifth when he was cashing a check at the branch office. He noticed all kinds of cops in there. Guys in suits talking to everybody and anybody. They were certainly detectives. Possibly FBI. He asked the guy in front of him about it and he said there had been some kind of huge robbery there three days before. It clicked in Williams's head that the license plate might be of help. It was just a hunch.

Agent Andy Oldham went out to see Williams at his office the next day. He brought along a lineup album containing twenty-four mug shots—photos of Grandstaff, Brown, Fennimore, and David's ex-brother-in-law, John Oliver, mixed randomly with twelve other total-ly unrelated men. This is standard police procedure in any law enforcement agency's handbook. Every precaution is taken to make sure suspects are not suggested by a photo lineup. Generally, the au-thorities try to find photos of men who look similar to the suspects, to make certain witnesses are making an accurate identification. As a rule, three photographs are presented for each suspect photo. The album had been shown to dozens of witnesses who had come forward after the robbery, claiming to have seen the van and its occupants. None of them had been able to make an identification.

It so happened Williams had missed the deluge of Grandstaff & Co. mug shots that had been littering the front pages and evening news. When Oldham showed him the photo album, he could not positively identify anyone, but he did point out five men whose features—in one way or another resembled features of the three men he'd seen in what he now said was a mid-sixties, light tan Pontiac Catalina. Williams noted that the car didn't appear to be in too good a condition.

Photo three, he said, appeared "similar" to the driver of the car. Also, number seven had eyes similar to the driver's, although the hair was all wrong. Williams also selected number eight. He lingered around the photo of John Oliver and also thought number fifteen had a forehead that struck him as familiar. Number fifteen was David Grandstaff. However, Williams said he could not positively identify anyone. The agent was disappointed.

But there was an up side. Williams had the file folder with the li-cense plate written on it and he gave the number to Oldham.

The FBI ran the license plate. It was a late 1970s gray Oldsmobile, which came up clean of warrants and tickets. It was registered to a Tom Kline of Phoenix. The agents would have called Tom Kline even though the car described by Williams was pretty badly off the mark. But when they couldn't find a Tom Kline, they decided to go one step further and find the previous owner. It was a little too odd that Tom Kline's address hadn't panned out. The man who'd owned the car be-fore Kline was one Artie Eliason, a quiet Phoenix car mechanic who was stunned when the FBI showed up on his doorstep.

A very nervous Eliason explained that the Olds had been in a car crash and towed to the station where he worked. A repair estimate was given that exceeded the car's worth. The car's owner had stalled and stalled on giving the go-ahead and the car sat in the station for months. Finally, the disgusted station owner was going to have it towed off for scrap. Eliason called the Olds's owner, offered him fifty dollars, and got himself a wrecked Olds, which he carefully, on his own time, repaired. He paid the most attention to the mechanics of the thing so the car would run well for potential buyers. He would worry about the aesthetics later. Anyway, he hoped to make a few extra bucks off the Olds. He'd done it before and now he hoped to God there was nothing illegal about it. The FBI guys just told him to go on with the story.

Eliason ran an ad in the *Arizona Republic* and several days later this guy named Kline showed up with another guy. Kline looked the car over as if he knew exactly what was going on. He didn't seem to care about the little dents and whatnot that Eliason hadn't gotten around to. It was funny, because that's what most people cared about. This guy was looking at the engine, the suspension, the working mechanics of the thing, and then he just got his head out of the hood and started to dicker. Kline knew what he was doing there, too. It was like he was a good old horse trader, checking the teeth, the hooves, and the flanks and coming out satisfied but not about to show it. Kline didn't get excited. He looked off at the right moments and pointed out flaws Eliason knew were there. Still, Eliason could tell the guy was ready to buy and wasn't all that concerned about the small issues raised. Eliason knew he did good work and he could see Kline knew it, too. He thought the dickering was a matter of principle, which Eliason could respect.

Eliason figured he'd put fifty man-hours into the thing and several hundred dollars in parts. He and Kline ended up agreeing on $1,800, which meant a nice profit for Eliason, and he was pretty pleased with the whole thing.

To make everything sweeter, Kline pulled out a wad of cash. Eliason told Kline he was going to have to go down and get the transfer paperwork completed at the Department of Motor Vehicles. Kline nodded and explained that he had to go, but he wanted the car title sent to his companion, Gene Kreuzinger, also of Phoenix. Eliason had hardly noticed this guy Kreuzinger until then. He couldn't even remember what he looked like. He'd just stayed in the background, shifting from foot to foot, not looking very happy. But Eliason couldn't see any harm in sending the title to an address other than the one on the title. What made the difference? The man had cash. He had ID. What could he, Eliason, do? Turn down the deal? The agents told him not to worry and left. Eliason stared after them with a queasy feeling.

It did not take the agents long to find Gene Kreuzinger. Kreuzinger was married to Bruce Fennimore's cousin and he was legitimate. He was listed in the phone book and working his own construction business. In Arizona, the season lasted year-round, if you could find men to stand the summer heat. There was more money to be made, so he'd relocated from Iowa.

Gene Kreuzinger was not unaware of The Boys from Iowa, although he didn't know any of them personally except Bruce. He had to admit, though, he found them all a little exotic. Intimidating, yes. Kreuzinger would never consider doing what they did. But they *were* real outlaws. When Bruce informed him that he was using the alias Tom Kline, Kreuzinger felt like he was having a little taste of the whole thing. Kind of exciting. Of course, he knew Bruce was on the lam. Everybody in a ten-state area knew.

He and Bruce and Jack Donlan would go out to the bars and mess around. His wife didn't even seem to mind. Bruce was the big man, lifting large bills from his wallet, pinching the waitresses. Kreuzinger had a decent time with Bruce and he didn't balk when Bruce asked to use his address for the title of the gray Olds. Didn't balk, at least, until the FBI showed up on his doorstep.

When the agents arrived all pressed and stern, Kreuzinger offered no resistance. He told them everything. He told them about the Tom Kline alias and gave the agents some idea of where Bruce might have stayed while he was in Phoenix. He told them he thought the car might be in San Diego. That's where he believed Bruce had flown in from. He agreed that he'd bought the gray Olds with Bruce but denied knowing anything about what the car would be used for. In fact, he didn't. The First National Bank had not yet been selected when the car was bought.

The Olds's license was now entered in the FBI's national crime computer as a high-priority wanted vehicle. On April 28, Tucson agent Larry Bagley called San Diego agent Jerry Barnett, asking if he would mind taking a spin through the parking area of the San Diego airport on his way home in an attempt to locate the Olds.

It was close to quitting time and Barnett was pretty tired. The airport was way out of his way home, so he tried to locate some of his people who might just happen to be in that area. There weren't any, so he tried to call in some favors from the local police department, but they were having none of it. They were all on their way home, too, and Bagley hadn't said the car was actually there. He'd just said it was a possibility. Nobody wanted dinner to get cold over a possibility.

Sighing, Barnett got his jacket. He'd known Bagley for twenty-five years and they'd worked together some. He guessed it wouldn't hurt for him to take an extra hour and look. Bagley would have done it for him. As it turned out, Barnett got lucky. He spotted the car in the first row he searched.

The windows were down and Barnett noticed a musty smell, as if the vehicle's interior was moldering in dampness. He didn't touch anything yet. He would need a warrant. But under the front passenger seat was what appeared to be the handle of a gun.

The FBI got a warrant for the car the next day. Inside they found a matchbook from the American 6 Motel in Tucson, a receipt from the Holiday Inn South in Tucson, and a Beretta .380 automatic—the gun Bruce had insisted on keeping when they left San Diego. Later, Barnett would discover that a San Diego undercover agent named Flores had run that plate the day after the robbery.

The gun was traced to People's Sporting Goods Store in Cheyenne, Wyoming. FBI agents were dispatched to question the owner, James Everett. Everett told Agent Judd Boher that a Tom Kline had purchased a .357 Colt Troop revolver on Christmas Eve of 1980. He'd also sold a Beretta .380 on that date to a George D. Bradley, who was using a Wyoming driver's license for ID.

Boher knew his suspects were well known visually to plenty of FBI agents around the country. Agents are often transferred from city to city and, in this case, there was an Agent David Boyer in Cheyenne. Boher got a duplicate of the Wyoming license registered to George Bradley and showed it to Boyer. Boyer said George Bradley was most certainly David Grandstaff. He'd seen him many times on the Wanted walls when he worked in Iowa.

Next, the FBI fanned out to sweep the hotels mentioned by Kreuzinger and on the receipts in the Olds. On April 30 they served a warrant on Archie Springfield, manager of the Holiday Inn nearest Sky Harbor Airport in Phoenix. They wanted his registration receipts, which innkeepers are required by law to hold for two years.

From Springfield they obtained registration cards signed by both Tom Kline and George Bradley in February 1981. The Tucson motels yielded cards for Bradley, Kline, and a Carl Simmons, which the FBI surmised was Doug Brown. Bradley listed a Buick with a license number and when traced, it was learned that car had been sold months earlier in Phoenix to a George Bradley. The license plate had also been recorded at the Tucson International Airport in the months before the robbery, along with the van painted like a telephone truck.

The receipts and the Olds, which were heavily fingerprinted, yielded the partial prints of David Grandstaff. Bruce had not wiped the car down as David had ordered.

Now they had Fennimore and Grandstaff together in Cheyenne and possibly Tucson and Phoenix. There was a problem, though. It was thought that Fennimore, Grandstaff, and Brown were probably traveling together, since they'd all jumped bond on the Phoenix robbery case. It would not be unusual for them to be in the same motels and none of the dates were close to the month of the Tucson robbery. If caught, they could charge them with gun and bond violations, but not with armed robbery. There was still no evidence of that.

They could not place their men in Tucson with any certainty. There were no incriminating fingerprints. There was no eyewitness identification. There was no trace of the money, nor would there be. The money had been unmarked. And The Boys were still missing in America, a fact that was making the American Bankers Association very nervous.

Bert Williams, however, was thrilled. The discovery made him a leading contender for the $25,000 reward offered by the American Bankers Association. He'd read about the reward in the papers after realizing that there had been a robbery at his bank. He and his wife discussed the situation far into the night.

The day after the car was discovered, newspapers and TV ran mug shots of the four wanted men again. After seeing them, Williams felt certain that these were indeed the men he'd seen in the car. Of course, there were four men wanted and he'd only seen three, but that didn't matter. One of them might have been eating breakfast or something.

After that, he began keeping a scrapbook and a diary on TUCROB. It was possible, he thought, that his story might make a good TV movie or even a full feature film. The Man Who Caught Jesse James sort of thing. Just in case he was approached, he wanted to have a full and accurate accounting of what had happened. In any event, he'd certainly be a star witness at a trial.

Williams made sketches of the parking lot and the men he thought he'd seen, which did not look like any of the photos in the FBI lineup album. He collected every newspaper article he could find on TU-CROB. He made diary notations of his contacts with lawmen and his personal ruminations about the matter. It was an exercise that would come back to haunt him.

Meanwhile, the authorities couldn't believe their good luck that came from one paranoid advertising man worried about his Corvette. Still, there were fundamental flaws in identifying the bank robbers. The FBI kept John Oliver on the list only because Charlie Virgil had been so dead sure there had been four robbers instead of the three described by the two bankers. Oliver had skipped town on a separate case and at a different time than Grandstaff, Fennimore, and Brown, but that didn't mean they couldn't have hooked up somewhere.

In any event, Roxanne Conlin was confident that Grandstaff, Fennimore, or Brown would surface somewhere. There were literally hundreds of agents aware of the case from coast to coast. The Boys couldn't avoid a dragnet like that forever.

30

On April 28—six days after TUCROB—the FBI was running down hotel receipts and car plates when Kathy Faller called her mother. She'd seen the mug shots of Grandstaff, Fennimore, Brown, and Oliver flash across the TV screen again. The attractive, blue-eyed, auburn-haired waitress now thought they rang a bell.

"I think I might have waited on those guys at Pinnacle Peak," she said.

"Well," her mother responded, "you better call the cops."

Faller called the 88-CRIME hot line, an anonymous tipster line set up by the Pima County Attorney's Office for informants. If the information offered garnered an arrest or a conviction, the tipsters were eligible for a reward. Kathy was not overly pleased when the operators asked her name, but she gave it anyway. There was no other way for the police to establish if she had information or not.

Faller wasn't due to work until the dinner hour. Her hours varied at Pinnacle Peak, but dinnertime made for the best tips. The steak house on Tucson's east side was enormously popular. Dimly lit and furnished with picnic tables covered with red-and-white-checked oilcloths, the restaurant offered on its menu three cuts of steak along with some pork ribs and chicken. The meal came with beans, salad, and bread and that was it. There was no dessert. At one time, anyone uppity enough to wear a tie to Pinnacle Peak had it snipped off by a hostess. The ceiling beams were covered with snipped ties that had been tacked up, some of them looking like they came out of the sixties. Some people objected to the practice, but the meat was excellent and the table turnover high. Faller estimated she waited on anywhere between seventy-five and eighty people on an average night.

FBI special agent Carl Gosting arrived at her house around 2 P.M. that day, accompanied by Tucson police lieutenant Jerry Reeves and Detective Michael Garigan. After the introductions went around, Gosting removed four photographs. The exact same photographs that had been flashed on the news and were at that very moment staring from the front page of the *Arizona Daily Star*, which was lying on Faller's coffee table in plain view of everybody.

Gosting wanted to know if these were the men Faller had waited on approximately a month before.

Garigan, a sixteen-year veteran of the police department, was disturbed. It was not approved policy to show potential witnesses only the photographs of the suspects. Particularly photographs that had just appeared in the press. In fact, Faller's 88-CRIME call had indicated that she'd seen just those photographs on television. It now seemed obvious that she'd also seen them in the paper.

Garigan did not approve of the procedure, but he said nothing. It was an FBI case. He and Reeves were just along for the ride. Still, it bothered him because he knew other witnesses had seen a police standardized book of twenty-four photographs. The lineup was available, but no firm identifications had been made from the book. Now Gosting was asking Faller if these were the men she'd waited on.

Faller held the photos like a hand in a poker game, studying each one. She ruled out Oliver. She'd never seen him before, she said. In fact, she'd only ever seen three men and they weren't always together. They'd only been together once, as she recalled, and then had come in two or three more times in pairs. One thing she was sure about, the one called Fennimore had always been there, and he'd been pretty obnoxious. He'd asked her out. When she told him she was married, he'd said that was just fine. He was married, too. Then he'd made a rude remark about the size of the diamond in her engagement ring. Was her husband so cheap, he couldn't get her a decent diamond? Faller was pretty angry.

The other thing she remembered was that this guy, Fennimore, always paid with $100 bills. One time, she'd brought the change. A $50 bill, a $20, and a $10. Fennimore had spread them out on the table like a card deck and asked her to pick the one she wanted for a tip. He said they had plenty more where that came from. Faller didn't say which bill she'd picked.

Garigan was even more concerned when Gosting did not go into specifics about the other two photographs. Faller had only said that she thought the other two had been with him. Didn't say she knew it or she actually recognized them. She just said the other two had been pretty quiet. She'd had no conversations with them. She thought another waitress might have waited on them as well.

The whole interview only took fifteen minutes from start to finish and Gosting was up and out of there. He told Faller he'd like to come by Pinnacle Peak that evening to see if any of the other girls might recognize the photographs. Faller said fine.

Faller was pretty excited. This was a real life cop story and it was obvious she'd picked the right guys. As soon as she got to work, she grabbed another waitress, Kimberly Aiken, and breathlessly spilled the whole story.

"The *FBI* is coming here tonight," Faller told Kim. "They want people to identify those guys we waited on who robbed the bank."

"Which guys?" Kim was pretty impressed.

"You know, the guys on TV."

Garigan accompanied Gosting to Pinnacle Peak that evening and again had pangs when Gosting took individual waitresses aside, showing them only the photographs of their top suspects. Again, he did not ask for physical descriptions. He didn't ask how certain any of the waitresses were. What he didn't ask said a lot more than what he did.

Several of the waitresses positively identified John Oliver. Kim Aiken identified all four men, even though Faller had said she'd only seen three at the most. Aiken said she remembered them because she'd once stopped by their table for a playful chat over some red tennis shoes one of the waitresses wore. She'd done that, she said, after Faller had mentioned they were so rude and obnoxious that she'd once run to the kitchen to wait for them to leave.

It didn't make a lot of sense to the Tucson cops, but it wasn't their investigation and they weren't about to start telling the FBI what to do. They just hoped they wouldn't be asked to tag along for the duration. There was plenty of other crime going on in town.

●

When Bruce flew to Miami after visiting Des Moines, he was unaware that David and Doug were there. He was also unaware that the FBI had just busted his alias wide open with the car sale and had a positive identification of him from a perky waitress he'd insulted in a steak house.

In Miami, he ordered a new Corvette, contacted Lee Pettit, and decided to play a little golf. It was a game David had taught him. He wasn't sure he liked it that much, but David seemed to think it was important. Then again, David thought a lot of things were important that Bruce couldn't understand.

There was that time in that restaurant in Des Moines. David was always wanting to go to fairly nice restaurants and Bruce wasn't used to it. David rarely said anything, but Bruce could always tell he'd worn the wrong clothes. It was just the way David looked at him. Then, a few days later he'd make suggestions about where Bruce might want to shop. He even offered to go with him a few times. It was confusing for Bruce. What the hell was wrong with Levis, anyway?

And David did not tolerate loud behavior. This was really odd because David was seen as the one guy in Iowa you did *not* want to piss off. In all the places Bruce frequented before David agreed to let him drive, the toughest guys were the loudest and the most demanding. But David never raised his voice, not even when the service wasn't the best.

Then they were in this restaurant with David, his girlfriend Sandy Wood, Bruce's wife, Sue, and a few other people. Bruce had been feeling left out because nobody was talking to him, only to David. Maybe he'd raised his voice a little bit. He must have, because David gave him one of those warning looks when David's normally flat eyes turned into fireballs. Nothing else in his face changed. His eyes just seemed to glitter and it seemed sparks might fly out of them and catch your clothes on fire.

Bruce had turned his attention to Sue. She hadn't been very affectionate lately and he'd wondered about it. Also, she'd made a remark to the effect that Bruce should take some of David's advice about his clothes. So he called her a fat hog and said that was why he didn't want to touch her. The table went silent.

"I think you should apologize to the lady," George Weir said quietly. Sue was on the verge of tears.

"Hey," Bruce said, thrusting his chin out the way it was done in real bars. "You're not fucking her. I am. I'll say what I fuckin' well please."

That had pretty much done it. David got up without a word, pulled the chair out for Sandy, and she also rose. He threw his cloth napkin down on the table in disgust. Cloth napkins, already. Another thing Bruce hated. He never knew what to do with them.

David was peeling off bills. The payment for a meal that hadn't arrived yet.

"I'm sorry, Sue," he said. Then he and Sandy just left. The others followed without a word.

It had really hurt Bruce's feelings. Just being left there like some kind of stupe. Now, Sue had filed for a divorce. She'd done it shortly after they'd left on the lam. Goddamn bitch. He'd given her nearly $10,000 from the Tucson robbery. It was damned ungrateful and it hurt him some, too.

Now in Florida, he was astonished to find David screaming at him again. It was true that David had asked him not to come back there, but where else was he supposed to go? He didn't know anybody outside of Des Moines and Phoenix. As for the Corvette, well, he'd always wanted one. He couldn't understand why David was so upset about it. It wasn't like the cops stopped every Corvette they saw.

Then David left abruptly. Bruce guessed David was angry.

He decided to call a waitress he'd met somewhere in his travels. He paid for a plane ticket for her to meet him in Atlantic City. Then he packed $30,000 in cash and got on a plane himself. If you've got it, flaunt it is what his real dad, Harry Flowers, always said. At least Harry liked him.

Bruce checked into the Playboy Club, showed the woman his suitcase stuffed with $30,000, and then they strutted downstairs to the gambling tables. He really liked the way the hotel gave them complimentary cocktails and food. It was the way he *should* be treated.

They each blew $7,000 that night on the tables. It made him feel better. Fuck those people and their damned manners. It was too high-falutin for Bruce. He was smarter than they were. He was cooler than they were. He wasn't going to get caught by any dumb cops.

After leaving Miami and Atlantic City, he'd go back to Des Moines. Where he'd be caught.

31

On May 25, a month after the Tucson robbery, an irritated manager of
The Car Barn in Los Angeles called the California Highway Patrol.
That Buick LeSabre had been sitting in his long-term parking lot near
the airport for almost a month and nobody had paid a thing on it. Lee
Foreman figured he was going to be out the money and he wanted the
cops to impound the car.

The CHIPS officers ran the Arizona plate first, discovering that it
was a top priority vehicle wanted by the FBI. The car was registered
to a George Bradley the FBI believed was David Lee Grandstaff.

Larry Bagley took the CHIPS call in Tucson and immediately contacted Agent William Stovall in Los Angeles. Stovall got a warrant
and went out to get the car.

It was as clean as driven snow. There were no prints anywhere. No
paperwork, no guns, nothing like what they got off the Olds in San
Diego. David had wiped the car down.

To make matters worse, there were no new leads. After involving
dozens of agents and hundreds of man hours, all they had for evidence
was a partial print from Grandstaff off the Olds found in San Diego,
a motel receipt, and the gun he'd bought illegally in Cheyenne. None
of those things proved anything about a bank robbery. They'd recovered some hair from the mask they found in the van, but without anything to compare it with, it didn't do them much good. This
investigation was shaping up to be one of the agency's more expensive forays and there wasn't a lot to show for it. They didn't even have
their suspects in custody. They had no idea where they were.

Then in late May, Roxanne Conlin got a call from the FBI office in
Des Moines. One of their paid informants had needed a little extra

cash and had disclosed that Bruce Fennimore was back in Des Moines. Apparently he had been back in Des Moines for days, driving a spanking new $30,000 Corvette.

Conlin was pleased. For some reason, she'd always believed Fennimore would surface first, although she didn't necessarily believe the part about the car. No one would be that conspicuous.

Naturally, there would have to be surveillance set up in an attempt to locate him. If he was stupid enough to be driving a new Corvette, he might not be savvy enough to make the FBI the agents. But the others might be with him—at least she desperately hoped they were. It was a long shot, but one thing she was certain about, the others would not be driving Corvettes and they *would* be able to spot the agents.

She instructed the agents to rent cars from around town. Cars that looked nothing like automobiles commonly associated with police agencies. Even the agents joked about "heat cars"—the dark-colored, often cumbersome American sedans with no individuality to them. Even civilians could easily spot them. Conlin had always thought it odd that these cars were still used for undercover.

She also instructed the agents not to look like agents. FBI agents, many of whom are recruited out of college, have a tendency to look square-jawed and squeaky clean, as if they'd never even had a drink in their lives. It was part of an upstanding image the agency had carefully cultivated, but it worked against them when dealing with men who had spent their lives getting to know it. Paint caps. Coveralls. Blue jeans. These were the clothes Conlin suggested. The agents went to work, watching known haunts, cruising by the homes of friends, relatives, and known associates of Bruce Fennimore. It took them three days to find Bruce. Doug, David, and John were never seen once, nor was there any hint that they were nearby.

Conlin decided to arrest Bruce rather than follow him. She felt certain the others would not be back in Des Moines, at least not yet. They always came back eventually, but the Tucson robbery made some kind of an arrest imperative. The arrest, however, would be more difficult than simply finding him. All of The Boys were considered armed and dangerous. Now, they might also be desperate. Because they had never appeared desperate before, Conlin had reluctantly decided not to add them to the Ten Most Wanted list after the robbery. They had never demonstrated viciousness. But she couldn't be sure what they might do with that kind of money at stake.

She enlisted the help of local and state authorities. She received the cooperation of anywhere between thirty and fifty officers total, and on the night of June 3, they decided to act.

Conlin sat listening to the police radio some blocks away from the Merle Hay Mall. Bruce had pulled in there about 8:30 P.M. and was sitting in the Corvette, parked near the Stuart Anderson Cattle Company steak house. He was apparently arguing with his girlfriend, Theresa Shay, who had helped break up Bruce's marriage. Theresa had been the Fennimores' babysitter of long standing, caring for Bruce and Sue Fennimore's two daughters. As she developed into her teens, however, she'd interested Bruce in other ways.

Bruce and Theresa were sitting in the Corvette, parked close to the restaurant entrance. It was a touchy situation. Theresa was not part of any of Bruce's outside activities, as far as Conlin knew, and they couldn't risk hurting her any more than they could risk the well-being of people going in and out to dinner. Four of the FBI rented cars were positioned around the lot. One of them, a green Thunderbird, was stationed in the middle of the lot, to Bruce's rear. Conlin could hear from the whispers that the agents could see a lot of gesticulating and what looked like yelling going on in the Corvette.

Suddenly, Theresa got out and slammed the door, stalking off toward the restaurant. At that moment, Bruce looked around the lot in exasperation—an expression that changed quickly when he saw Agent Robert Reaney leaping from a van parked nearby with his gun drawn. Reaney yelled at Bruce to halt and identified himself but Bruce had already put the Corvette in reverse.

In the Thunderbird, Agents John Koziol and James Donlan saw the movement. Koziol, who was driving, threw his car into gear, squealing forward as fast as he could go, which he remembered ruefully later was not very fast. His intention was to ram the Corvette from the rear to prevent Bruce from leaving, but Bruce had already gotten the Corvette in motion. The two cars collided, spinning the Corvette around in a full circle, nearly crunching Reaney who was still trying to get to the driver's door. The spin left the Corvette's nose pointed at the parking lot exit. In a split second, the car was careening out of the lot with smoking tires and a rooster tail of sparks flying from its damaged rear end.

It took a while for Koziol to get the Thunderbird restarted. Its front end had been heavily damaged by the impact and was much worse off than the Corvette. Conlin heard him cursing as the engine coughed in protest. Other agents and the local police were already in hot pursuit, radioing madly to the other officers parked around the area. Conlin heard some of the agents laughing giddily as they took up the chase. There was plenty of adrenaline.

Koziol finally got his car started, but it wouldn't move very well. It chugged and balked along the city streets like a dazed fighter with a head wound. Meanwhile, Bruce was reaching speeds of 120 mph in residential streets as the cops tried desperately to figure ways to cut him off. At one point, he spun up onto a lawn, hitting several tricycles that had been occupied by toddlers ten minutes earlier. He turned his headlights out, hoping to become invisible, but eventually, his own car gave in to the wounds suffered in the lot and came to a halt. Grabbing two suitcases off the floor, Bruce vaulted several fences as cops from several agencies screeched to a halt in front of the disabled vehicle. Smoke rose and radios crackled hysterically as bewildered residents appeared on porches to watch a small army of men with guns drawn fan out, some going over the same fences and others looking for avenues to stop the escape.

Bruce threw the suitcases over another fence, hoping to retrieve them later. The woman who walked outside and saw them was the grandmother of Tucson detective Jeffrey Saunders, who at that moment was assigned to the Tucson bank robbery.

Bruce went in a different direction, but there were too many police and not enough places to go. Tired, frightened, and winded, he collapsed in a backyard. He was tired and sick at heart. The last six months had been a living hell. Far from being romantic, being on the run had been a nightmare of bad hotels, constant movement, and total loneliness. He missed his friends. He missed hanging around the auto parts stores, talking mindless crap. He hated not being able to show his face in familiar bars. Panting, he waited silently in the darkness. Surely they would find him. Incredibly, officers were all around him, but never saw him. He waited quietly.

A frustrated group of agents and officers began congregating on the streets in small clusters. It looked as if the son of a bitch had gotten away. They would continue a house-to-house search, but he might have actually evaded them. Not that he would get far. He would probably be picked up in a day or two. But for now, he seemed to have disappeared.

About a half dozen officers who had clustered at one end of the block were discussing the situation when a lone figure materialized in the chaos as if he'd been beamed in. He walked casually, in no hurry to reach them, but it was clear he was walking over to the group of lawmen. Alarmed, one of the cops ordered him to stop and leave the area. A police investigation was under way and it was no place for the curious.

"You don't understand," said Bruce. "I'm the guy you're looking for."

Shocked and completely unconvinced that he'd heard correctly, the cop yelled again for Bruce to clear out. Bruce repeated his message. This time, there was a reaction as the group leapt all over him. There was a brief struggle, during which Bruce protested constantly that there was no need. Then, in an abrupt change of heart, Bruce refused to answer any questions or provide an ID. It didn't matter. One of the cops milling around recognized him from previous arrests.

Conlin, listening to her radio, smiled. Then she went home. Much later, she would have other problems. Tonight, though, she would let Bruce stew. She was sure he would find accommodations at the Polk County Jail less than pleasant. It might help her in the the morning.

●

The morning of June 4 found Des Moines agent Dave Oxler in a good mood. An agent for twenty-five years, Oxler had been interested in The Boys for quite some time. Conlin remembered that he had even taken money from his own accounts to help out a sting operation. The Boys had not used their usual fence in a Phoenix jewelry store robbery. They had gone instead to Las Vegas where things really got fouled up after a series of gangland-style murders. The murders had made it impossible for them to get rid of their jewels, so they had come home. The FBI had been tipped off that Mike Gabriel had gone local, but they couldn't get any seed money to make the buy. Finally, they'd managed to put enough together with Oxler's personal help. They'd gotten Gabriel in the act, but searches of Grandstaff's, Brown's and Fennimore's homes turned up only marginal evidence. It had been enough to make the lesser charge of interstate transportation of stolen goods, but the men hadn't bothered to wait around for trial. Now, though, he had one of them in arm's reach and in serious trouble. They might be able to make Bruce cooperate.

Conlin also skipped her usual wake up with tea period and went right to the federal building interrogation room, where Bruce waited. His attorney, Tim Pearson, was waiting in the hallway outside the interrogation room. Conlin couldn't tell whether it was a good or bad sign that Pearson was there. She knew him, of course. And he might be there willing to deal. On the other hand, he might just be there to make sure Bruce didn't say anything he didn't want to. It was hard to tell. She'd just have to see. Conlin, Oxler, and several other agents entered the room. One of them threw the hood ornament from the wrecked Thunderbird on the table.

"You owe us for that car," the agent told Bruce.

"Hey, man," Bruce replied, "*you* hit *me* . Take care of your own problems. You should be talking about paying for *my* car."

Conlin thought Bruce looked very relaxed. Very self-assured. He did not seem the slightest bit interested in his surroundings, nor did he seem fazed by his situation. She thought him rather nice looking, in a cocky kind of way. She guessed him to be younger than the others. He was possibly in his early to mid-thirties with a mop of curly, black hair and striking, blue eyes. She wondered if the hair was permed. Some of the older mug shots showed the hair to be straighter. She introduced herself.

Bruce looked at her, tilting his chin upward. "I know who you are," he informed her.

"Bruce," Conlin began again, "we want to help you. You're in a terrible mess."

"Yeah, well, I've been there before."

"You're going away for a long time, Bruce. We want to help you with that."

"I want to see my lawyer."

"He's right outside, Bruce. You can see him whenever you want."

"Well, I want to see him now. Alone."

"Where are they, Bruce?" one of the agents broke in. "Where are David and Doug?"

Bruce stared at him. "I ain't sayin' nothin' until I see my lawyer."

Conlin nodded. It was a good sign. They brought Pearson in.

32

Near mid-June, Conlin was wondering what Bruce Fennimore was going to do. So far, Fennimore's overtures had not interested her much. He'd told all about the robbery, but they knew all that. It was no mystery where his money had come from. He'd said so—through his attorney—days after his arrest. When they'd picked the suitcase with $400,000 up at Harry Flowers's house, Fennimore had folded completely, naming Grandstaff and Brown as his accomplices. Flowers had also said Bruce had done the robbery with Grandstaff and Brown, but hadn't reported it because he was afraid of the two free men. Brown later ridiculed this assertion, scribbling in the margins of police reports, saying that he and Flowers had often won money from tourists at blackjack and that "I've always thought that old man's genes ought to be frozen for posterity." Conlin was actually more inclined to go with Brown's rendition.

Flowers, who owned an Emery Freight franchise, was Bruce's real father or stepfather or something like that. Nobody, not even Bruce, seemed sure about the relationship. One day Bruce claimed Flowers was his biological father and the next said something else. One thing was for sure, Harry Flowers did little to clarify the lineage. He had several houses and seemed financially well off. He'd posted a $40,000 bond for Bruce on the Phoenix robbery charge (which bail Bruce had forfeited when he went on the lam) but otherwise seemed more inclined to hang around with Doug Brown's gambling associates than with Bruce. It must have been weird for Bruce, growing up with a mother who told him nothing and her lover—a cop who taught Bruce the car-theft trade. It almost made Roxanne feel sorry for him.

Then there was Harry Flowers's innocent act when the FBI had come to retrieve the $400,000 Bruce had left with him days after TU-CROB. He first protested that he never guessed at any ill origins for the cash, then later said Bruce had called him and told him about it. Well, Harry Flowers was full of shit, Roxanne thought. Bruce probably called him from Tucson to report his accomplishment, hoping for approval. And the FBI suspected that The Boys used Flowers's shipping business to transport stolen goods. This would never be proven.

Actually, Roxanne herself had not fully realized the magnitude of the robbery until she posed for the press with the stacks and stacks of bound currency mounted several feet high on her desk, and that was just Bruce's cut. In the photograph, even she looked amazed.

Even the FBI was overwhelmed. They first attempted to hand count the cash taken from Bruce, then realized it could take them weeks to get it right. Three agents booked four seats on United Airlines from Des Moines to Washington, D.C. Three seats were in the agents' names, the fourth in the name of D. Bagg, which was the duffel bag needed to carry all the money. It was their little stab at humor.

A special, electronic money-counting machine was rented from a bank in Washington. It took nine hours to count the cash. The FBI fingerprinted every single bill with no results.

And herein lay part of Roxanne's problem. It didn't really make any difference to her that Bruce was talking—through his attorney—about the mechanics of the robbery. She needed *meaningful* information—to wit, where Grandstaff and Brown were. Maybe Bruce really didn't know where they were, but so far, he'd even refused to testify in open court in the event of anyone's capture.

She did not think that any of the more accomplished in the group would talk when they were finally caught, as they certainly would be. Based on the rap sheets she'd seen, she figured Grandstaff, Brown, See, and a half dozen others would sooner have their tongues ripped out than turn informant. Some of them had taken raps for crimes they'd never committed just to keep a friend out of jail. Even Michael Gabriel, whom she'd just successfully prosecuted for the Phoenix jewelry store robbery, had given information on himself only and then only through his attorney. His comments would be useless against the others.

But Bruce Fennimore. Bruce was different. First of all, his cocky demeanor did not fool her in the slightest. She could see the man was insecure. She suspected that he couldn't read. Every time she put a piece of paper in front of him, he pretended to peruse it, but there was no eye movement from left to right as if he were actually reading words. Then, he'd always ask for privacy with his attorney before answering. She guessed his attorney, Tim Pearson, was reading the documents to him.

Secondly, Bruce's rap sheet showed he'd never done any hard time. A little jail, yes. A little lying before the grand jury, which he'd done for George Weir. Roxanne actually found that understandable. If she were up against George Weir she might lie, too. Weir was nobody you wanted to piss off. The last man who'd tried to inform on George had nearly died. Someone had taken him into a field and shot him. Only he had managed to crawl through the weeds to relative safety before they could finish the job—or so the story went. There had never been a conviction or even a charge.

But mainly, Bruce looked to be a car thief. A petty, braggarty car thief who'd been mesmerized by the big guns in town. He'd tried for a long time to become part of the circle. Because of his driving skills and expertise at stealing cars, he'd finally been admitted. But he was not really in their league. Roxanne figured he was terrified of prison. And she had a lot of leverage. He'd confessed to the Tucson robbery and had the bond-jumping rap hanging from the Phoenix jewelry store. He was looking at fifty years. Yes, she had a lot of bargaining leverage.

But so did Bruce. True, they'd recovered his money. But the way the investigation was going, they were going to need him to testify to convict anyone else.

Roxanne had been doing a lot of ruminating about The Boys lately. When she'd first taken the U.S. attorney appointment, she'd assumed the people she'd be prosecuting would be *different* from the "good guys." She'd be able to spot them in the hallway and hear it in their voices. Their shifty, mean eyes would give them away. They'd look somehow *dirty*.

It was true that plenty of defendants did look unsavory. But The Boys didn't. They were well dressed. They were polite, at least in court. She knew that they were plenty abusive to the police, but she half suspected that cut two ways. But although she never really got to know Grandstaff or Brown well, she actually had become friends with some of the others. It had been a revelation to her that these people were, in fact, just like her in every way except their work. Outside of armed robbery, they were completely law abiding. They didn't even have traffic tickets.

When the decision had been made not to put the fugitives on the Ten Most Wanted List after the Tucson robbery, it had been based in part on the fact that they had never *hurt* anybody physically. After getting to know Mike Gabriel, Roxanne was convinced that the last thing they wanted was to hurt people and that's why the jobs were so carefully planned. No surprises. Nobody bursting in they didn't know about, endangering the whole enterprise. Still, she'd often wanted to ask them what they would have done if problems had arisen. They went in, after all, with loaded guns.

She had trouble thinking of Gabriel brandishing a pistol. A robust man with dancing, blue eyes, Gabriel was everybody's idea of the life of the party. Once, while she was trying to put him in prison, she'd slipped on the courtroom floor and he'd jumped up—a perfect gentleman—to steady her.

"Please be careful, Roxanne," he'd said. She'd seen no hint of sarcasm in his eyes.

During his trial, Gabriel chatted amiably with her. He was out on bond, working the restaurants he would surely lose, but he looked relaxed. Resigned might have been a better word. He was not going to run away like the others and Roxanne almost started feeling sorry for him.

When the Arizona authorities levied their own charges in the

Phoenix robbery, she refused to allow them to arrest him during his trial. They were stupefied.

"Excuse me, ma'am," said one incredulous officer who'd flown up from Phoenix. "We have a warrant here for his arrest. It's signed and it's dangerous to leave him out of custody, knowing he has these additional charges."

"He hasn't run yet and I don't believe he's going to," Roxanne informed them curtly. "I don't see any value in letting the jury know that he's been taken to jail, when this whole time they've seen that he's free. It could prejudice his case."

The two Phoenix cops raised eyebrows. "Counselor, isn't that *his* problem? You're the prosecutor here."

"I have as much interest in seeing that this case is not reversed on appeal as anyone. And let me remind, you gentlemen, that you are in *my* jurisdiction. It's *my* decision."

Roxanne didn't figure that anyone was too happy with her. Certainly not the two Phoenix cops who had to wait through the duration of the trial, glaring dourly at her whenever she walked by them. Gabriel remained out on bond until he was sentenced. In the interim, he threw a going-away party at the Chapter 11 bar, and invited Roxanne to attend.

"Are you crazy?" Oxler shouted when she said she might go. "That is just nuts. He could be lying in wait there for you. He could be trying to do anything. . . ."

"I don't think so, Dave. Besides, I have personal assurances from his attorney, who is an old friend of mine. We went to law school together."

"So what? I didn't say your friend was going to get you!"

In the end, Oxler went with Roxanne, fully armed and as mean as a snake. He didn't speak to anyone, but struck a menacing pose in a corner where he could see the entire room. Everyone ignored him.

"Thanks for coming, Roxanne," Gabriel said. "It means a lot to me."

"Mike, I don't mean to sound like a dope. But I just got done putting you in prison. Why on earth would you thank me? Why don't you hate me?"

Gabriel shrugged. "You were just doing your job. I don't take that personally. I did my job and I got caught. Why should I cry when I'm asked to pay the penalty? I always knew it was there. Nobody forced me to do a thing. I just like you, that's all."

Roxanne left, shaking her head. She had to admit, she was impressed. It wasn't often that she heard defendants talk like Gabriel. And she did feel bad for him. Not only did he now have this federal sentence, but he was going to get a state sentence as well when the Phoenix authorities got done.

She knew, as all prosecutors know, that part of the reason the Arizona charges were levied at all was to squeeze Gabriel. The Phoenix people wanted the other robbers. They would threaten Gabriel with a lifetime in prison over a period of weeks in an attempt to break him. The federal sentence was more than enough time to do for the crime he'd committed. But the state authorities would threaten to "stack" the sentences, forcing Gabriel to serve one after the other if he didn't turn the others over.

It was exactly what she was preparing to do with Bruce Fennimore.

●

On June 15, the FBI sent another telex to twelve cities and the director's office. It alerted agents around the country who had been scouring for clues on TUCROB that a deal with Fennimore was imminent. They needed the deal, because nothing else was turning up.

Law enforcement had expected problems. The Boys were suspected in a dozen major robberies nationwide and had been indicted for only one. The reason was, there was no evidence. No trails. No witnesses and no informants. Nobody in the community wanted to inform on The Boys. So after they'd found the car and gun in San Diego and traced the gun to Cheyenne, leads had dried up despite hundreds of interviews and countless man-hours. The investigation was shaping up to be one of the more expensive in the agency's history.

David and Doug were now the only remaining suspects in the case. The agency had been forced to drop John Oliver from the list when he'd been able to prove that he'd been in Springfield, Missouri, the day of the robbery. It was too bad. Oliver was suspected in a half dozen, minor unsolved robberies. Had they been able to nail him for TUCROB, he would at least get his just deserts.

John wasn't exactly on the lam like David and Doug. But he wasn't on the right side of the law, either. Since the $1.5 million Olsen jewelry store robbery in Phoenix, John hadn't worked much with David. He was now divorced from David's sister and some of The Boys felt that his exits from the job sites were getting a little too panicky. During the Phoenix robbery, he broke into a run in the parking lot, breaking a cardinal rule about nonchalant departures. David had never forgiven him for attracting the attention of a couple of construction workers. They weren't able to identify him later, but it was still a close call, even though John never got indicted for the Phoenix job. Mike See, who wasn't there, did.

●

Knowing it wouldn't do any good, Oxler contacted The Boys' friends and family members, all of whom knew and detested him. But it was generally felt that the TUCROB money would be shipped home in shoe boxes via one method or another. And somebody had to pick it up. Maybe somebody would slip. There was a chance.

Grandstaff's sister, Sharon, now a restaurant hostess, told him she hadn't heard from David in eight months and didn't expect to. End of interview. Sandy Wood, an old girlfriend of David's who managed a restaurant, told the agents she had nothing to say as soon as they identified themselves. She slammed the door. Kelly Grandstaff and his wife, Pam, a house painter and a schoolteacher, respectively, ordered the agents off their property unless they could produce a warrant. Mike See, one of the original clan, laughed in their faces.

Oxler then turned to the Brown clan. Dale Brown, Doug's younger brother, refused to speak. Lori Brown was a real long shot. Not only was she Doug's sister, but she was now David Grandstaff's girlfriend. Oxler turned to Clyde Brown, the clan patriarch.

Clyde Brown was a well-known Des Moines character who made his money running bars. Rotund, shrewd, and unflappable, he was affectionately called "Brownie" or "One-Eye Brownie" because his left eye was glass. Clyde was generally known for his quick-buck stories, but no one held it against him because it was a well-known fact and everyone had fair warning.

Officially, Clyde listed his occupation as an aluminum siding or tombstone salesman. No one who knew Clyde questioned his flexibility.

Clyde had been involved in few violent episodes. The ones he had been in were directed against him. On one occasion, one of his best friends set him up to be robbed at a poker game he was to host. The starting pot was around $25,000 and Clyde was held at gunpoint for several hours until all the players arrived to have their pockets emptied. Clyde eventually found out who had set the whole deal up—and taken the money. But it didn't prevent him from playing with the man again. Clyde did not believe in grudges. Money could be made or lost anywhere. It was easy.

When Oxler showed up at his house, Clyde was not particularly concerned. Oxler had been there before and he was not difficult to handle. The man was so obsessed, he didn't think straight. As a gambler, Clyde knew obsession was an unaffordable pastime. He didn't allow it in himself but was perfectly pleased to take advantage of those who did. Clyde invited Oxler in graciously and offered him a drink. Oxler declined the alcohol but accepted an iced tea.

"So what brings you around, Dave?" Clyde asked congenially, when they were seated in the living room.

"Clyde, I think you know the answer to that question." What a joke, Clyde thought.

"I haven't seen my son, if that's your problem." Clyde shook his head sadly. "It's a darn shame about that boy. I tried and tried to bring him up right, but it just didn't take." Clyde sipped thoughtfully on his iced tea, warming to his subject. "Broke his mother's heart, too, poor thing. Especially when he got Dale involved in that *awful* jewelry thing out of Phoenix. And Dale and Lori were doing so well up there in Vegas. Dale going to school . . . Lori with a good paying job . . ."

"Let's skip the testaments about your children's characters, which are self-evident. And about your poor wife. I'll bet your leaving her for a younger woman did wonders for her state of mind."

Business was business, Clyde always thought, but this was getting personal. A man's family was not material for what Oxler had come for. He began to anger, then restrained it.

"Well, Dave, we all make mistakes, you know. Nobody is perfect."

"Certainly not in this neighborhood," Oxler replied tartly. "So I'm gonna ask you again, Clyde. Where is Doug? I *know* he's contacted you. He always does. Now don't make me go out and get warrants and phone records and things like that. Just tell me when you heard from him last."

The man was starting to lose it, Clyde thought, watching Oxler's cheeks flush. It was not going to be hard to push him across the line.

"Dave," Clyde said condescendingly, "I want to help. I really do. I just don't know how. If you want to go get pieces of paper, you go right on ahead. I certainly can't stop you. And you know I'll cooperate in any way possible. I have nothing to hide. I'm a simple businessman. More iced tea, Dave?"

Clyde watched Oxler explode. "Goddamn you! Goddamn all of you!" Oxler was on his feet, breathing hard and pointing. Clyde remained seated. "You tell that little son of a bitch I'm going to get him if it's the last thing I do! You tell that son of a bitch son of yours that I'm gonna get him and make sure he goes to prison for his entire life! Do you hear me? For his entire life, that son of a bitch."

Clyde put his glass down. He no longer felt like being civil. "I think you better get outta here now," he said.

Oxler left. Six years later, he'd have to recall his threats in open court.

●

On June 22, Bruce Fennimore finalized his deal with the government. The government would allow him to plead guilty to federal charges involving TUCROB and the Phoenix robbery. No other charges would be brought. He would plead to a total of thirty years, but the sentences would run concurrently, making him eligible for parole in six. He would also be allowed to keep his Corvette, purchased with the TU-CROB money, as well as several thousand dollars not connected to TUCROB.

In return, he would talk to the FBI through his attorney, Tim Pearson. He would not testify in open court. It was an old trick, Roxanne Conlin knew. Talking through a third party so that anything could be denied on the stand.

"I never said that, Your Honor," the wide-eyed defendant would say. "My lawyer must have gotten it wrong."

She agreed to the arrangement because it was the only conceivable way they could get anymore information. Within days of Fennimore's arrest, Pearson had come with an offer. If his client turned over all the money from Tucson, would they go easy on him? Well, Conlin had said, they'd *think* about it. No guarantees. After all, they needed some kind of a good faith effort here. She didn't bother to tell Pearson that they needed the money to make a case on him, even with a confession. Defendants can recant confessions.

●

The deal Fennimore got was not the one he wanted. He'd wanted a severely short sentence in a nice, country club prison somewhere in a balmy climate. Conlin could not see her way clear to do this because he could not—or would not—tell them where Grandstaff and Brown were. He would not testify against them when they were finally apprehended.

Fennimore's deal would later fall under quite a bit of scrutiny. On paper, he received thirty years, but the machinations of the federal parole rules meant he would serve less than half of that time. In addition, he was allowed to keep his Corvette and some cash that had obviously come from the robbery. His "friends and family" would not be prosecuted for their roles in the cover-ups and Fennimore himself would not be prosecuted for at least a dozen crimes he admitted to— implicating most of the other Boys—in the process of his negotiations.

In an uncharacteristic move, Bruce requested to be sent to Leavenworth Penitentiary, which had a reputation for violence second only to the Marion prison in Illinois. Perhaps he thought David Grandstaff's acquaintances there would protect him. In any event, he set about bragging over the TUCROB robbery immediately, also saying that he'd committed the crime with two "Latins" from Miami. Nobody in Leavenworth believed this, but the effort gained him a certain grudging respect, despite the fact that his personality grated on the highly structured hierarchy. And as Roxanne had suspected, Bruce quickly decided that prison was not his cup of tea.

●

In Walnut Creek, California, a pretty blond woman of twenty-four was arrested for narcotics possession. She had never been arrested before and she was frightened, nearly hysterical. She called her boyfriend, Jimmy Smith, who had cut the cars from the Tucson robbery to pieces.

"What will it take for you to let her go?" Smith asked the cops. A long-time felon, both he and the police were familiar with the procedure.

"I don't know, Jimmy," one cop said languidly. "It depends on what you've got."

"She's never been in trouble before. She's just a kid."

"I'm all broke up inside. I'm gonna cry any minute now. What have you got?"

Jimmy Smith had agonized over this decision for hours. But he loved the woman. "Maybe David Grandstaff."

The cop picked up a phone and dialed an extension. "Run me a David Grandstaff." He spelled it. He rocked in his chair as if Smith weren't present, waiting for the answer. When it came, his expression changed. He replaced the receiver carefully. "All right. Let's hear it."

Jimmy Smith drew a deep breath. He had no intention of giving David over. But it was true that he knew his whereabouts because David was funneling money through him. If he could figure out a way to give enough credible information without leading them to David, he might be able to get his girlfriend out of this jam. It wasn't going to be easy running the cops around in circles. Jimmy had no idea how it would work out.

33

THE SPRINGS

In early September, 1981, David Grandstaff traveled to Colorado Springs and treated himself to The Broadmoor, one of the most regal hotels in the country. It was out of character, but he felt he deserved it.

Having come to Colorado Springs from Las Vegas, David had seen enough of silly dreams for the time being. He was feeling solitary, even pensive, as he pulled his blue Monte Carlo under the curved, arched driveway to the mammoth hotel. Valets dressed in snappy, military-type uniforms swarmed around him, one accepting his keys and several going for the luggage in the trunk. David quickly took possession of a smaller suitcase, making sure he did not lunge for it in an obvious way. The others he left to the bellhops, tipping each man generously.

At the turn of the century, The Broadmoor was perhaps the most prestigious hotel in the country, and the yawning lobby still carried that feel. Ornate brocade wallpaper whispered stories of robber barons and gunfights. High-backed, velveteen chairs seemed more suited for grand ladies in flowing silk dresses with matching parasols than for the mostly elderly women who occupied them now. The men behind the brilliantly polished oak counters lacked only waxed mustaches to bring the setting back a hundred years.

No sound but the tinkling of china plates in the adjoining dining room disturbed the mood. It was a dining room that would serve fresh raspberries in a pure silver dish with heavy cream as an appetizer for breakfast. When he arrived in his room, there would be freshly cut roses on the antique desks, some of which alone were worth what a family of four might spend on an entire summer vacation. Dishes of mixed nuts, fruits, and candies would be replenished twice a day by invisible maids trained to sense when someone was in the room. And there would be no noise. No one at The Broadmoor talked loudly. There might be an occasional ballroom dance, but that would be as raucous as it would get.

By rights, David should have felt uncomfortable at The Broadmoor. The people staying there were, after all, the people he had railed against his whole life. They were the rich. The comfortable. The safe. They hadn't struggled and they had built their fortunes, he thought, on the backs of others.

But somehow, that did not phase him this time. He was neither concerned with their presence nor intimidated by the surroundings. It was as if they did not exist. He arrived in his room to find his bags neatly laid out and took one look out his picture window, which afforded a wonderful view of the mountains behind the hotel. There wasn't snow on them yet, he mused. It would come soon. Then he carefully removed his silk shirts, noting which ones required ironing. He hung everything in order—first shirts and then pants —and then arranged his Nunn Bush shoes on the floor. The dressier pairs had wooden shapers in them.

He took long walks around the hotel lake, roaming the sidewalk over and over again as he once roamed the walks at Leavenworth and Atlanta. He watched children feed the ducks and geese. Canadian geese seemed especially plentiful, he noticed, and he remembered he had read somewhere that they mated for life. Such an odd thing in animals, even human ones. He didn't believe it. He thought life mating was either the result of some shared misery or shared need. It was blind to call it anything else.

He thumbed through magazines in the lobby, casually watching the guests come and go. He sat sipping weak drinks on the back deck, basking in the autumn sun and letting his mind slip into nothingness. He found a gym and worked out, purging the Las Vegas poisons from his system. After three days, he was ready to go. He'd stayed too long already.

It had been five months since the Tucson robbery. He was tired of running. He had to start thinking about Connecticut and lying down for an undetermined amount of time. Still, he wasn't ready. It seemed too much of a step—too big of a break. He decided to risk calling Doug at Linda's apartment in Los Angeles. If they hadn't found him by now, it meant Bruce hadn't said anything about her.

He found a pay phone and called, telling Doug he must have a wrong number. He asked Doug if he'd reached 555-9957 and Doug said no, but the number David had given was the pay phone number he was calling from. Doug went to a pay phone on the corner and called back.

"It must be telepathy," Doug said. "Linda and I were just planning a vacation in Vail. We could meet you in Denver for a few days."

David said fine and placed one more call to Walnut Creek. He told Jimmy Smith where he was going and asked after his business interests. Smith said everything was fine, then inquired how long David planned to stay in Denver. No more than two days, David told him, without mentioning Doug. Jimmy Smith hung up, beads of sweat accumulating around his forehead. He would wait three days to call the FBI agents, who were still dangling a drug charge over his girlfriend's head. In three days, David would be gone. David always did what he said he would. The agents would find traces, but no bodies.

●

David checked into the Sheraton by the airport. Doug and Linda took a hotel down the street. The men met that first afternoon for a vigorous game of handball in the Sheraton's gym. The two bank robbers sweated and grunted in a competition much more serious than the matches played by the businessmen and lawyers around them. They wore sweatshirts and gym shorts instead of matched outfits and when they were finished, their sweat had soaked their clothing. They left the court without speaking to each other as some of the nicer players shot covert looks.

David changed his room from the ninth to the second floor. He didn't like heights. He believed the air was thinner at heights and thin air muddled the mind. He also did not like the lack of escape routes from the ninth floor.

He showered and dressed carefully, trimming his mustache to a razor line, then inspecting his shirt for unwanted creases. When he was satisfied, he left his room and descended to the lobby. He flirted for a moment with the girl in the flower shop, a potential affair he'd decided against. Then he left the hotel to meet Doug and Linda at Cafe Giovanni's, one of the finest restaurants in the West.

●

Jimmy Smith was again taking heavy pressure from the cops. They needed more information from him before they could do anything for his girlfriend. Sure, lots of his leads had panned out. They'd followed David's trail from Oregon and Washington to Miami and Arkansas, but they'd always been a day late and a dollar short. They needed action.

Smith whined that he was doing the very best he could. He had given them more than they'd gotten themselves so far, hadn't he? He couldn't be responsible for David's movements every second. The man was a wraith. But he thought that, just maybe, David would be in the Sheraton Inn in Denver on September 9—the next day. He wasn't there now, but he would check in on the ninth. The cops grunted and left. Jimmy sagged into his chair in terror. David was gone from Denver by now, he was sure. But the stress of this thing was killing him. And he was starting to be less and less afraid of the cops. David would never understand what he was doing and David was infinitely more scary than a jail sentence.

●

"I've decided to stay over a night," David informed Doug and Linda as he laid his napkin across his waist. A $250 bottle of wine rested on the table. "I figured we'd get pretty messed up here tonight and I didn't want to drive wasted."

Doug grinned at him. "What would make you think that?"

"You know, a highway patrol guy pulled me over on the way up here," David said languidly. "I was a little worried that one of us was gonna have a bad day."

"I hope you didn't expect it to be you." Doug was perusing the menu.

"I knew it wouldn't be me."

Doug grunted his approval. "What's next?"

"Don't know. Maybe go up to Connecticut. Maybe go back down to Miami."

"All this moving around is fucked, David," Doug said. "Sooner or later, somebody's gonna spot you. You better just go lay down like you planned. At least until they forget about this thing."

"They ain't never gonna forget about this, Doug. This is *dollar justice* we are talkin' about. You can rape their daughters and beat their sons and they'll give you five years. But, by God, don't take their money. That's an automatic twenty-five to life. I done time in the joint with guys that had crippled people for life and got out long before I did. Believe me. They ain't gonna forget."

Doug shrugged. "Doin' okay so far. I got to tell you, it looks like you were right about that prick Fennimore. He must be keeping his yap shut."

"I'm sure The Boys are treating him real good in Leavenworth."

"Yeah, well, I've seen other cretins with nothing to complain about inside run to the man anyway. Bruce isn't the type to be able to do hard time. He needs his bragging places and cars and bar fights. There isn't anybody in Leavenworth that's gonna put up with a braggart."

"Like you said"—David was getting an edge—"he's doing okay so far."

"Just so far," Doug grumbled.

●

At midnight, after serving them the racks of lamb, chocolate mousse, several more bottles of wine, and brandy, the restaurant's staff stood in a row by the door, watching the three remaining guests laughing and carrying on as if they were going to move in. It had been a long night. Earlier, the table next to the group, who had left only a half hour ago, pulled out some joints and lit up. The two tables had passed the marijuana around, causing the maître d' to have heart palpitations. He was now very close to an anxiety attack.

"I guess we've kept these folks up long enough," David said, motioning for a check. A waiter dashed over with it, running back to his post by the door as if he expected to be snake bitten. "Oh my," David said without interest as he looked it over. "Are you catching this or am I?"

"Wel-l-l," Doug said, attempting to blow smoke rings with his cigar, "seeing as there are two of us, I'll get it." Doug reached for the bill, looked it over, and said, "What is the tip on an eight-hundred-and-sixty-dollar bill?"

●

David slept in the next morning, had a leisurely breakfast, then met Doug and Linda. They drove Linda to Stapleton Airport. She was flying back to Los Angeles. Doug would drive the Bronco he'd just purchased.

After dropping Linda off, David and Doug retired to David's room to discuss politics, religion, and their respective futures. David allowed that, yes, he was probably through with armed robbery, but "you can't say when the last time for anything is until you're dead." Around 2 P.M., he called the front desk, asking for a short extension on his checkout time. The clerk said fine.

●

At 4:15, Denver FBI agent Brian Jovick got a call from his superior, Andy Sibley, saying that David Grandstaff was supposed to have checked in at the Sheraton that day. The source was out of California and somewhat reliable, but he'd been wrong before. Would Jovick take a run out there and check it out? Grandstaff was supposed to be driving a blue Monte Carlo with Iowa plates. Just check the parking lot for it.

●

At 6 P.M., David and Doug agreed it was time to roll. David said he'd just run down and pay the bill, then come back up for the formal good-byes. Doug said fine, he had to use the bathroom anyway.

In the lobby, David went out of his way to stroll by the flower shop for one last look at the pretty girl. He approached the shop feeling queer about something he couldn't put his finger on. Poking his head in the door, he gave a rakish wink and saw the girl was ashen and trembling, her hands gripping the glass counter in front of her as if she'd be blown away by gale force winds if she let go.

David felt the first shot of adrenaline pump into his muscles as he withdrew from the shop, which he now realized was empty. The lobby, too, didn't look too populated. The hotel had not been terribly busy, but there should have been somebody else there. Casually, he began an ambling pace toward the front desk, sliding his eyes about the lobby without turning his head. He noted six or seven men involved in various activities. There were no women.

His only hope would be to make the FBI agents believe he was not suspicious. Possibly he could get into the parking lot and disappear between cars. He stopped once to flip through a magazine. He did not think even the FBI would be hungry enough to try to take him there. There was always a possibility that some unwitting guest would stumble into the whole mess. No, they would try to get him outside.

At the desk, clerk Ron Davis's hands were trembling and his shirt was sweat-soaked. The man could not seem to concentrate on getting the change right and kept recounting it. The head clerk, Bernie Mustoe, seemed to keep stepping backward, as if to be ready to turn and flee to the office behind him at a moment's notice.

David was disgusted with the FBI. What purpose did it serve to scare these poor shitkickers half to death with tales about what a dangerous desperado David was? He was sure they'd told him that he carried machine guns and hand grenades and wouldn't hesitate to cut the guy's throat. These poor saps were terrified so that some agent could feel important going through the whole routine. David thanked Davis in a gentler voice than he usually employed and turned toward a hallway that led outside. He had to pass the main front doors to get to it.

●

Agent Jovick watched Grandstaff pay his bill with growing trepidation. He had been aware of Grandstaff for months now—ever since he'd talked to Agent Bagley in Tucson about the robbery there. Then, of course, Jovick was case agent in the February $100,000 robbery of the Western Bank in Denver. No evidence there to suggest Grandstaff and Brown, but nobody was confused by that.

Grandstaff, Jovick knew, was considered to be one of the most sophisticated robbers in the country. According to the reports Jovick had read, Grandstaff was familiar with all manner of weapons, including automatic weapons. He was expert at controlling groups of people—a "takeover" as the reports called it. By this time, Grandstaff must be a desperate man. If he were successfully prosecuted on the Tucson job, he'd never see the light of day again. Therefore, it stood to reason that he might try to shoot his way out rather than be taken. It gave Jovick the willies and his department had taken no chances. There were approximately fifteen agents in and around the hotel, all armed to the teeth.

It had been Jovick's intention to arrest David outside the hotel, where he assumed David would go after paying the bill. Jovick had to make a quick and unpleasant decision when Grandstaff passed the front doors, heading down a hallway with an exit to the parking lot. Anything could happen in that hallway. But he gave the signal anyway and seven armed agents came rushing from their positions.

●

David saw drawn guns and the blur of movement before he was overcome by a web of grappling arms. He knew who they were, but anyone else might not have, since they didn't announce it. It was annoying. Also, his attempts to inform them that he was not armed were drowned in all the screaming they were doing. Everyone was yelling at once, which made David wonder what they ever learned in their academy. Several agents tripped over one another's feet and went sprawling across the floor long before they finally got David facedown on the carpet. He didn't understand why they wanted him on the floor in the first place. He hadn't put up a fight.

Finally, they got the cuffs on him and hoisted him up. "Where's Doug Brown?" he heard one of the agents yelling over and over again as if he were having a breakdown. "Where's Doug Brown!"

"You boys must be speaking Iranian," David said calmly.

Jovick would never forget the response and the cool personality required to make it. He was slightly unnerved as he hustled David to the car for transport to the Denver County Jail and he didn't attempt to speak with him again. He could tell it would be pointless.

PART V

THE BEST REVENGE

34

HIRSH

It took the FBI four years to indict for TUCROB and even then it was iffy. They had a partial print of David's on the car Bruce had not hosed down and left in the San Diego airport. They needed Bruce—it was their only hope—but he hadn't agreed to testify in open court until 1984. It was unclear who he was afraid of.

Meanwhile, David and Doug stayed in prison over the Phoenix jewelry store robbery and their subsequent bond jumping. There were several escape attempts, none of them successful. The FBI believed Doug Brown spent a half million dollars of the TUCROB money in the efforts. They would bring that up at trial. For now, they were just glad to get a grand jury indictment.

●

"Afternoon, boys," FBI agent Larry Bagley said cordially. He stood in the basement holding cell in the federal courthouse in Tucson, looking happily at Doug, David, and David's attorney, Richard Hen-

ry. Henry, a former FBI agent, shifted uncomfortably, a gesture that
was not lost on David.

The agent accompanying Bagley mutely moved to a corner of the
small, green room, folded his arms across his chest, and stood with
feet apart in a stance of menace. A tough guy, David thought wearily.

Bagley shut the cell door and began ruffling through the papers in
his hand. Doug looked at the wall as if he didn't know anyone else was
in the room. David could see that Doug's cuffs were on too tight, but
he knew Doug was not going to say a word about it. For that matter,
David wasn't going to say anything about his own cuffs, which were
slowly cutting off the circulation to his hands.

David had hired Henry because he thought the attorney might still
have inside connections in the FBI that might prove useful. So far, all
Henry had done was simper about what a great case they had—how
they could really beat this thing. He'd produced nothing to back that
up and in David's view, the evidence so far meant he would die in
prison.

"Let's see what we've got here," Bagley was saying, studying his paperwork. "We've already gone over the grand jury subpoena." He
looked up with questioning eyes. "Your position on that hasn't
changed? You still refuse to appear?"

When the question died in silence, Bagley said, "You realize you
will be hit with a contempt of court charge if you do not appear?"

"I'm fucking terrified," Doug said in a dead voice.

David turned flat eyes on the agent. He thought about asking if
Bagley was trying out for a career in stand-up comedy but decided
against it. He was worn down from being kept in isolation and he had
been refused a shower again for the third day in a row. David had been
wondering how they knew that uncleanliness was the worst punishment they could have inflicted.

"Okay," Bagley said briskly. "Suit yourself. The judge is on the
bench now and she'll be issuing the citation as soon as I phone her.
Which will happen as soon as I leave this room."

Doug remained motionless. David didn't bother to look at his attorney. The bastard was obviously not going to say a word. David tried
to remember how much he'd already paid him.

"Next," Bagley said, going to the next set of papers, "we have a court order for both handwriting exemplars and hair samples. The order requires you to sign your names as George Bradley and Carl Simmons and also allows us to cut a small portion of hair from each of you." Bagley looked at Henry. "Would you like to see the order, Counselor?"

David's blood boiled as Henry shook his head. He wasn't even going to go through the motions.

Had it been $10,000 that he'd asked to be wired out? David thought.

"All right, gentlemen," Bagley said stoically, producing pens and paper and laying them on the table. "If you would be so kind."

"Have you lost your fucking mind?" Doug asked, still immobile. "Do you really think we're gonna do this?"

David sighed, looking at the FBI agent as if they were all reasonable men here.

"We've given handwriting samples a hundred times before. They're all on file in your department. We're not gonna sign nothing for this trumped-up case and that's the end of that story."

Bagley shifted his weight. The situation was embarrassing. He could not force them to write, but he had the authority to take the hair samples, by force if necessary. They could not resist under the circumstances.

It was still a creepy situation. But Bagley nodded at the agent in the corner.

David did not move as the second agent combed through his hair, carefully picking up loose strands and depositing them in a plastic evidence bag. The agent was gentle—tentative—as the comb stroked lightly over the top of David's head. If David had closed his eyes, he could have imagined that Virginia were there, lightly running her nails over his scalp. He did not close his eyes. And he knew the light touch stemmed only from the agent's discomfort at having to touch another man. David wondered how much they paid the man. He ignored the feeling that he was a monkey being groomed in a zoo.

Doug offered no resistance when the agent combed his hair out. His eyes remained fixed on the wall and he could not tell what the man was thinking.

"Well," Bagley said, "unless you have changed your minds, I think that concludes our business."

"Have a nice day," Doug said. Bagley got the hell out of there.

"You're fired," David told Henry as the guards came to take him back to the Federal Correctional Institute (FCI). Henry, David thought, looked relieved.

●

David was talking to Doug through the slits in his cell door. He couldn't see Doug. He couldn't actually see anything because the slit was just large enough to pass a plate through. He could hear him fine, though.

"Well," Doug said, "I guess we should figure out what we're gonna do. Not that it matters. You'll go back to fucking little boys and I'll go back to reading."

David rolled his eyes. He had no idea why Doug felt the need to say the outrageous things he did, but he'd grown accustomed to it.

"We ought to have at least one private attorney," Doug said. "We can get a public defender to help with the investigative costs. Let the state pick up the costs of some of this mess."

David agreed, but gave no answer. If he was going to die in prison, he was not going to carry any question marks with him. He was not going to have a voice rumbling around in his brain saying, "What if you had gotten a good lawyer?" He began interviewing.

●

David gathered the names of some of the best attorneys in the state. They filed into the prison one by one, each demanding huge fees, which was expected. What was not expected was their rap. Each one told David in full earnest that he or she could get David acquitted. It made David sick. The lawyers were willing to let him believe they could defeat a case based on fingerprints, hotel registration cards, gun traces, and, most important, the firsthand testimony of a participant in the crime. They were willing to lie about his chances simply because they thought he had so much money, he could support their offices for months. After all, when they lost, David would not be in any position to come back for a refund.

Robert Hirsh was the final attorney on the list. He swept into the interview room with a small entourage of clean-cut, serious-looking men David guessed were either law students or recent graduates. Hirsh flopped into a chair opposite David with a casual grace that bespoke utter self-confidence. There was a recent ketchup stain on his tie and the first words out of his mouth were the pronouncement that David's case was almost impossible to win and he should think about a public defender instead of a high-priced racehorse like himself. The results would probably be the same,

David hired him immediately.

●

After some twenty-five–odd years of practice, Bob Hirsh's name was instantly associated with either the just Knights of Camelot or the Four Horsemen of the Apocalypse, depending on your point of view. Prosecutors and police both hated and envied him for his phenomenal success record (although he was the first attorney contacted by the Tucson police union when they ran into bargaining difficulties). Neutral and liberal judges admired his keen—almost psychic—grasp of the law. Even conservative judges who hated ruling in his favor had to admit that he possessed a near-brilliant legal mind. Judge William Druke once was almost certain he could deny Hirsh's motion to suppress evidence in a drug case when Hirsh stood and delivered a complex, compelling argument that caused the judge's expression to change from passive indifference to profound concern. Worriedly, Druke looked at the prosecutor for deliverance from what would certainly be a reversal of his opinion if he ruled against Hirsh. But the prosecutor merely stood up in exasperation.

"Your Honor, I don't even know what he's talking about," the prosecutor said, flapping his arms to his side.

Judge Druke looked at him with disgust and tried—over Hirsh's objections—to argue the prosecution side himself. He ended up ruling in Hirsh's favor. Hirsh had not even researched his own motion. He had winged it.

But Hirsh's grasp of the law was not even considered his strong suit. The attorney had the ability to walk into a room, observe the con-

tents—the way they were arranged, the way they were cared for—
and make an assessment of the person who resided there. Whether
they were jealous, intelligent, self-conscious, selfish or generous. He
had been known to accurately predict how frequently a person
brushed their teeth. It was not unusual for him to size up someone he
met in person within ten minutes, right down to family background.

This played well with juries. Unlike his adversaries, Hirsh rarely
argued the law to juries. Arguing the law was reserved for pretrial
motions. Before juries, he argued *motives*. He argued personalities.
He argued *life*. He always ran with his best instinct.

His success record showed that juries seemed to agree with him.
Of seventeen murder trials, he had lost only one. Several of his vic-
tories involved temporary insanity defenses.

Longish, shock-white hair topped a six-foot-two-inch frame that
is better described as relaxed than lanky. Hirsh was rarely seen sitting upright in court. He melted into his chair. He slouched forward
to write and he leaned his entire frame against the defense table to
talk to his client. The result was not slovenly, but exuded a kind of
power of ownership, as if he were sitting in his own living room going through a serious but familiar exercise.

He could not be called good-looking, but he was striking. His features were angular and pronounced and the bright blue eyes had been
called "strange." When he walked into a restaurant, people looked up,
whether they knew him or not, although a large number of Arizonans
did know him, at least by sight.

He was gregarious. He enjoyed creating a party atmosphere in
whatever establishment he was in, involving total strangers in the fes-
tivities. The strangers, once over the shock of having Hirsh sit down
univited at their table, always seemed to have a great time.

This did not play well at formal functions, so Hirsh rarely attended them. If he'd played a little closer to the establishment, he would
not have lacked invitations. But the fact is that he cared little about
what the establishment thought of him. When he debated in public, it
was always against the status quo. He did not overlook opportunities
to insult cops or prosecutors. One young prosecutor was nearly reduced to tears when Hirsh swept into a courtroom for trial and examined a meticulous diagram of the "scene of the crime" the young
man had spent three days preparing.

"What's that, Kevin?" Hirsh asked languidly. "A diagram of your brain?" The gallery erupted in laughter. Sensing an audience, Hirsh continued the parlay until the prosecutor fled the courtroom.

Yet no one seriously questioned his personal commitment to the causes he chose. He spent too much unpaid time on them. Few knew that he was subject to periods of insomnia and depression.

In 1985, in what even the police called a tragic accident, Hirsh hit two elderly women jaywalking at night in a torrential, Arizona cloudburst. One of them died. The police never considered pressing charges against the attorney and even allowed him to go home from the scene. But Hirsh spent weeks in his office with the blinds drawn, alone. He refused calls and conversation. He gave away his car. Worried sick, his staff spoke in whispers, wondering if his spirit had finally been broken. But when he emerged from his cave, Hirsh seemed unchanged. He did not mention the accident. He asked for a file and a dictaphone. He bought a new car. Survival and optimism. Optimism and survival. Hirsh had lectured friends about it a hundred times.

●

Now looking at Grandstaff at the FCI in Tucson, Hirsh made his appraisal. The potential client was cuffed, abnormal for the circumstances of an attorney/client interview. He was surrounded by unusually heavy security. He was being held in solitary. The guy had captured sombody's attention.

The potential client was clean. Unusual. He didn't complain about his circumstances. Unusual. Hirsh checked the haircut and the posture. From blue-collar origins originally. Maybe a little below. Not very much education. Probably a dysfunctional family. Probably involving some degree of alcoholism. But he'd done something about it. Hirsh was liking what he saw so far. This was not a bad man. That didn't mean much in the legal system.

Hirsh had just lost a righteous case that should have—under any justice—been won. The *Sanctuary* case, which involved priests and nuns who transported to the United States Central Americans who were about to be executed. The U.S. government had sent paid informants into the churches where the refugees were harbored. It killed Hirsh that he could convince twelve people that killing your wife was okay, but he couldn't make them believe in the innocence of lambs. The weeks following the loss had been among the lowest in Hirsh's life.

Hirsh evaluated David's case as a plea bargain for sure. He told David that up front. David shook his head. No deals. You will be paid. Hirsh said okay.

MINKER

Jeffrey Minker took the call from federal district court judge Bilby knowing in advance he would comply with whatever request awaited on the other end of the line. Bilby was one of the most respected men on the bench. It wouldn't be sane for a lawyer with a solitary practice to pass up an opportunity to please him.

The son of a restaurant manager who took the drastic step of moving his family from Reading, Pennsylvania, to Las Vegas in the early fifties, Minker was a motivated man. His brother, Alan, now a superior court judge, thought they'd be able to ride horses to school. Minker remembered comforting him when his brother discovered there were buses in the West.

That's about as much as Las Vegas rubbed off on him, despite the drama teacher at Las Vegas High School who wore slippers and a bathrobe to class and was always attended by his pet poodle. The same teacher instructed his students to visit the casinos, study the faces of the gamblers there, and return to mimic the emotions. Minker complied happily, but still decided to sell shoes to get through law school rather than go into the theater.

A tall, athletic man with black hair and chiseled features, Minker preferred quieter pursuits than the ones offered by his adopted hometown. He enjoyed art, music, and gourmet food and was more likely to take a vacation exploring the tombs of ancient Egypt than to take a wild beach holiday in San Diego. In this, he was the complete opposite of Bob Hirsh, who was not adverse to boisterous parties and the occasional questionable companion. But the differences ended in the courtroom. Both attorneys were aggressive, astute trial lawyers. They were unaffected by fifteen-hour days and unintimidated by prosecutors or judges. When they took a client, they would work until they dropped. Minker made it a point to take a number of cases each year for free. He felt he ought to pay society back for his own good fortune, even though he did it himself.

Bilby was aware of this, and the phone call in May of 1984 was a request that Minker take Doug Brown's case as a court-appointed lawyer. The case was so high profile and potentially volatile, Bilby wanted the best representation for Brown he could get. Contrary to popular belief, judges do not like reversals and appeals dragging into eternity. The best way to avoid it is to get a good attorney who is not going to make the mistakes that constitute legal error. As Bilby would later admonish Bob Hirsh after an irritating day in court, "technicalities are the cornerstone of the legal system and we all know that very well."

Minker didn't know anything about the robbery except what he'd read in the newspapers and that had faded to a dim memory. Something to do with a telephone van and the largest bank robbery in American history. He had expanded his practice more and more into the civil arena anyway and wasn't paying much attention to what he considered to be the media's shamefully breathless crime stories. But he agreed to go out to the Federal Correctional Institute off Wilmot Road and interview Brown. He had not filled his self-imposed "free case" load yet that year.

The thirty-mile drive down I-10 to the prison in the middle of nowhere was a chore in itself. It took twenty minutes to get out of town and another thirty to reach the front gates. But usually when you got there you got quick service. You got ushered into the attorney/client interview room after a cursory inspection and within minutes your client was in front of you. That had been Minker's experience with the feds, in any event. What he found this time surprised him.

In the first place, he was thoroughly searched. Not his person, but all the paperwork he carried with him. This was not standard prison etiquette, especially for a well-known, local attorney who was meeting a client for the first time and completely above suspicion anyway. Then, it took a half hour for the guards to produce Doug Brown and when they did produce him, he was shackled from hand to foot. There were also four guards with him instead of the standard single escort. They did not uncuff his hands once he was seated in the interview room, as was normal. They did not leave the immediate area, which was their right. But under usual circumstances the escort would have gone to the Coke machine for a nice break or something. Minker couldn't understand it. The man in front of him was clearly going nowhere.

The man in front of him also clearly had the attitude of a cornered animal. Doug Brown's blue eyes were icy balls of hatred, which Minker found weird, since he had ostensibly come to help the man. Brown held his body rigid—poised—as if saying he would be willing to attack even given his obvious disadvantages. The pose said that the possibility of even the worst kind of punishment was not enough to break him.

Minker dragged out his paperwork and began his questions, but Brown's answers were sullen and nonresponsive. Sometimes they were aggressive and sarcastic. Even personal and insulting. Minker realized with some surprise that Brown actually considered him an enemy. Part of the system. Which was true enough. Minker considered himself a good citizen who would never deliberately sabotage the system. But he couldn't understand how Brown could think he wouldn't defy it under the proper circumstances or at least try to gentle it a little. Didn't Brown understand that he took on the police and prosecutors in court every day? That he wasn't there to punish him?

Apparently not. And after about an hour, Minker decided not to try to explain it. In that time, Brown's attitude had not budged one iota and one thing Minker did not feel obligated to do was to justify himself to a man who might receive Minker's considerable services for nothing.

When he left, Minker felt more puzzled than insulted. Here was a man facing a life sentence who was trying to alienate the one person the court might see fit to help him. It didn't make sense. Brown was clearly intelligent. Well above average, Minker thought. And he had smiled once—a fleeting smile over some past memory he hadn't seen fit to divulge. Brown had hidden the smile instantly, as if Minker might rob him of a precious treasure if he knew its root. But Minker had thought it was a winning smile. One that suggested a different person from the one in the handcuffs staring with all that contempt. It was a mere suggestion, though, Minker thought, shaking his head. The guy had really been pretty creepy.

Getting into his car, Minker thought he'd probably take the case despite his potential client's unpleasant personality. Minker hadn't filled his self-imposed quota yet. And besides, bank robbery cases were a dime a dozen in Tucson, no matter how big they were. The courts were clogged, the District Attorney's Office busy with a myriad of huge drug-smuggling cases, which certainly took priority with the "War on Drugs" being waged by the Reagan administration. The security precautions with Brown had been odd, but maybe understandable given what a jerk he was. God only knew what he did to piss the guards off if he treated his potential attorney like a pariah.

But District Attorney Dan Knauss had never met Brown or had to put up with his routine. Knauss had other concerns. All in all, Minker thought a plea agreement would appeal to Knauss far more than the prospect of a time-consuming trial against two defense attorneys Knauss could count on to put up a huge fight. Not only would the prosecutor's aspirin consumption go up, but his hard-won budget would be dented as well. Bank robbery as an image paled in comparison to Nancy Reagan's portraits of cocaine dealers lurking around elementary schools.

Happily, Minker thought he might only have to talk to Brown a few more times before he negotiated a deal with the U.S. Attorney's Office. After all, Brown's record indicated he had never physically hurt anybody. He didn't appear to be vicious. Looking at it now, Minker thought he might be able to get the idiot a ten-year cap, which, added to the sentence he was now serving, would at least get him free again before he died.

That thinking was about to change.

36

It got established pretty early that neither Minker's nor Hirsh's client was going to go for a deal, particularly if it meant testifying against each other, which was pretty much the only way you got a deal from the authorities.

Minker and Hirsh were disappointed, but they were hired guns, after all. They decided to expend energy and take some trips to interview family members, friends of Bruce, and past colleagues who might be receiving their room and board courtesy of the federal government. Why not? Bruce was the key to the case and the government was known to treat its keys with signed checks.

Flying into Des Moines the first trip, Minker was appalled. The place was to him what Alabama is to New Yorkers. It was worse than just unsophisticated; Minker found it scary. It seemed that everybody he talked to had some uneducated remark to make—and those were the authorities he went to first to get court records on Fennimore's divorce. Looking at some of the cops, Minker kept conjuring up visions of back room interrogations and rubber hoses. He wondered if some of The Boys' stories about this could be true. He could well see how a group of robbers could have banded together in such a place without an ounce of remorse or guilt. He wondered how much longer he could endure the grilled cheese sandwiches he was forced to eat because his palate couldn't take any of the other "home-style cookin'."

Hirsh was not as offended by Des Moines, but he was harder to offend than Minker as a rule. Hirsh had brought along a girlfriend, Kim, because she was originally from Iowa. He thought she might be a help. But it turned out there was a lot more to Iowa than Des Moines. The little, one-street town Kim had grown up in was a hundred miles and a whole separate planet from David's hometown and Kim spent most of her time in the hotel room.

Some of the witnesses Hirsh and Minker wanted—Bruce Fennimore's ex-wife, Sue, for one—were discovered in these tiny towns most of them were born in before making their big break for Des Moines. They looked exhausted, answering their doors for the two attorneys as if the rigors of living in a town of 150,000 had sucked the blood out of them. When they were too worn-out to take the traffic lights anymore, they headed back to Perry or Minas or wherever they were from.

The towns were picturesque in an antiquated sort of way. Many of them looked like time had been frozen for seventy years. Old Coca-Cola signs—long disappeared from most cities—still swung from gas stations that looked like they might still be privately owned by old guys with pipes who spent their time whittling on the front stoop. But the effect was claustrophobic to people who actually traveled outside of their own state. There was no escaping your neighbors, whom you would see as often as three or four times a day just in the course of normal living. Everybody knew your business and if they didn't, you were considered queer—even dangerous. Minker did not like the looks he received on the streets. Strangers in town. Brother. How long would it take the information to get around. An hour, he thought, tops. He didn't have to speculate about how these folks felt about Jews. But they probably hadn't actually ever seen one. Neither he nor Hirsh made an issue of their religion, but there was always an uneasiness in a place like this.

He was relieved when Sue Fennimore answered the door at the address the investigator had turned up. She was a bit frumpy but had a pleasing face. Or could have had. The face was marred by worry and poverty and the eyes carried the same dull suspicion Minker had encountered elsewhere. The difference with Sue was that there was also a look of resignation, as if she would take without comment whatever bad thing was about to happen to her—just as she'd been doing her whole life.

She let them in. After some gentle reassurances she talked. She told about living with Bruce the car thief. Bruce the robber. Bruce the brawler. Bruce the womanizer. No, he'd never hit her. But her life with

him had been nothing but psychological abuse—often public abuse.
The children had been ignored. There had never been any money for
her, although there was always plenty for the girlfriends. Finally, she'd
left.

Yes, she knew David Grandstaff, Doug Brown, and the others, but
not well. They did not actually socialize with Bruce. He often complained that The Boys felt superior to him—a creepy car thief. This
was important information for the defense. Fennimore was repre-
senting that he was never out of their company and therefore knew
all of their business.

●

When the attorneys left, they just felt sorry for the woman. They
hoped it would not be necessary to drag her to Tucson, as she'd begged
them not to. Perhaps the damning divorce papers Minker had dug up
in the courthouse would be enough.

●

The Brown family was more spritely. Lori Brown was astonishingly
beautiful, well groomed and well dressed. She could have been the
model she'd once aspired to become, but for her short stature. It almost made Hirsh regret bringing Kim along. This was a woman he
wouldn't mind kicking around with.

Lori didn't have much to say and Minker realized it was because
she didn't know what she was supposed to say. She hadn't been
briefed. That was all right. She was a tangent anyway. He'd probably
only end up using her for emotional reasons. Loving sister. Aspiring
wife and mother. Like that.

Clyde was more helpful. Both Minker and Hirsh could see a shrewd-
ness in his eyes that belied his "Who me?" attitude. Hirsh particularly enjoyed these sparring contests: getting information from people
who didn't want to give it and who knew the ropes. Clyde had been a
gambler his whole life and he knew a poker game when he saw it.

But Hirsh could also see that Clyde actually wanted to help his son,
he just didn't want to jeopardize his own position in the process. He

spoke freely about his run-ins with Oxler and other FBI agents and his belief that they followed Lori constantly, thinking David or Doug would contact her. The girl had many sleepless nights over it, Clyde said sadly. Looking at Lori, Minker doubted it. She did not look like an innocent to him, which was probably why Hirsh was drooling over her.

Then Clyde got around to the good stuff. Local car thieves. Burglars. Hustlers. He dropped the names casually, as if he weren't aware he was talking.

If it ever got back to these guys that the attorneys knew who they were because of him, Clyde could always deny it. Meanwhile, these were guys who could talk about what a horror show that punk Fennimore was. Clyde wondered idly if his ex-girlfriend, Susan Smith, was still sleeping with the idiot before he'd jumped bond in 1980. Anything was possible where Susan and men were concerned. Clyde still had trouble believing she'd left him for Mike See. He kept this to himself, however. He did not necessarily want to embarrass the woman and she probably didn't know anything anyway.

One by one, the defense team tracked down Bruce's former associates. What they got was a litany of double-dealing, betrayals, thievery, and general poor character—even for the witnesses. Even witnesses who purported to retain Bruce's friendship hedged badly when asked to defend him. They probably didn't know what kind of a shitstorm they might be getting into and Hirsh did not feel compelled to enlighten them. Let them worry about their own hides. If the prosecution tried to use them as character witnesses, Hirsh would crack them like walnuts. Unlike Clyde, these mechanics and petty burglars were completely mystified about how the justice system worked.

When the attorneys left Des Moines the first time, they felt they had something to at least talk about. Not enough to win, but enough to put some fear into the mind of U.S. attorney Dan Knauss.

●

Minker's utter relief at departing Des Moines was soon replaced with the shock of meeting Bobby Gene Jones, another paid informant for the federal government who claimed Doug Brown had paid him to break him out of jail.

As per the defense team's request, the government had dragged him down from one of several witness-protection programs he'd been in over the years. Bruce Fennimore was making his debut appearance in the program with Jones. They were both kicked back in their chairs, flanked by their new friends in the FBI, and watching both attorneys with complete contempt.

Hirsh would get to Fennimore soon enough, but Jones was Minker's problem. He was the only government witness who could substantiate Fennimore's claims that The Boys wanted their former associate murdered, but he was only going to accuse Doug Brown. There was no question that Jones had visited Brown at the Nevada County Jail. Minker could not argue that Jones didn't even know his client. He could point out, however, that Jones had only reported this threat in 1984, three years after his meeting with Brown and only *after* he'd met Fennimore. Only *after* Fennimore confided he was worried about getting kicked out of witness protection because the authorities didn't believe there was a threat. There was also Jones's record, which Minker had perused the night before. The sheer volume of it had stunned him.

Now looking at Jones, Minker felt shivers of disgust. Soft, pudgy, and aging, the man looked at him through thick glasses that made his eyes appear mutated. There seemed to be some kind of sickness coming off him. There was a vacancy in Jones's face that bespoke an utter lack of morality. Next to Jones, Brown looked like royalty.

Unlike Hirsh, Minker was not given to tirades about his government. But this was too much. It was getting Minker angry that the government used *his* tax dollars to support this guy. Even went so far as to give him $5,000 to open a jewelry store that would likely be stocked with stolen goods. Minker understood the informant system as well as anybody. But they'd gone too far on this one. Way too far.

Minker began with the arrest record, which began in 1950 and continued to the present date, although Jones was at the moment serving one of his numerous prison dates. The offenses included arson, bank burglary, bombings, simple burglary, weapons charges, money laundering, loan-sharking, assault, and a variety of lesser offenses, many of them committed while Jones was a working informant for the FBI. Were it not for that, Minker thought with disgust, this asshole would have been in prison.

Minker finished his points, then watched Hirsh coddle and bamboozle Fennimore for a while. Fennimore seemed to be having a great time, holding court before all these FBI agents, prosecutors, and famous defense attorneys. He really thought he was an important man. It was pretty pathetic.

"Jesus, could you believe that guy?" Minker asked as he and Hirsh left the courthouse.

Hirsh shrugged. "I really don't think a jury is going to want Mr. Fennimore going out with their daughters."

"Not him, Bob. Jones. Bobby Gene Jones. God, what a disgusting human being, if that's what he is."

Hirsh was grinning. He thought Jones's record was hilarious. He thought the government's hypocrisy was hilarious, too. Sometimes Minker took things too seriously. "Cheer up, Counselor. Optimism. They couldn't have handed you better cannon fodder if they were working with us."

"I hope they're all not like him," Minker said dejectedly. The prospect of interviewing the two dozen inmates on David Grandstaff's list and having them all be Bobby Joneses was not appetizing.

"Well, we should probably go to Leavenworth together," Hirsh said, now serious. "Most of them are there. Then we can see about splitting up to do the interviews in the state prisons. And by the way, we have to make another trip to Des Moines. Sean Duval, aka Roderick Hunt, has managed to get released. He says he's got something important for us and he wants to meet there."

Minker groaned. Des Moines again. And now it was November. It would be bitter cold. He'd probably have to eat the cheese sandwiches frozen.

●

As it turned out, Minker did most of the Leavenworth interviews. Hirsh went on the state joints, with an agreement to meet in Leavenworth and then fly to Des Moines for the meet with Duval. It was okay with Minker. It would save time. For a case that was supposed to be a simple plea bargain, this was getting tiring. Hirsh had a whole staff of people to keep his practice afloat while they gallivanted all over the Midwest. Minker was a sole practitioner. His business could suffer. Besides, he missed his wife, Barbara.

Minker didn't know the security setup at Leavenworth, but it again seemed like a very long wait to bring each of the men to the interview room. When they came, they were heavily guarded and Minker had to bicker to make them take the handcuffs off. Then he wondered why he had. These were the toughest cons he had ever seen, Minker thought.

He thought about it all the time he spoke to the men, one by one. This was the netherworld, a group of people who didn't look any different, didn't speak any different, but who were different and had created their own society. Some of them had really good personalities. Like George Weir. George was so . . . well . . . *gentle*. He almost spoke tenderly about David, asking how he was—how they were treating him.

"Not too good, I'm sure," Weir sighed softly. "But he'll come out okay. All of us are here to do anything we can."

It was a real us/them mentality. In a way, it was reminiscent of how cops think when they go out in the morning. It was strange to think of George holding a gun down someone's mouth—this quiet, humorous man who was now talking about his five children.

Minker tried to shake it off and get back to work, but when George Ripley was led in, it all came back to him. The man nicknamed Popeye had to be nearly seventy years old. He got his nickname when he lost a leg during a high-speed chase and resulting accident. His latest bank robbery sentence was recent—within the last few years. This guy was robbing banks in his late sixties. Minker couldn't restrain himself from asking the question.

"What are your plans when you get out, Popeye? What are you going to do?"

Ripley looked over as if trying to decide whether Minker was toying with him. "There's only one thing I *can* do, Counselor," he said finally.

Jesus, this is what the system comes to, Minker thought. A seventy-year-old cripple who doesn't have a single skill except bank robbery. Something is wrong.

At the Leavenworth airport, Hirsh and Minker compared notes. Some of the inmates had backed out. They had parole hearings coming up and they were certain they'd be denied if they helped David Grandstaff and Doug Brown. Hirsh thought that was probably a good bet.

Some wanted to be paid. Hirsh hadn't even bothered to talk to them once the demand was out of their mouths. It was out of the question. And they were looking for reliable witnesses, not ones that changed their minds like that. It was going to be hard enough to sell this as it was.

All in all, they had a list of about fifteen men who had solid stories neither attorney had been able to shake. The fifteen were nice-looking—or at least didn't present images of murder and mayhem. They were articulate and they were system savvy. Hirsh did not think they wanted to call all fifteen, but they'd go over it later, culling out only the cream of the crop.

●

Leavenworth was a good five- to seven-hour drive from Des Moines, so the attorneys decided to splurge and hire a light plane. On the way, the weather turned ugly.

Neither Minker nor Hirsh had ever thought about dying more seriously than any other healthy men in the prime of their careers. But they thought about it that day.

The pilot would later call the thunderstorm that enveloped the tiny craft the worst of his twenty-year flying career. Lightning flashed all around them, one bolt coming within inches of Minker's window. For a moment, he thought he'd been hit, then realized he was still alive. Astonishing blasts of wind tossed the plane around like a piece of confetti, sometimes hurling it hundreds of feet downward, only to blast it upward again. For the men in the plane, there was little to do but attempt to hang on to their seats while the pilot struggled lamely with his instruments, hoping to outrun the evil thing before it could kill them.

Minker, at least, was certain of his own impending death. Battling a losing war against nausea, he tried to remember if he'd put all his affairs in order. He was pretty sure he had. That would be at least one burden Barbara would not have to bear.

He felt sad for Barbara, but he knew she would survive. He felt dumb to be dying for a court-appointed case and a client who hated him. It was strange how calm he was.

When the plane landed, no one spoke. Ashen faced and trembling, Hirsh went off to see about a car. Minker tried desperately to control his heaving. He did not want to start a spate of uncontrollable vomiting, but it would take hours before the impulses finally left him.

●

Sean Duval entered the attorneys' hotel room with the aplomb Hirsh had expected from David's description. The lone robber who had eluded the FBI over and over again was highly intelligent, but could get on your nerves for that very reason. Personally Grandstaff liked him, but he had a tendency to be more arrogant than necessary. "Well," Hirsh thought, "I guess so. A guy as small as this one who walks into bank vaults alone and holds a half dozen people at bay while he cleans the place out has to have plenty of confidence."

It was typical for Hirsh to judge the person and for Minker to judge the deed. Looking at the smallish man with bland, Irish features and off-reddish hair, Minker thought, "Wonderful. I almost die and the first person I get to talk to is a cocky convict."

"What do you got for us, Sean?" Hirsh asked, getting right on it. He was eating as usual. As usual, bits of food and condiment were falling on his shirt. As usual, he didn't notice.

Hirsh's greeting was not brusque and not patronizing. It was matter-of-fact and even—like Sean was an equal. Hirsh did not have trouble communicating with nebulous characters. They seemed to sense that he was interested in the reasons they did things, not the things themselves. Also, there was a hint of a criminal about Hirsh, too. Looking from Minker to Hirsh, Sean walked to Hirsh.

"Shit!" Hirsh exclaimed. He'd just noticed a large mustard stain on his shirt. "Dammit!" He began whirling around the room, looking for something to dab it with.

Minker said nothing. This scene was repeated daily. Anyone who knew Hirsh knew it was useless to point that out to him. He would forget about the mustard stain in a few minutes. The cleaners would deal with it later.

Momentarily confused by Hirsh's shift of attention, Duval glanced at Minker. He decided to wait for Hirsh, who had failed to find a cleaning solution and was looking at the stain with a pained expression. "Well?" Hirsh asked without looking up.

"I signed an affidavit for David when he was in Leavenworth—" Duval began.

"Yeah, we have it." Hirsh now looked directly at Duval. "You gonna testify for us to that effect? That Bruce told you it was two Latinos that did the thing with him?" Hirsh felt it was important to be a little challenging when asking about testimony. Most people didn't understand what a frightening experience it could be.

"Of course," Duval said mildly. Duval understood.

"Okay, good. We'll get you a subpoena to make it all legal. Anything else?"

Now Duval looked pained. "Of course there's something else. I wouldn't have hauled you guys up here just to tell you about that."

Hirsh ignored the assumption that Duval could haul him to a five-star restaurant, much less 1,500 miles to the hinterland. He waited. Duval produced several pieces of paper, holding them just far enough away that Hirsh had to move forward to get them. Brother.

The sheet on top appeared to be an immaculately drawn map. Hirsh had always been impressed at how neat some of the older convicts were. If they got a smudge mark or stain on anything they were working on, they often threw it away and started over. Maybe they were just killing time, but it showed a certain compulsiveness that was interesting. . . .

"It's a map and floor plan," Duval broke the rumination.

"Of what?"

"The bank." A hint of exasperation now.

"The Tucson bank?"

Duval nodded, pleased with himself. Hirsh looked confused. David had said Duval had never been to Arizona. Then he tumbled to the point.

"Fennimore helped you draw this map when you were in Leavenworth with him in '82?"

Duval nodded again, triumphant.

"So that *you* could *rob* it again?"

"Let's just say I certainly had a professional interest in that kind of setup."

Hirsh turned to Minker. "Well, well, well. Looks like our reformed, upstanding government witness was helping bank robbers plan heists even while he was negotiating his deal."

"I didn't say that," Duval said, smiling. "I said I had a professional interest."

"As long as you say it on the stand," said Hirsh. Minker put his face in his hands.

"Counselor, would I be here if those weren't my intentions?" said Duval.

"Are you hungry?" asked Hirsh.

37

KNAUSS

In November 1985, U.S. attorney Dan Knauss was still getting bombarded with defense requests in *United States* v. *Brown and Grandstaff*. Given the attorneys, it was not unexpected, but he'd really expected them to start making plea agreement noises before this.

The case had initially been assigned to one of his deputy attorneys, but Knauss had decided to try this one himself. Given his responsibilities as head of the Tucson office, Knauss hadn't been active in the courtroom for some time. That didn't concern him, even given the defense team's extensive trial experience. This had been one of the most extensive FBI investigations in history and he had faith in the meticulous work FBI agents always brought in. Even if he was going up against two of the most aggressive defense attorneys in the region.

Hirsh. Brother. Minker was at least civilized during interviews and pretrial motions. But Hirsh would be constantly zinging his agents with little side remarks, pissing them off and making them unmanageable. Knauss himself even got irritated when Hirsh did it to him and he was used to it. Even before the trial, Knauss would ask Minker to speak to Hirsh about cutting out the sarcasm. Minker would, but it wouldn't change Hirsh's demeanor a wit.

Right now, Minker was asking for rough notes. It wasn't enough that they had every agent's reports. Minker wanted the rough notes. Well, all right. Knauss would see if he could find them.

●

It was now a little more than four years after Brown and Grandstaff were arrested and almost two since Knauss had managed to get indictments on them. That only happened after Bruce Fennimore agreed to testify in open court. Bruce didn't like prison much.

Knauss personally disliked Bruce. The guy was a thief and a whiner to boot. He was always getting into trouble in the institutions he landed in. No matter how hard the authorities tried to please the idiot, he couldn't leave it alone. He kept acting out. It put Knauss in a bad position. Fennimore always called Knauss, or Agents Oxler and Bagley. They'd had to haul Fennimore's butt out of trouble a few times, something that had obviously not been lost on Minker and Hirsh based on the questions they were asking. There was that time at the Phoenix prison when Knauss had had to appeal to Washington, D.C., to force the warden not to transfer Fennimore. He'd caused such upheaval, the warden couldn't stand it anymore. Bruce didn't want to leave Phoenix because it was warm and he had family there. Knauss had reluctantly intervened. He'd have to pay for that some on cross-examination. Special treatment. Government coddling of a liar. Et cetera. It was an old argument and one Knauss was used to.

But the law and order business wasn't always pretty. Criminals didn't associate with upstanding folks like the ones that would be on the jury. He'd explain that to them, as he'd done in a hundred cases. Knauss would patiently explain—as did every prosecutor in his position—that the state didn't *like* dealing with such men. They *had* to because such men were the only ones who knew people like the defendants.

"Ladies and gentlemen," he might say, "men like the defendants do not go to dinner at their local minister's home. I'd love to bring in a minister to testify here, but a minister didn't rob a bank with these men." It was a pretty canned argument. Most of the time, juries bought it. They would in this case once they realized what a crime wave these guys were. Knauss couldn't believe the defense was calling *other convicts*. They were practically making his case.

Of course, they created another irksome problem. In one of a myriad of pretrial defense motions, Judge Richard Bilby had already ruled that Knauss could not introduce any evidence about the defendants' criminal records. This was standard and Knauss had known it would happen. In the United States, you only put people on trial for the offense in question—not for their past.

This case presented special problems in that the defense was calling witnesses from various prisons who had known each other for years because of their criminal activities. How was Knauss supposed to establish where these guys all met without going into the fact that both Brown and Grandstaff had extensive records? How was he supposed to show their motives for lying? George Weir would probably commit suicide before he would say anything about David Grandstaff.

Well, it was probably a moot point. The jury was going to be able to see these guys were in custody. The U.S. marshals had extra security lined up for them. Nobody was going to be mistaking them for choir boys.

Knauss's biggest problem with the case would be placing The Boys in Tucson around the time of the robbery. There were hotel registration cards signed under their known aliases placing them in town within a few weeks of the robbery, but nothing within a few days. The jury might not care about the aliases, since it would be a known fact that they were fugitives from the Phoenix robbery charges and fugitives usually took aliases. Also, it might not matter that they were in town at some point, since they were not challenging that fact. They were merely saying that because they were in Tucson did not mean that they robbed a bank.

Of course, Bert Williams could place them within ten days of the robbery, but there were serious problems with his identification, namely that he had not made one at the time, but now said he could. Hirsh would harp on that, especially in light of the fact that Williams received the $25,000 American Bankers Association reward. It was a clear motive for improved memory, but Knauss thought it was manageable.

Likewise manageable was Kathy Faller, the Pinnacle Peak waitress. At the time she called 88-CRIME, Faller could only positively identify Fennimore as having been in the restaurant. Now she was saying different. And there was that small problem with the photo lineup. She really should have been shown something other than the pictures that had appeared on television and in the newspaper that morning but . . .

The fingerprints on the car found in San Diego were a cinch. The FBI had positively identified them as Grandstaff's and Knauss did not anticipate a problem there. No problem with the handwriting IDs on the registration cards. No problem with the gun purchase in Cheyenne. No problem with the victims. Knauss doubted the defense team would mess with them much. They couldn't make any ID and they were too sympathetic to rip apart on the stand.

●

A year after he'd managed to get the indictments on Grandstaff and Brown, Knauss knew he was about to face one of the most important fights of the trial. Hirsh and Minker had filed motions to suppress evidence seized from the two men when they were arrested in Denver. That included some $57,000 found in Grandstaff's suitcase and $120,000 found in Brown's Blazer. The money had been processed and fingerprinted a dozen times and there was no way to link it to the Tucson robbery. The specter of it, however, would be important at trial.

Essentially, Hirsh and Minker were arguing that the agents had no right to search either Grandstaff's hotel room or Brown's Blazer without warrants. Of course, the agents had eventually obtained warrants but not before they'd taken possession of the car and room. The defense argued that even though the two men had been arrested, there was still a "reasonable expectation of privacy" under the law and the agents had no right to relieve the men of their keys.

It didn't seem like much to Knauss, but court rulings could be unpredictable and he wasn't about to leave anything to chance. That left three areas. The money from the Denver arrest, which was coming up, and his main witnesses. Bruce Fennimore, to testify about the robbery, and Bobby Gene Jones, to testify about Brown's attempt to have Fennimore killed. Big problems. Both of them were scumbags. Even being around them made Knauss queasy. But he needed Fennimore for obvious reasons and he needed Jones to show that Fennimore's life had, in fact, been in danger. That was the *only* reason he'd decided to cooperate, Knauss wanted to show. The defense team would harp incessantly on the deals he had made and Knauss wanted to be able to show that wasn't his only motive in this thing. Jones was a horrible criminal. But those were the breaks.

●

Hirsh and Minker were not unhappy with the way the pretrial motions had been going, but they still believed the case would wrap up in some kind of a plea deal. They didn't know just what, yet, but they had time to think about it. They still had to file the motion to suppress the cash found during the Denver arrest. It was a matter of principle and Hirsh thought he had a pretty good argument.

The rest of it was going as well as could be expected. When he and Minker had interviewed Fennimore, the man had been just as surly as Hirsh had expected, based on David's extensive correspondence. Bruce had refused to be tape-recorded, which Hirsh would use to his advantage if there ever was a trial. He'd answered a lot of questions with "Could have been" or "I suppose so," prompting David to write on the edge of a police report: "For a guy who knows the whole story, he sure has to guess a lot."

About waitresses Kathy Faller and Kimberly Aiken, who said Bruce's group was loud and obnoxious, David wrote: "These crazy women must have been on drugs. I have *never ever* comported myself the way they describe in a public place." Knowing him better now, Hirsh could believe that. When he'd had Faller on the stand during pretrial motions, he'd actually gotten her to admit that only one of the trio she remembered was obnoxious. In fact, she hadn't even talked to the other two. That would come in handy when she pointed at Doug and David at trial, if there was a trial.

Likewise, Hirsh had made some unexpected discoveries about Bert Williams. What a piece of work that guy was. Him describing to Knauss his adrenaline rushes and intense fear; scary eyes in a passing car and whatnot. He was a regular chatterbox for Knauss. But when Hirsh had risen to question him, he'd clammed shut in a New York minute. In fact, Hirsh had begun his questioning by asking him why he'd refused to talk to defense investigators for more than a year.

"In fact, you've spoken to the FBI every time they've asked you to, have you not?" Hirsh asked

"Is there anything wrong with that?" Williams had snapped.

Hirsh liked it when prosecution witnesses acted hostile. It made it look like they had something to hide. So he'd pursued the line of questioning, asking whether he'd talked to Knauss also.

"What do you mean, talked to him?" Williams had answered sullenly. "He said good morning and—"

"Listen to my question, sir," Hirsh had responded patiently. "We'll do a lot better if you listen to my questions. Have you talked to Mr. Knauss (about this case) in the last week?"

"Do you mind if I consult . . . if I look at my schedule in my pocket secretary?"

Taken aback, Hirsh said, "You don't recall, sir? You don't recall independently?"

Normally, Hirsh would have just said "Yeah, go ahead." But even he had been surprised Williams wanted to check dates. Was the guy so paranoid about having his $25,000 taken away, he thought a mixed-up date would disqualify him? Didn't he realize they weren't going to take back money they'd already given him?

It was too much. It also signaled that Williams would do or say just about anything to protect his bank account. And then it turned out that not only did Williams keep all his little dates in his pocket secretary, but he'd also kept a file from the moment he thought he might be eligible for the reward. This was a grand tidbit. When he got the typed transcripts from the hearing, Hirsh highlighted the section in three different colors. Plea agreement or trial, it would go to Bert Williams's motives either way. It was a personality trait that could be understood without legal explanation.

●

On July 17, 1985, the attorneys did battle over the issue of the Denver money. The onus was on Hirsh and Minker. They would have to punch some serious holes in the arresting agents' activities to get results. Even though the FBI wanted Grandstaff and Brown in the worst way, the agents hadn't done anything blatant, thank God. Knauss would sit back and do damage control. Shore up any loose holes the agents might open up. They were professionals, but it was Hirsh, after all. Hirsh might get to them.

He did get to a few. Brian Jovick answered sarcastically on a few occasions. Hirsh asked how Jovick knew Grandstaff had come down to pay a bill at 4:30 P.M. and Jovick said, "Because I was there." Another time he looked up innocently after Hirsh interrupted an answer and asked, "Did you ask me a question?"

All in all though, the agents did fine. Hirsh elicited that the agent who entered Grandstaff's room did not know Brown was there when he entered, meaning that he had no right to enter without a warrant. A couple of agents hedged on this, saying they had vague information Brown *might* be in the Denver *area*. It was a little embarrassing because the one agent, Sibley, made it clear that his informant told him he had no idea where Brown was. All the other agents would have received their information from him. But Hirsh didn't belabor this and Knauss was prepared to accept the premise that they did not know. He was ready for that argument.

Hirsh began, "I'll lay this out in a nutshell. What we have is (Agent) Lisotto goes down to the room, he's got no warrant, certainly there are no exigent circumstances. . . .

"Here, the discovery of the materials to be seized and searched comes about as a consequence of Lisotto's illegal entry into the room. There's simply no way of getting around that."

Knauss was ready. "In this case, the defendants were federal fugitives, they had been charged with severe crimes. . . . They also knew Grandstaff had purchased a firearm under an assumed name in

Wyoming; a lot of firearms and violent crimes were involved in this. They did a very logical and correct thing to do with the information they had . . . and I suggest that this is a legitimate protective sweep search and they were legitimately in the room at that time."

Knauss's argument was that this case fit legal precedent that allowed officers to make a protective sweep when they felt they might be faced with violence. But there was a sinking feeling as Judge Bilby responded.

"When you say legitimate protective search, you know, it would be pretty clear if this were a house and Mr. Grandstaff and Mr. Brown were known to be living or habitating in the house and Mr. Grandstaff walks out and is arrested in the front part of the house and they had information that Mr. Brown was there. I would think that they certainly would have the right under those circumstances to make a protective sweep.

"But what if they had a house that was Mr. Grandstaff's house, you had no knowledge that Mr. Brown was in the house or lived there, but just that they had allegedly committed some crimes together . . . do you have a right to go and make a sweep of that house?"

The issue now became whether Grandstaff had an "expectation of privacy" because he had contracted for the hotel room, which legally is the same as occupying a house. However, Grandstaff had overstayed his checkout time. The way Knauss looked at it, that negated his contract. The way Hirsh looked at it, Grandstaff had made verbal arrangements to pay extra for the extra time, which put the contract back into effect. And if that didn't, the fact that he'd already paid the extra amount when he was arrested did.

They called Bernie Mustoe, the checkout supervisor at the Sheraton, to settle the question. Unsure of what he was expected to say, Mustoe squirmed under questioning but finally admitted it was hotel policy to consider the room private until after the guests had left, whether they overstayed their checkout time by a few hours or not.

Mustoe was especially cagey with Hirsh, which irritated the attorney. Hirsh was trying to find out if the supervisor had noticed the condition of David's hair when he checked out. David had said it was wet, because he'd informed the desk that he only wanted to take a shower before he left.

Hirsh asked, "We neglected to ask you this question, sir. When Mr.

Grandstaff came to the front desk, did he appear to have shaved and showered?"

Mustoe shifted uncomfortably, looking to Knauss for guidance. "His hair was still damp. That's . . . that's all I remember."

"You *do* remember his hair was damp?" Hirsh pressed.

"It looked like it had . . . you know, either . . . from sweat or a fresh shower . . . I don't have any—"

Hirsh cut in. "Maybe it was the perspiration of the anxiety of staying at your hotel."

Knauss pressed his hand to his forehead. People in the audience smiled covertly. Mustoe fled the courtroom for the flight back to the safety of Denver as soon as he was excused.

●

Days later, Knauss got the bad news. Bilby had ruled against him. The evidence seized in Denver would not be allowed in trial.

Knauss sighed. This meant an appeal to the Ninth Circuit in San Francisco. It could take months—even more than a year. But he had to do it. He could not let this kind of a precedent stand. Given the conservative mood of the courts these days, he thought he had a good chance of overturning Bilby's decision, even though judges don't like contradicting other judges.

In the meantime, he might as well go ahead and approach the defense team with a deal. They'd made their points and he'd made his. He could proceed without the Denver evidence, so it wasn't like they had him over a barrel. But they certainly had chopped a hole in it.

It was time to talk turkey. Get to the points they all knew were coming anyway. He'd talked it over, and he had his offer.

●

It was Minker who brought it up at one *of the* myriad of interviews the defense team had requested—*and* Knauss had set up.

"What's your bottom line *here*, Dan?" Minker asked casually.

Knauss paused for *effect*. "Twenty-year cap. *If* they give the money back."

Minker *thought* it over. A twenty-year cap in the federal system meant doing about ten years. If you added that to the eight or so they already had to do for the Phoenix robbery and the bail jumping, it came to about eighteen. They'd be out somewhere in their mid- to late fifties, which was a hell of a lot better than the 270 some-odd years if they were convicted at trial. That meant death in prison. And both Minker and Hirsh knew The Boys weren't going to get offered anything better. The FBI had fought too long, too hard, to get them.

"We'll mention it to them," Minker said, rising to leave.

●

As usual, it took forever for the guards to get David and Doug to the attorney interview room. As usual, there were enough guards around to stop a small riot and, as usual, they did not remove the handcuffs from either man.

As much as Minker had come to hate his own client, this treatment irritated him. To tell the truth, the government's handling of the entire case was irritating him. The more he went over this Bobby Gene Jones thing, the madder he got. They had no business paying tax money to a crook to open a jewelry store with stolen merchandise. He was almost beginning to see Grandstaff's point.

"Can't you do anything about getting us some yard time?" David was asking Hirsh. "I've got to have some exercise."

David's tone was respectful, conciliatory, understated. It galled Minker even more. Brown never showed him anything but contempt.

"We have an offer," Minker broke in briskly. And he laid it out. Assuming a professional demeanor he had to struggle to achieve around Brown, Minker went over the sentence structures, the possibilities of parole, good time, and appeals, and the potential sentences if the deal were not accepted. Then he got to the part about the money. Minker looked at Doug, who was staring off at a wall.

"You'd have to tell them where the money is," Minker said without inflection. "They want it back."

Brown turned his head languidly and fixed his ethereally blue eyes directly on Minker's. David watched Doug warily. Minker felt like he was gripped in a tractor beam from one of those *Star Wars* episodes. The effect was intense.

"What money?" Brown asked, also without inflection.

David thought the response was an acceptable compromise on Brown's part. Any deal, even a twenty-year cap, would make them old men before they got out. What would be the point? Minker should realize that, as Hirsh did by virtue of his unusual silence. Doug stared at Minker awhile before turning away. Minker found it impossible to break away first.

Minker didn't remember what David or Hirsh said, if anything. He just remembered getting into his car thinking, "Jesus. We're going to trial on this thing. And we're gonna get stomped."

38

CONNER

Now that the appeal was in the hands of the Ninth Circuit, the flames could be doused. Minker went back to his practice. Hirsh went back to his. Knauss tried to pick up the paperwork at the U.S. Attorney's Office.

Doug and David were transferred, first back to Iowa where David orchestrated two failed escape attempts. One involved sawing off cell bars, replacing them with painted, carved soap bars until a big enough hole could be cut. Everyone agreed it was ingenious and would not have been detected but for a riot near the cell block where he resided which resulted in one of the more serious shakedowns in the Polk County Jail.

The second was more harebrained, but came close to working anyway. One of The Boys' teenaged sons used a pulley and rope to come down off the roof of the jail to David's cell. He was to cut the bars open with hacksaws, then swing with David to the ground on the rope.

He was detected but got away and has never been charged. David and Doug were immediately transferred to maximum facilities in Chicago. They were now traveling in their own private planes, guarded by a dozen U.S. marshals, shackled hand and foot. Even trips to the bathroom were supervised and the shackles were not removed. It was a bitch trying to take a piss with your hands cuffed tightly at your belt buckle, but David just ignored it. It was just one of many things he'd learned to ignore and the deep breathing exercises helped. After going Around the Horn for a while, he got back to Leavenworth. Doug was sent to the federal penitentiary in Lompoc, California.

David was embraced after leaving the admissions area. Men who would sooner fight than be labeled homosexuals held him, pressing packs of cigarettes and forbidden candy bars into his hands. They asked if he needed anything—anything at all. Nobody had to mention the rigors of the last few years in solitary.

David said no, he'd get some books. Maybe a little heroin but he wasn't interested in getting into the swing of things just yet. He inquired if all the commissary had been taken care of from the street. Had everyone's accounts been held up-to-date? They had, he was informed. Well, that was a relief. No double cross from that end yet. He just wanted a little peace right now. Get back into an exercise regimen. He was worried about the condition of his body. The men said they understood. Cool. When you want something, just let us know. They drifted off to give David time with George Weir, who stood quietly with Danny Davis. Almost a million years ago Davis had comforted David after Ronald Agee had drowned in a city reservoir and David had gone into a rage. David nodded at them, stashing the "welcome home" gifts. David felt too embarrassed to say anything. George smiled at the floor. Some things didn't change. David was one of them. The big dope would never admit he was affected by anything.

"Come on," George said quietly. "Let's get you something decent to eat. I convinced a cook to give me some bananas. Potassium. Your favorite fucking vitamin. Or whatever you call it."

David nodded, feeling his mouth salivate at the mention of the cherished food. "You're still killing yourself with those goddamn Pepsis, aren't you, George? When are you gonna get smart about this?"

"At the moment," George said, "you don't look a whole helluva lot smarter than I am. Do you want the fucking bananas or not? I can always sell them."

David started walking. Danny Davis shook his head, smiling. He left some distance between himself and the newcomer so that he could watch the corridors. It was always possible that some of "the youngsters" had experienced a crack-induced brainstorm, causing them to believe they could waylay these bank robbers and extort money from their families. It would not be a very bright idea, but it wouldn't be bright to ignore the possibility of a knife lunging from some corner up in front there, either. Danny was close enough to get there in time, if it happened. No one was getting any younger and it was getting harder to recover from such injuries. Already, the prison doctors had argued that Davis should have his leg amputated due to diabetes. He had wisely refused. Years later, his leg was still fine. And nobody in Leavenworth was going to take advantage of any of The Boys without blood being spilled. They would help who deserved it, and fight who didn't.

●

Doug Brown handled his situation a little differently. Like his father, he read a poker game well. Doug was not adverse to violence, but if you could pay to avoid it, why not?

Linda made weekly trips from the Marina Del Rey area up to Lompoc. It was about a seven-hour drive one way but she didn't mind. She was not working now and neither was Dale Brown, who was now living with her. Maybe a watchdog. Maybe not. It wasn't sexual. Doug wanted it that way and it was fine with her. She didn't have to worry about things like electric bills, credit cards, or nice weekend vacations to take the edge off. And Doug needed his books and his commissary. There were people in Lompoc depending on him. She made the trips.

●

On December 15, 1986, Hirsh got a letter and a newspaper clipping from David. The article described bank robber Terry Lee Conner's re-arrest after his third successful escape from custody.

> *Bob,*
>
> *Hope you find this article of interest. I'm sorry for Conner's sake, but maybe we can benefit from his misfortune. Maybe we should try to get a statement from him before he gets away again. He will be taken to Marion, Ill. but will be bounced from jail to jail during the next few months. The way it looks, he will be tried for at least three new bank robberies. Anyway, let me know if anything might come of this or any other change in the case. Hoping to hear something. Have a Merry Christmas and Happy New Year.*
>
> *David*

Hirsh had mixed feelings about the letter. Terry Lee Conner had contacted David years earlier, through the prison grapevine. Although the two bank robbers had never met, they knew each other by professional reputations and had a mutual respect for the way they comported themselves in prison. They were both stand-up. Conner had read about David's indictment for TUCROB in 1984, while he was serving time for his own bank robberies. Through a series of prisoner transfers, Conner got word to David that he knew David was innocent of the charges, because he had committed TUCROB himself. He was willing to testify to that effect. The defense team had meant to interview him in 1985, but Conner and his partner, Joe Dougherty, pulled off an ingenious escape from U.S. marshals while being transported from one prison to another before the attorneys could get to them. Now he'd been re-arrested.

Conner would end up being one of the most interesting criminals Hirsh had ever met. Hailing from an impoverished and dysfunctional family, Conner had been determined to leave the past behind. After graduating from high school, he'd done the only thing available to him—taken a job in a fast-food restaurant in Yuma, Arizona. He'd married, but trying to support a wife on a fry cook's salary had been uncertain and at one point he was so hungry he'd broken into a church and stolen a mess of fried chicken stored for a planned picnic. The subsequent burglary charge got him probation.

Undaunted, Conner went back to work, moved up through the ranks until he felt he had enough capital and experience to open his own fast-food restaurant. He called it "Burger Boy" and he supervised the operation twelve to fourteen hours a day. The hours ruined his marriage but made the restaurant successful and he opened another and then another. In all, he had seven "Burger Boy's" between Arizona and the California line before the recession hit in 1974. It was something he hadn't counted on.

Overextended and unable to make payroll, Conner went to a number of banks for loans. He was unilaterally turned down. Depressed and feeling responsible for the people he'd employed, Conner sat alone one evening in his now-bachelor apartment trying to come up with a solution. He decided he would rob a bank. If the motherfuckers wouldn't loan him the money, he'd take it from them.

The first robbery occurred in Flagstaff, Arizona—about a seven-hour drive from Yuma. It was astonishingly easy. He came back with the take, made payroll and continued operating his businesses.

But the recession had not gone away and he soon found himself unable to cut the payroll checks again. The second robbery was easier. The third and fourth times better still and on the fifth run out he was caught. He went to prison for eight years.

Conner returned to Yuma where he made another stab at the restaurant business but this time it didn't click at all. Conner didn't have much interest in the business anymore and life in the small town bored him. He got involved in the Mexican black market business, which is not illegal on the U.S. side of the border. Appliances, electronics, cars—anything that can't be reliably manufactured in Mexico was bought in the United States and sold at a profit to the south.

Unfortunately for Conner, he partnered with Dwane "Bucky" Walker, who would later become the subject of a Vincent Bugliosi book and a TV movie. Walker, who would later also walk a prison yard with Doug Brown, had informed Conner that he'd escaped from the federal penitentiary at McNiel Island after being sentenced for stealing a yacht in Hawaii. He did not tell Conner that the couple that owned the boat had disappeared, one set of bones having been washed ashore in a foot locker on a remote island. When the FBI found Walker in Yuma on August 8, 1981, they also found Conner, who was returning a typewriter to Walker's hotel room, completely unaware that the area was surrounded.

Conner denies that the guns and drugs found among Walker's possessions had anything to do with him. Although he's been accused of running drugs, he steadfastly denies it. However, he was on parole and associating with Walker violated his conditions. He was returned to prison.

"Some dates you never forget," Conner would later tell prosecutor Dan Knauss. And that date was November 20, 1981 when Maricopa County officials in Phoenix mistakenly released Conner from custody. He simply walked out of the jail, thinking somebody would have to realize the blunder at any second and gun him down. But they didn't. He teamed with Joe Dougherty and the two went on a midwestern bank robbery rampage, often using the technique David Grandstaff had thought of fourteen years earlier—taking bank managers hostage at their homes and then walking them to the bank vaults at opening times.

Re-arrested in March of 1983 during a botched job in Chicago, Conner and Dougherty were again returned to an Oklahoma prison, but not for long. While being transported by two U.S. marshals for a court appearance in Oklahoma City, Conner unshackled himself with a homemade key he concealed between his teeth and gums, and the two outlaws convinced the marshals in the front seat that they were armed, although they were not. The lawmen were handcuffed to a tree and the bandits escaped with their car and weapons, taking a family hostage for several days until they could be sure the police were no longer combing the area for them.

The pair was on one of the first segments of *America's Most Wanted,* although Conner today finds the program—and subsequent written accounts of his career—laughable. A balding, slim man with wire-rimmed glasses and a soft voice, Conner denies that either he or Dougherty ever threatened anyone with violence and were, in fact, apologetic to their victims. Some newspaper accounts do report that both men fixed coffee and washed dishes for their hostages and there is no evidence they were armed with grenades and plastic explosives as some have suggested.

Those types of weapons were never found, but Conner and Dougherty did enjoy another eighteen-month robbery spree before Conner was recognized at a motel in Arlington Heights in Illinois and Dougherty in a laundromat in Antioch, California, in late 1986.

●

Conner believes he is serving 249 years plus two life sentences—consecutively—because he was such a grave embarrassment to both the FBI and the U.S. marshal service. But he had been drawing hefty sentences even before then for kidnapping bank managers—then a life sentence on its face. Escape seemed like a good alternative but that was easier to accomplish from outside a prison than from within. Especially from within the penitentiary at Marion, Illinois, considered the Devil's Island of the federal system, and where Conner was eventually held in maximum security twenty-three-hour lockdown.

Conner had admitted to the Tucson robbery in 1981, after David and Doug's arrest. He'd gotten word through friends of friends, finally reaching George Weir at Leavenworth through a kind of bizarre telephone game that took months to accomplish. His two subsequent escapes—and the fact that David and Doug weren't even charged until 1984—made his confessions somewhat moot. Not that anyone believed him anyway. Conner had confessed to a dozen crimes. The police believed he did it only for the opportunity to be transported around the country, testifying for other bank robbers, in the hope he might get lucky again.

Conner only smiles at the suggestion and gives a little shrug, like a schoolboy caught in a minor offense. He allows that, barring an earthquake that could rip Marion in two, his travels are his only form of entertainment and hope. Hope being crucial to the well-being of a caged mind, Conner in 1989 again made his confession to robbing the Tucson bank with Bruce Fennimore and another man.

●

Unbeknown to Hirsh and Minker, the man Conner named had been murdered some years before in the Florida everglades by disgruntled business associates. His body was never found, although his fate was common knowledge in the federal system. You just don't rip off Colombian drug dealers and expect to live.

News of the Conner confession made the attorneys uncomfortable as hell. They never said it out loud, but both of them knew they were putting on dubious testimony, even though neither had any direct proof of its falsity. Mere suspicion did not obligate either lawyer to air his beliefs. They were pretty sure Dan Knauss would pick up that end anyway. But they dragged their feet making concrete plans to interview Conner. Neither Minker nor Hirsh wanted to do it. They didn't have to. A friend of Doug's flew to Marion under the guise of an "investigator" for Doug's case. When he left, Terry Lee Conner knew most of what he needed to describe TUCROB inside and out. In the end, Hirsh interviewed Conner after he'd been transported to Tucson for only one hour just prior to his testimony. He found Conner to be intelligent, entertaining, and witty and Hirsh couldn't wait to get away from him. He didn't want to know how Conner knew—down to the color of the money bags—what had gone on in that bank.

●

As The Boys inside and out of the federal system continued marshaling their forces, there was an unexpected break. Garvin "Bubba" White was transferred to Leavenworth. Shortly after his arrival, he found himself coincidentally in the company of Danny Davis and George Weir, who had come in from a handball game as White was going to his cell. After White found out who they were, he had a very interesting story to tell.

White, a private pilot, had initially been incarcerated for flying loads of marijuana from points south into Miami. He was strictly contract, flying for the actual owners of the drug for a fee, but he was hit with a hard sentence anyway after he would not inform. He compounded the problem by staging an escape attempt that resembled something the A-Team might have tried on prime-time television. His two teenage sons, armed with high-powered rifles, posted themselves in strategic areas around the Florida prison where White was being held. While they kept the guards' heads down with a barrage of fire, White and two others made a break for the wall. They were all caught and White's two sons, who heretofore had been mild-mannered high school students, went to prison with him.

In the course of his travels around the federal system, however,

White had celled opposite Bruce Fennimore in Texarkana, Texas—
one of the places Bruce had roomed while the authorities tried to find
a permanent home for him where at least some of the other residents
could stand him.

During his stay, Bruce told White he had masterminded TUCROB
and had used two Latino accomplices from the Miami area—the same
story he told over and over when he first arrived in Leavenworth.
Bruce bragged he could get out anytime if he would just finger Grandstaff and Brown and said the FBI was making him daily offers on the
subject. He also allowed as how he still had a good chunk of money
the dopey feds never got from him, and he was thinking about going
into the drug business when he got out. Would White want to throw
in with him? They could steal an airplane together to get started.
White found the whole thing amusing, but accepted copies of Bruce's
address book so he'd know how to reach him in the future.

"Would you testify to that?" George asked White carefully.

"Course," White replied easily. "It's true, ain't it?"

"If Bruce says so," Danny Davis said with a grin.

●

White contacted Hirsh by mail and Hirsh readied the subpoenas.
White was a fine catch. He wasn't an armed robber. He'd never known
any of The Boys and therefore had no motive to lie for them. And he
corroborated the stories from Leavenworth that would most certainly be attacked for their veracity.

Bubba White was treated very well in Leavenworth.

39

RICE

James Rice got his summons for jury duty in November of 1988. The forty-year-old landscaper and handyman disliked people who shirked civic responsibilities. He never had. He always voted. He gave old clothes away to the Salvation Army and he never cheated on his income taxes. Ordinarily, he would have welcomed the chance to participate in the justice system.

But his eight-year-old child had asthma and Reaganomics had precluded his ability to pay health insurance. Rice was working two jobs to pay the outrageous hospital bills. He could not afford a lengthy trial at twelve dollars a day—the going rate for jury service. It was an anguishing proposition for him and one he hadn't expected to have to make. He thought he had enough problems without this.

Rice was lucky in that one of his employers, at least, agreed to pay his salary during the trial. He and his wife, Barbara, discussed the situation and decided that he should serve on the jury. They did want to live up to their responsibilities as citizens.

●

Arriving at the federal courthouse in his customary bib overalls, Rice was a bit overwhelmed. He'd never served on a jury before. Never even been in a courthouse. He'd been arrested once as a teenager for buying liquor on a Sunday in a state with "blue laws." He hadn't appreciated how the police had bullied and pushed him around that time, but it was long ago.

Still, he couldn't help thinking about it as the men in the imposing uniforms started herding the prospective jurors through the polished corridors. It seemed like there were hundreds of people, all getting jammed into a waiting room until their names could be called for the various trials going on around the building. Some people looked bored, as if they'd done this before, and some must have done it before because they'd had the presence of mind to bring books and magazines. Most, though, looked like Rice felt. Like they were sheep in a pen, stupidly waiting to be called to their slaughter. It was November, but November in the desert is mild—usually with temperatures that straddle the fence between air-conditioning and heating. On this day, the powers that were had elected to use neither system and the jury room was close. Rice started to sweat.

Eventually, he and about seventy others were led upstairs to a large courtroom that was air-conditioned. A snowy-white-haired gentleman with reading glasses sat on what looked like a throne at the front of the room. The judge's bench towered over the rest of the room, but he had a comforting, fatherly appearance that put him more at home. This was more like what the movies showed.

Two long, shiny tables sat at opposite ends of the room, facing the judge's bench. At the one to Rice's right sat four men. It was hard for Rice to take his eyes off one of them. The man was tall and limber with shock-white hair. He moved with such authority and athletic ease that he seemed not much older than Rice himself. In fact, Bob Hirsh was fifty-three.

Next to the tall man sat a man in a cardigan, rocking slightly in his chair. He turned once to look behind him and Rice caught a glimpse of his intense, dark eyes and razor-cut hair. There was no expression on his face. To Rice, the guy looked like a cool dude. Very much in control.

The guy next to him was a different story. Rice didn't like the looks of him at all. Doug Brown.

Next to the kind of creepy guy was a man with black, wavy hair sprinkled with gray and an aristocratic face. Because he and the tall man were in suits, Rice assumed they were attorneys. The guys dressed casually next to them must be the criminals. And the blond guy with the glasses at the other table must be the prosecutor. Rice didn't know what to make of him, but he didn't like him any better than he did Brown. Rice didn't know why.

In the jury room, they'd all been given questionnaires to fill out asking about their backgrounds, their jobs, and stuff like that. Rice had been uncomfortable about filling them out, but he didn't want to make a scene, so he'd done it. He saw now that the attorneys were bent over them, reading with deep concentration. The tall man with the shock-white hair was particularly riveted and seemed to be in his own world as he went through the pages, sometimes lifting his eyes skyward as if he were trying to see a picture on the ceiling.

Now the judge was asking questions. He introduced himself as Judge Bilby and said it was going to be a very long trial. Anyone with family hardships, religious views, or prejudicial personal opinions should leave. The crowd started thinning out as one prospective juror after another had a problem. Rice was glad he had such reasonable employers. This was getting pretty interesting.

When there were only about twenty people left, the judge started asking the jurors to answer individually instead of just raising their hands. The questions got pretty weird, too. Rice didn't know what to say when they asked what kind of bumper stickers he had on his car. For some crazy reason his ancient arrest flashed across his mind and he thought Mothers Against Drunk Driving knew about it and had informed the judge, because he had been joyriding the night he bought the liquor. Shaking that off, he said his favorite sport was football and answered all the rest of the questions, hoping his voice wasn't trembling.

The question he was asked that made the most impact, though, was whether he would be capable of believing the defendants were innocent until all the evidence was in. That just because they were sitting there with marshals all around them, would he be able to say, "These men are innocent." Also, would he be able to render a not-guilty verdict if there was just a "reasonable doubt" in his mind. Not a total doubt. Not a belief that the men didn't do it at all. But a "reasonable doubt."

Rice liked that. It was the way they'd taught you it should be in school. What he'd found out was that the system hardly ever worked the way they taught you in school. But maybe it would here.

He had to take another look, though, at the defendant he didn't like and check with his own mind to see if he could. He decided he could and said, "I really don't care where they are sitting. I'll go by the evidence. If I were in that chair, I'd want somebody like me to decide, you know?"

Surprised by his own mini-speech, Rice looked around the room. The tall attorney was staring at him intently, then turned and scribbled something on his legal pad. Rice hoped he would be picked.

●

Hirsh watched Rice with interest. The guy looked like a farmer, but he didn't talk like one. Maybe he would be okay. Hirsh made a note of it.

Hirsh sometimes used psychological firms to evaluate potential jurors. He had in this case. They had pretty much come up with the obvious. No bankers, no Nordic people, no stockbrokers. We need people who question authority. Nonetheless, Hirsh did what he always did and went with his own opinion. He put a bank teller on the jury. His reasoning was that she was Hispanic, had probably never been given a raise in the seventeen years she'd worked for the bank, and would be happy to know somebody had robbed one. It was the same logic David had used on Charlie Virgil.

40

Hirsh and Minker had their normal 6 A.M. breakfast together the day of the trial. Minker had been up as usual until 10 P.M., orally delivering his opening argument to the paintings on his walls.

It was a technique he'd developed by accident. In the early years of his practice, he'd simply written his arguments out and gone from notes. After a few years, however, he decided that the words that looked so good written down didn't *sound* as good when spoken. There was a difference between the written and spoken word.

He missed Barbara, but was almost relieved she'd had an opportunity to go to Egypt on an archaeological dig. She never complained about listening to his orations, but it was going to be a long trial. At least one of them should be having fun.

Minker liked to think of a trial as an orchestra. There were the facts, there was delivery of the facts, and there was the way you delivered them—much like a sheet of music. He was the conductor and, if he did not do it right this morning, the audience would walk out on him. He missed Barbara again.

Hirsh's view of a trial was not quite as poetic, but it was just as realistic. He saw trials as contests and contests were meant to be won.

Early in his career, Hirsh had been mystified by what seemed to be at least a partial public perception that the defense attorney should merely be present and not fight as hard as he possibly could for his client. These people seemed to believe that criminal defendants were not entitled to defend themselves. The very people who cried foul when a defendant was acquitted were the first to hire him when they themselves were caught in difficulties.

●

U.S. attorney Dan Knauss got to the courthouse early and began arranging his exhibits. There was a small book's worth and he wanted to be clear on what was where. He was still messing with the papers when the jury filed in and James Rice watched him with a kind of growing distaste. "A man of privilege," Rice thought. "I wouldn't get a glass of water from him if I were crawling."

Hirsh and Minker swept into the courtroom in a serious mood, but they did not arrange papers all over the defense desk. Rice liked the fact that they did not act like schoolboys trying to impress the headmaster. They were there for a fight.

Knauss rose for his opening argument. In excruciating detail, he plowed through all the facts, talking, Rice thought, as if the twelve people in the jury box were complete idiots. In truth, they were simply bored.

Knauss then moved to the robbery. This was slightly more interesting, but there was a lot of talk about bags and descriptions that didn't mean much. Knauss talked about his main witness, Bruce Fennimore, explaining that Bruce was not necessarily a nice guy, but he was telling the truth and they would be able to put it all together and believe him on their own. Well, thought Rice, he had that right.

●

Hirsh stood, taking a last-minute look at his notes. He looked every juror in the eye before moving toward them. Right away, the jurors started shifting and straightening. The climate had changed.

Hirsh nodded at Knauss without looking at him. "Counsel," he said by way of recognition. "Ladies and gentlemen," he said to the panel."Let me tell you as a starter to all of this, when you hear from the U. S. attorney . . . I wasn't at the bank on April 22 any more than you. I don't know any more than you do. So when the lawyers make an opening statement to you and show you what they think the evidence will show, this is the *hope* or the expectation of the lawyers on the case."

Rice liked that.

"The central witness that the government presents to you that makes the claim that Grandstaff and Brown were the robbers is absolutely a man who has the carrot in front of him. That has a substantial inducement to give testimony in this case. And the inducement is not money. It's something more important than money. It is his liberty interest that he has at stake and you're going to hear a lot about that.

"I'm telling you there is no case here absent the testimony of Bruce Fennimore. And I think that when you evaluate the truthfulness of the claims, you simply will not be able to accept it and you will render a verdict of 'not guilty.' Thank you for your attention." Hirsh sat down and reclined in his seat. He did not stare at Rice the way the prosecutor and FBI agents were.

Minker got up.

"Before I get into what I consider my formal opening," Minker began, "I'd like to go over something briefly. We live in—as you're well aware—we live in a unique country and we have a unique system of law. And one of those you are taking part in today and that's the criminal justice system. And different from almost every other country in the world, in this country when someone is charged with a crime the *government* has to prove its case to the satisfaction of twelve jurors beyond a reasonable doubt.

"I got involved in this case more than three years ago. . . . I am here today, as is Mr. Hirsh, to present the defense point of view. And the point of all that is that when the government says to you that we have proven our case beyond a reasonable doubt and asks you to return a guilty verdict, that you make sure the government has been put to its test. So as defense counsel, that's what we are doing here. . . ."

Rice was feeling pretty patriotic when it was all over. He was ready.

●

Kenny Kauzlarich and the group from Iowa thought Hirsh had done a pretty good job. They couldn't really be sure, not having ever sat through a trial before, but it seemed like he'd kept everyone's attention real well.

But that wasn't why they'd come. They'd come for Bruce, who was now entering the courtroom. Kenny thought he looked as stupid as ever with his chin thrust forward as if he were hoping somebody would take a poke at him. That wasn't as surprising as the suit, though. Kenny had never seen Bruce in a suit. Not that it was a suit like the attorneys were wearing. It was a kind of green and the lapels were too wide. Bruce wasn't wearing a tie, and the shirt was open à la John Travolta to expose a series of gold chains. The whole effect took Kenny aback, disrupting the hard guy stare he'd planned for Bruce. Kenny was sure Bruce's clothing was new, because he was certain Bruce had never owned clothes like that.

Rice looked at the open shirt and flinched. David had to make an effort to keep his face straight and Doug turned his head. Hirsh and Minker watched impassively. Knauss seemed to be reading everybody's minds. He brought up the suit on direct examination, eliciting that the FBI had bought it for $240.

Hirsh was amused. They'd spent hundreds of thousands on this case, but they couldn't bring their witness into court in anything but a cheap green suit. It spoke for itself. No need to harp.

FENNIMORE

"Now you testified that you spent time in Arizona," Knauss said after going through a litany of evidence. "What was your purpose for being here?"

"David, Doug, and me came looking for things to rob," Bruce answered.

The answer was pleasing. The more often Knauss could get Bruce to say the defendants' names, the better. Hirsh had been objecting like a banshee when Bruce had been saying just "we."

"And what were you looking for in particular?"

"Originally, we came looking for armored cars."

Knauss went on, asking about the techniques for picking targets and how would-be robbers gauge the difficulty of any one job. Bruce sounded stumped at the last question.

"I don't know. We looked for them to be in behind somewhere where nobody could see or where . . ."

David rocked slowly in his chair, never taking his eyes off Bruce. Doug rolled his eyes theatrically, prompting Minker to throw him a sharp warning look. Rice was getting a little pissed off at the man he now knew as FBI agent Larry Bagley, who sat next to Knauss. Bagley, Rice thought, kept staring at the jury as if they were his personal, dim-witted servants.

"When you were down here, were you always with Mr. Grandstaff and Mr. Brown?" Knauss pressed on.

"The majority of the time I was, yes."

"But not always?"

Knauss needed to make this point, because his own evidence reflected the men were not always together. However, Bruce screwed up, insisting that they were together almost all of the time, and Minker was on his feet demanding a full accounting. This testimony did not jibe with Fennimore's previous statements.

"Well . . ." Knauss said, grasping for a comeback.

"Well, I think that's proper cross-examination for you, Mr. Minker," Bilby announced, ending the crisis.

Carefully, Knauss now took Bruce through a number of areas. The man was easily confused by dates and times and tended to make bad gaffes while trying to recover. Knauss was as gentle as possible, moving him through his meeting Doug's girlfriend, Linda, who was now scheduled to testify as an alibi witness. He moved him through the Pinnacle Peak meals, which took some doing, since Bruce had apparently forgotten those episodes entirely. He named nearly every restaurant in town as ones he'd frequented except that one and Knauss had to be careful not to put words in his mouth. Finally, Bruce tumbled to the place. It was a relief.

Knauss was careful to include David's and Doug's names as companions in each incident he mentioned and then moved on to a detailed description of the actual robbery. Bruce testified about clothing, car movements, following bank employees home, tying bank employees up, and every subsequent move the robbers made. Doug's temples throbbed as he stared relentlessly at his former partner. Bruce, who had been studiously avoiding the defense table, was forced to pass by it on his way to a large exhibit—a map of the bank—where he had been asked to show vehicle locations. Inadvertently, he looked down and caught Doug's eye. Bruce's neck nearly snapped, he jerked his head away so quickly. Catching the motion, David glanced at Doug. He gave a brief nod and returned to his rocking. Juror Rice thought it a cool move. If Rice had been Grandstaff, he'd have wanted to come over the table at Fennimore.

Finally, nearing the end of direct examination, it was time for damage control. Time to get to the issues Hirsh would certainly pound and get to them first. First, the issue of remorse. Knauss asked Fennimore about his arrest.

"Well, I just drove out of the parking lot and they (the police) didn't know where I was. I parked the car a couple of blocks away and I was walking to a friend's house. As I'm going there, I'm meeting different police cars and that. Nobody seemed to bother me. . . .

"I got out of the area and decided to straighten up. . . . I just felt like there had been too much happening with my family and things like that. I came back and cleaned up."

Now the touchy area. Government protection and the deals Fennimore had gotten for his testimony. Anytime an informant gets a deal, there is the implied problem that he's lying to get out of prison earlier.

Knauss went into the charges against Fennimore at length. Then he quickly left the charges that had been dropped, concentrating on the ones he'd been sentenced for. Fennimore listed his sentences for TUCROB, possession of stolen property, and a few other minor offenses.

"Were all those sentences to be served consecutively?" Knauss asked.

"They was stacked up on top of one another."

"So in other words, you have a total of thirty years." Good. Let that sink in for the jury. Thirty years is hardly a deal. Knauss went on.

"Now, in December of 1981, did you attempt to have your sentence reduced?"

"Yes. I did."

"Was it reduced?"

"No. It wasn't."

Finally, Knauss addressed the issue of the ill-gotten gains the jury might think Bruce still had stashed away somewhere. Brother, those gold chains certainly weren't helping this one.

"You have tax problems?"

"Yes."

"Have you been offered any help?"

"No. You said that would all be up to the IRS."

"Do you have the money to satisfy those needs?"

"No. I do not."

"Do you own any real property?"

"No. I do not."

"What happened to the Corvette you were allowed to keep?"

"I sold it. I had a ten-thousand-dollar note to the bank that my father had signed on. I sold it and give him the money in cash. Then I had . . . I been locked up six years. It's gone. I gave some to my kids. Some to my ex. I spent a little."

"Okay." Knauss was pleased after he got in that Bruce had to be bought a suit because he also owned no clothing. He'd also gotten in the fact that the man had done quite a bit of time in prison. He ended his direct examination. There would be plenty of time for re-direct, as he expected Hirsh and Minker to keep Fennimore around for days. He wasn't wrong.

●

Knauss could not have known that Hirsh was smirking about the clothes and Minker was smirking about the family support bit. Minker had an entire court file on Bruce's abuses toward his wife and children.

Hirsh got up and wasted no time in attacking Knauss's final points.

"Now, I want to get a few things straight here, sir," Hirsh said. "You are eligible for parole in February of 1988, is that correct?" The date was three months away. Not thirty years.

"Yes."

"And at that time, you will notify Mr. Bagley, Mr. Oxler, and Mr. Knauss, is that correct?"

"Yes."

"And you expect them to be present at that hearing, in accordance with the agreement you have with the government, isn't that right, sir?" Knauss himself had admitted to this, although he'd downplayed it.

"Yes. Yes." Bruce said nervously.

Hirsh went on to outline the terms of the agreement. If Bruce testified satisfactorily at the TUCROB trial, the prosecutor and two FBI agents would give favorable testimony to the board about his cooperation and rehabilitation. They would not guarantee his release, but they would be present to help it along. Hirsh jammed the point home.

"And in fact, sir, they're (the government) going to give an assessment about how well you've cooperated with them, isn't that a fact, sir?"

"I believe that. Yes." Bruce apparently did not realize that he'd just freely admitted his best reason to lie.

"And the parole board can set you free right then, isn't that true?"

"I hope they will," Bruce said meekly.

Hirsh moved on. He could see Fennimore was trying harder to grapple with this change in their previously cozy relationship than with the questions. Ill-prepared witness, Hirsh thought.

Peter Carlson, the prison warden at the Federal Correctional Institution in Phoenix, would later testify that Fennimore had been a "cancerous personality," had disrupted his institution and that Carlson had tried to have him transferred to a different prison to avoid altercations or worse in his protective custody unit, where Bruce was housed.

Bruce did not want to leave Phoenix because he enjoyed warm weather and Carlson would also testify that he'd been prevented from making the transfer after a call from Richard Davis at the justice department, asking him not to. As a "favor," Carlson would testify that he obeyed the order. But Hirsh now brought out that while Bruce was having his troubles with the warden, he made forty phone calls to Dan Knauss and agents Bagley and Oxler.

"Didn't he (Knauss) say he was going to intercede for you?" Hirsh asked.

"I believe he called Washington," Bruce said proudly.

"Called Washington," Hirsh repeated. "That's higher than Mr. Carlson, isn't it?"

"I believe it is," said a pleased Fennimore.

Hirsh began going over all the points Knauss had raised. Where Bruce had gone after the robbery. Who he had seen. What cars had he bought. Had David or Doug ever been with him on a single one of these trips back to Omaha or Des Moines? Could any of the Iowans he'd visited place them together? No. No. And "No" came the answers. And Bruce was starting to get testy.

Bruce admitted knowing he was wanted for TUCROB when he got back to Iowa, but for some strange reason denied seeing newspaper accounts about the event which, at the time, were front page news every single day. Hirsh started to bore in. Not on the law. On the personality. Bruce was simply being recalcitrant and Hirsh wanted to give him his fullest opportunity to show it off. After ten minutes of questioning about the newspapers, during which time he expected an objection from Knauss at any time that never came, Hirsh delivered a zinger.

"But at least you were alerted to the fact that your picture had been in the paper," Hirsh said in a compromising voice.

"Yep." Bruce shifted confidently with his victory.

"And you claim not to be curious enough to get a newspaper and find out what the newspapers were saying about you? That was of no interest to you, Mr. Fennimore?"

"Well, I read a newspaper that he (a friend) had in his possession."

Looking startled, Hirsh exclaimed: "Oh! You *did* read a newspaper!"

"I didn't see the Des Moines paper *first.* That's what you asked me. I saw the Omaha paper *first.*"

It was one of many remarks that would make the jurors glance at each other sidelong. It was an idiotic distinction their children might make in an argument.

Hirsh now moved through the tedious hotel receipts, the road bills, the car receipts and Fennimore's use of the alias Tom Kline—all important because of the last hotel bill. He also asked with each person Bruce met with, were Doug or David with him. The answer was always no and then Bruce did it again.

"And Dave Bell," Hirsh said, checking his notes. "You saw him too."

"I don't know a Dave Bell," Bruce said defiantly.

Hirsh was momentarily confused. "You don't know anybody by? . . . Is it Craig Bell?" he said, finding the correct notation.

"Yeah."

"Oh. Craig Bell," Hirsh said sarcastically. "You got me on that one, sir."

Hirsh returned to Bruce's movements around Des Moines directly after the robbery. Again Hirsh made an error in the sequence of events and again Bruce corrected him. His tone implied that the attorney was too dense to remember that Bruce made a stop at his mother's house to drop off $400,000 in a suitcase, asking her to bury it. Hirsh couldn't have been more delighted.

"How old a woman is she sir?" Hirsh asked.

"About sixty-two."

"And she is a single woman?"

"Yes."

"And you give her a suitcase full of money."

"I give her a suitcase. Yes."

"Well, it was full of money, wasn't it Mr. Fennimore? And you tell your sixty-two-year-old mother to bury the suitcase in the backyard. Is that right, sir?"

"Somewhere along them lines."

Hirsh asked whether Bruce had discussed TUCROB or his fugitive status with his mother while carrying out the task.

"I only seen her for a few minutes," Bruce replied.

"You mean you'd been on the run since November of 1980. You went to Des Moines and saw your mother and told her to take the suitcase and bury it in the backyard."

"Yes."

"And then left and said 'Goodby Ma.'"

"That's right."

"Did you at least leave her a shovel, sir?"

"I figured she had a shovel," Bruce said, sticking his chin out.

In the jury box, Rice turned to the juror next to him.

Then it was time for lunch.

42

Before the jury filed back in, Hirsh sashayed over to the witness stand and leaned casually against the rail. He was a foot from Bruce's face.

"Hi, Bruce," he said. "You want to take a look at these notes I've made to make sure they're accurate?"

Bruce fairly rocketed from his chair trying to move away. Hirsh smiled faintly and wandered leisurely back to the defense table, waiting for the jury. No matter what the crime, Hirsh had never liked an informant.

●

Hirsh started in slowly again, going through the events after the robbery. After finishing with the three days Bruce had spent in the Des Moines area, he turned to Bruce's trip to Miami where he'd met again with Lee Pettit, bought his Corvette, met with David Grandstaff, then taken a trip to Atlantic City with a married woman.

Departing from his careful rebuttal of Knauss's direct, Hirsh at no time mentioned any of Bruce's meetings with David in Miami over this period. The only person who could corroborate it was Lee Pettit, the tall cowboy who Bruce said had received $10,000 for purchasing the TUCROB van in Phoenix. For some strange reason, neither the defense nor the prosecution had been able to locate Pettit in more than three years. For some strange reason, the prosecution never made an issue of it. For some strange reason, Bruce made the same comments about his father and the $400,000 he'd left there as he'd made about his mother.

Hirsh then turned to Bruce's arrest on June 3, 1981, attacking

Bruce's testimony that he'd turned himself in to "come clean."

Hirsh: "Now, let me ask you this, sir. On direct examination you told the jury that on the night of June fourth you thought things had gone too far and you just got tired, is that right?"

"I think things did get out of hand, yes."

Referring to his notes, Hirsh added that Bruce had said the same thing in a court-ordered pretrial interview. Bruce had consistently refused to talk to the defense lawyers unless ordered and then refused to be tape-recorded. Hirsh hammered on that for a while and then returned to the arrest.

"Well," Hirsh went on, "let me talk to you about that, sir, for a moment. Your decision to turn yourself in. The fact is that on that particular evening you were out with Theresa Shay in your new Corvette."

"Yes."

"And you parked over at the Merle Hall Mall in front of the Cattle Company Restaurant."

"The Merle Hay Mall," Bruce corrected him.

David rocked slowly in his chair. The answer was almost the key to Bruce's lunacy. He really thought he owned Des Moines. Because he'd been associated with The Boys and gotten into a few bar fights, it was the only place the guy felt important. Again, David cursed himself for not seeing it. Of course Bruce would have returned there to bask in his glory. To play the big man. And now he was willing to look like a moron before an entire room of ex-friends and strangers just to prove he knew the name of a two-bit shopping mall.

David was tired. He hadn't been sleeping more than a few hours a night and he'd taken up smoking for the first time since he'd quit twenty years ago to make money off the damned things in Anamosa. The authorities were dragging in inmates from all over the country, subpoenaed by Hirsh for the defense. All of them had been given rough trips by the U.S. marshals and all of them wanted to catch up on old times to ease the pain. David wanted to be left alone to read his legal briefs and newspapers in preparation for the next day's rigors, but his first obligation was to them. He watched Fennimore again, wondering what it must feel like to feel no sense of obligation. Bruce was in the process of denying that he left the Merle Hay Mall at a high rate of speed because he knew the FBI had him surrounded.

"Well, sir," Hirsh was saying, "something caused you to back out of there in a big hurry, isn't that right?"

Bruce hedged around a bit, finally admitting that he actually had seen the FBI agents in the van and noticed the other cars in the lot, though he steadfastly denied knowing that he'd nearly hit an agent on the way out. He was forced to admit realizing that his own car had been hit by agents in the rented T-Bird. That was a hard one to ignore.

When Hirsh reminded Bruce that—in the process of turning himself in—he'd doused his headlights after leaving the mall parking lot, skidded through a residential neighborhood, and run up onto a lawn over a child's tricycle that moments earlier had been occupied, Bruce said it "could have happened," but he just didn't remember. It was becoming one of his favorite answers.

Bruce tried to mitigate his desperate escape from the mall.

"The only activity that was going on was in the mall itself. Nobody chased me down the street or . . . They had no idea I'd left the mall."

Considering the fact that Bruce had been rammed by a police vehicle and nearly hit an agent before tearing off with a rooster tail of sparks behind him, the answer stunned even Hirsh. "The police had no idea you'd left the mall, sir?" he asked incredulously.

"They didn't find the Corvette for fifteen minutes," Bruce replied stubbornly.

"You mean you outsmarted the police? Is that what you're telling us?"

"I don't know that I outsmarted anybody. I'm just telling you the fact that—"

"How is it that you know that they didn't know that you'd left the mall for fifteen minutes, sir?"

Finally, Knauss got up. "I'm going to object. He didn't say that about the mall. He said that about the car."

The judge sustained the objection, but it was a day late and a dollar short and Hirsh dismissed it with a simple "Oh, I misunderstood."

He then proceeded to outline everything Bruce had done that evening, from running through backyards to dumping suitcases full of money into hiding places to throwing away all of his identification to, finally, refusing to talk to the police when he was arrested.

"For a man who is turning himself in, Mr. Fennimore, you are doing one heck of a job," Hirsh concluded.

Moving right along, Hirsh returned to Bruce's plea agreement, in which a series of charges against him were dropped in exchange for a "statement."

"You would agree that you got one heck of a deal in Des Moines, Iowa, in June of 1981?"

"I think so."

"And all they wanted in return was for you to give a statement."

"Yes."

"And you had to come up with names."

"Yes."

Now moving again to Fennimore's past record, Hirsh said, "Prior to your incarceration, do you remember having to go to a probation officer for a pre-sentence report?"

"No," Bruce said, again with the chin out. "I didn't go to him. He came to see me."

"Oh! You are right, sir," Hirsh said, dripping sarcasm. "*You* are right. *He* came to see *you*."

Hirsh went into lengthy questioning about Bruce's car thefts and odometer alterations. He consistently referred to the practice as "swindling honest folks," knowing full well that many people on the jury probably had been taken in car deals before. Bruce never objected to the term and at one point replied that he'd made a pretty good living at the gig. He said it with a touch of pride that filled James Rice with disgust.

Hirsh now made what was to become a tactical error by bringing up a series of crimes, including the Dahl's Market robbery and others, which Bruce had admitted to in police reports. Knauss would now be able to go into those robberies on re-direct, because Hirsh had opened the door.

"Now, isn't it true, sir," Hirsh said, "that until 1981 your life was about nineteen years of continuous criminal activity?"

Bruce sparred around a bit on that one, finally admitting that he'd been involved in "some crime," which had not been mentioned to the probation officer who came to interview him before he was sentenced.

"In fact, you did not tell the truth about your background, did you?" Hirsh prodded.

"I told him that I had been in the car business, didn't I?" Bruce said sullenly.

"You told him you were an honest, righteous car dealer."

"I don't think it says anything about being an honest and righteous—"

"Well, you didn't tell him you were a crooked car dealer, did you?"

"No. I didn't. But I didn't tell him I was an honest one, either."

"Oh, you mean—"

"I didn't tell him either way."

"Oh. Okay. So you told him you were in the car business, but you didn't tell him 'I was in the crooked car business,' so therefore you told the truth."

"I think I told you I skirted around some of it."

"Oh. That was a skirt."

●

If Bruce understood the world of hurt he was in, he was not showing it. For the next day, he continued to argue with Hirsh on small points without ever once denting the real implications. Hirsh had him admit he'd thrown a beer bottle at a waitress, to which Bruce replied he'd actually thrown it at her table and it had subsequently ricocheted off into a plate glass window near her. Hirsh asked about a grocery store robbery in which thirty people were forced to lie on the floor—like "cordwood," as Bruce had described to the police. Bruce argued with Hirsh as to whether they'd been on their faces for ten minutes or fifteen.

"Then in 1977 you were involved in an armored car robbery," Hirsh went on. "Remember that one, sir?"

"Refresh my memory," Bruce challenged.

"Well, that was the one where the courier was kidnapped and at your request he was tossed out of the car while the car was moving. Remember that one?"

"No. I don't remember that."

"You deny it?"

"I don't deny it. I just don't remember it."

"You mean it just slipped your memory? That a courier was tossed out of a moving car?"

The jury panel looked perplexed. Rice caught Bagley looking at one of the women as if to say that all of this were mere hocus-pocus. The woman looked quickly away.

●

Bruce chuckled happily when Hirsh confused the sequence of assaults Bruce had made—one on a cab driver and the other on his own attorney.

Hirsh: "And what's worse, sir, the time that you were charged with assaulting a cab driver, you even assaulted the lawyer that was defending you because you got mad at him."

Fennimore: "That's not true."

"You did not assault your own lawyer?"

Fennimore (laughing): "You just said at the time I assaulted the cab driver, I assaulted my attorney. . . ."

"Oh. Okay. *After* you assaulted the cab driver, you assaulted your attorney."

Minker began collecting his notes. Hirsh had only a few more points to make.

For good measure, Hirsh pointed out that of a $1 million cut, Bruce had seen fit to give only $10,000 to his wife and children, who were practically destitute at the time. Hirsh implied that Bruce had attempted to set David up by leaving a gun David had purchased in a car Bruce had driven alone to San Diego, parked at the airport, and knew would be found.

"Not *we,* sir," Hirsh thundered when Bruce tried to include David and Doug in the disposal of the car. "Not *we! You! You* parked the car all by yourself!"

Next, Hirsh hammered away at Bruce's assertion that David and Doug had been with him at the Holiday Inn North a day before the robbery. The registration card, Hirsh brought out over and over, was signed by Bruce and listed an occupancy for one person in one room. Still smarting from Hirsh's outburst, Bruce started waffling on when David or Doug might have been at the hotel.

"They may have been, but I'm not positive about that. They may have had a room off the swimming pool someplace. We stayed so many different times at so many places. . . ."

"Yes," Hirsh jumped in. "But this is *two days* before a three-million-dollar robbery and you can't tell the jury whether they stayed in the same room?"

"We went to rob that bank several different times."

"I understand, sir. I understand your claim. You can't tell the jury whether these men stayed in your room?"

"Not, uh . . . truthfully, I can't tell exactly where they were at."

"Well, sir, you didn't sleep in the same bed, did you?"

"Hell no!" Bruce was clearly flustered by the question. "We drug mattresses. . . ."

"Well, there were two beds in that room, weren't there?"

"I assume there was."

"All you do is make assumptions, is that right?"

Minker was ready. Hirsh had only one last coup d'etat. In a pretrial interview, Bruce had told the defense team that—with all the aliases he'd used—he'd never been tripped up on a story. He'd always been able to keep his lies straight.

Hirsh: "But you were never caught in any lies."

"I believe I did tell you that."

"And you were a successful liar."

"Yes."

"Thank you, sir."

Hirsh wheeled toward the defense table, wondering why in the hell Dan Knauss had allowed his star witness to be bludgeoned so badly. In two days of testimony, Knauss had objected only a few times and those had been lame. Hirsh hoped the prosecutor didn't have any tricks up his sleeve. As it turned out, he did.

●

Jeffrey Minker's cross-examination of Bruce Fennimore gave him the darkest days of the trial. No matter how hard he tried, he just couldn't seem to get going. He couldn't get anywhere and it wasn't because Bruce was doing such a good job. Minker knew it was his fault.

The first night, Minker gave himself a stern talking to and rehearsed more of his questions in preparation for the next day. But the next day, nothing had changed. Minker just couldn't seem to make the big points. The jury was fidgeting and finally Minker just sat down, depressed. Doug Brown looked at him scornfully.

Knauss got back up for his re-direct. He did not address any of the character flaws Hirsh had brought out. After all, he'd already conceded that Fennimore was not an angel. What he did do left the defense team speechless.

Knauss proceeded to list every robbery Fennimore had ever confessed to—about twelve in all—and asked after each incident, "Did you commit this robbery alone?" Fennimore replied in each case, "No."

The tactic, Hirsh felt, clearly violated the court's ruling that previous crimes be excluded from the trial. Yet neither he nor Minker felt they could object to the questions in front of the jury. It might lend credence to Knauss's clear inference that David and Doug were the partners in those crimes.

At the recess, Hirsh demanded a mistrial.

"It's pretty obvious to anyone listening that Grandstaff and Brown were supposed to be the participants in these and Mr. Knauss is circumventing a court ruling by asking the questions as he did. In other words, 'this is our little secret that Grandstaff and Brown were the participants.' "

Hirsh said the introduction of prior bad acts was absolutely improper and there should be a mistrial immediately. Knauss countered that Hirsh had questioned Fennimore himself on the other robberies and added:

"There is an inference that Bruce Fennimore is a one-man crime wave. And the fact is, he didn't do it alone."

Clearly concerned, Judge Bilby said he would take the motion for a mistrial under advisement. Hirsh was not unhappy with that. If Bilby ruled against him, he would have excellent grounds for an appeal. And he expected to be forced to appeal after this conviction. Meanwhile, the show would go on.

●

The government now brought in the victims of the robbery: Bud Grainger, the bank manager; David Harris, the assistant manager; and Charlie Virgil, the janitor who'd been snatched from his truck. This was mostly a matter of form. The men had not seen anything useful, and the stories of what they had seen differed so drastically from one another as to be almost a liability for the prosecution.

Charlie Virgil, for example, was adamant that there were four robbers, not the three described by Grainger and Harris. Hirsh harped on this constantly, pointing out that Virgil had spent the most time in the bandits' company. In an effort to excuse his own witness, Knauss pointed out that Virgil must have been terrified. Wouldn't the stress alone have caused some problems with perception, Knauss asked? Virgil, who had been accused of the crime, questioned for days, and threatened by the police with a lifetime in prison, replied:

"I wasn't terrified until you people got ahold of me."

Knauss quickly sat down.

David Harris gave steady, calm, and unremarkable testimony, responding only to the questions he was asked. Bud Grainger often interrupted the questioning attorneys with little details he'd forgotten. Knauss allowed Grainger to deliver lengthy descriptions uninterrupted. He must have believed there was a sympathy factor for the aging man who'd been terrorized and Knauss guided him along like a health professional helping an Alzheimer's patient.

Hirsh found it condescending and even tiresome. But he was not about to object and make the jury think he had no sympathy for the victim.

"We are not going to lay a hand on him," Hirsh muttered to David, who nodded his approval. He'd noticed the way Bilby catered to Grainger and he did not want Hirsh to anger the judge with pointed questions.

Minker had also noted the judge's shepherding of Grainger, but had decided not to lay hands on him for other reasons. Minker felt Grainger was engaging in a kind of therapy to rid himself of the robbery experience. Looking at his own client, he could well imagine why such therapy might be necessary.

Several jurors were not as charitable. They felt Grainger's tearful breakdowns were a tad melodramatic. After all, thought Rice, the thing happened more than five years ago and nobody was hurt. Rice also thought Grainger's accusatory stares in the direction of the defense table were uncalled for. Hadn't the man said he never saw the faces of the guys who accosted him? Why was he looking at them as if he wanted to throw a stick of dynamite in that direction. Innocent until proven guilty, Rice thought. And you weren't going to be able to prove guilt by this testimony.

Rocking in his chair, David wondered how many times and at how many parties Grainger had told the story of his harrowing brush with death. Probably added years to the guy's life, David thought. Given him something to live for. Unlike the prospects he himself was facing.

43

On a misty morning in November, a U.S. marshal jet was revving up at a tiny airstrip outside Marion, Illinois. The jet had been positioned at the farthermost end of the strip, far away from buildings or any other signs of human life. It sat near acres and acres of lonely farmland, surrounded by a dozen marshals armed to the teeth with pump shotguns held upright in a ready firing position. Some marshals also kept a hand on their side arms. The U.S. marshal service was taking no chances with Terry Lee Conner.

A small caravan of marshal vehicles crawled slowly up the runway, making their way from the federal penitentiary some miles away. There were marshals in the front cars, marshals in the back cars, and four marshalls surrounding Terry Lee Conner, who was shackled hand and foot for his trip to Tucson to take responsibility for the largest robbery in U.S. history. Conner had a small smile. For a robber whom the press had branded as the "gentleman bandit," he had certainly become a dangerous outlaw.

"You guys must think I'm Houdini and Rambo rolled into one," he remarked good-naturedly to the marshal next to him.

The officer sighed. It *was* a bit embarrassing. And for all the precautions, most of the marshals actually liked Conner. He was personable and intelligent. But that didn't change the fact that he'd escaped twice, once by taking guns away from colleagues and handcuffing them to a tree. It could have been life threatening.

"Terry," the marshal said, "if you get away from us again, they'll disband the agency on the grounds of sheer stupidity. We couldn't afford to leave anything to chance."

"Well," Conner said mildly, "I congratulate you on your thoroughness. If you need a recommendation, feel free to ask."

A half dozen marshals accompanied Conner to Tucson in the sleek jet. He was the only prisoner on board, and they weren't picking anyone up for a return trip. "Mighty impressive," Conner thought. "If they'd just loaned me the money they're spending on this flight when my businesses were in trouble, I wouldn't be here now."

When Conner got to the prison in Tucson, there was a screwup. At least it would be called a screwup later. The inmates say they wielded the same influence with some guards that is practiced all over the country to get drugs and other contraband inside, namely money. Conner ended up in a cell next to David Grandstaff, and they chatted uninterrupted until the "mistake" was discovered two hours later. Newspaper clippings and other written material were passed back and forth. It was generally assumed that Conner was getting a refresher course on the visit he received from Doug Brown's friend months earlier.

●

George Weir, Garvin White, George Ripley, and Sean Duval (who had returned to prison since the motel meeting with Hirsh) were also being rounded up from prisons around the country. In all, about fifteen inmates would be brought to Tucson, but not all of them would be called to testify.

Transport security did not approach the level ordained for Conner, but it was still unusual. There were two or more marshals per prisoner. The men were not allowed shoes, but given slippers called "bus slippers" by the inmates. Shackles were not removed during flight, a fact George complained about loudly.

"For Christ's sake," he said with annoyance. "Do you think I'm going to jump out of an airplane at thirty thousand feet? How am I supposed to take a piss like this?"

Arriving at the far end of Tucson International's runways, George saw a large bus, a half dozen marshals' cars, and the heavily armed officers, the desert sun glinting off their upraised shotguns.

"Jesus," White said, leaning over George to peer at the spectacle. "What creep do you suppose they're expecting?"

It had not occurred to George, either, that the welcoming party was for them.

Inside the prison, the men were escorted to solitary, four guards to a man. George thought things were really getting out of hand. They hadn't removed the foot shackles and it was difficult to walk. Once inside the cells, they were made to squat down and stick their hands between the bars before the cuffs were removed. It was a security procedure used for only the most violent and high-risk prisoners. George was irritated.

"Where the hell do you people think I'm gonna go, anyway?"

"Orders," the guards said curtly.

"Man, these guys have been worried about your arrival for weeks," a resident prisoner next to George informed. "They are scared shitless of you."

George did not believe that. He believed the treatment was being meted out because the government was aggravated that (A) the men had banded together to testify for Grandstaff and Brown and that (B) it was a lot of trouble moving them around. He did not expect the treatment to improve and it didn't. Once, George was taken outside in abnormally freezing temperatures to exercise and was not provided shoes or a jacket. The guard began to complain about the cold in twenty minutes, but that just egged George on. He was due an hour and if he had to suffer, so did his keeper.

Over Knauss's objections, some of the TUCROB inmates' jail experiences would come out at trial. Juror Rice, who generally thought the men were far more interesting than some other witnesses, did not approve of what he considered to be petty and unfair retaliations. Bilby agreed, although more privately. Not only did he allow the testimony, but he made some orders for change in conditions.

44

Hirsh did not spend an undue amount of time on Detective Michael Garigan or Agent Carl Gosting, the lawmen who'd shown the four photographs to Kathy Faller after her 88-CRIME call. They were unfriendly witnesses, accustomed to testifying, and Hirsh didn't want to give them a chance to demonstrate their contempt for career criminals. Besides, he only had one significant point to make with either of them.

Hirsh: "Now, it's not the procedure of the Tucson Police Department to simply show one photo of one suspect to witnesses when you're doing a photographic lineup, is it, sir?"

Garigan: "No. It's not our procedure."

Hirsh: "You have strict procedures in that regard, don't you?"

Garigan: "Yes. We do."

Hirsh: "In other words, in order to make it fair, the police endeavor to pick out five or six similar-looking individuals and put all of them in a photographic array. To give the victim or the witness a fair opportunity to pick out the one that he or she can identify. That's the process, isn't it?"

Garigan: "Yes. It is."

Hirsh: "Now, this was not a police department investigation, was it?"

Garigan: "No. It wasn't."

Hirsh: "It was an FBI investigation, wasn't it?"

Garigan: "Yes. It was."

Hirsh: "Now, did you talk (to the agents) about the feeling that this might be a suggestive showing of photographs?"

Garigan: "No."

FBI agent Gosting received the same questions.

Hirsh: "And in fact, sir, isn't it true that the usual custom of the FBI is to provide witnesses with a minimum of six different photos when you do a police lineup?"

Gosting: "The usual practice, yes."

Hirsh: "And in fact, there was a book in your office that had been prepared with the twenty-four photos in it. That would be for each of the four suspects there would be six photos for a total of twenty-four."

Gosting: "Yes."

On re-direct, Knauss brought out that Gosting couldn't remember if he'd known about the book the day he went to see Faller. And Garigan said he made distinctions between victims and witnesses when doing lineups, saying there was a different standard for witnesses, of which Faller was one. Hirsh slouched in his chair, watching the men. When they were finished, he had no further questions and they were dismissed.

●

Knauss continued with his stream of law enforcement witnesses—he would call nineteen over the five-week trial—but one of the most important was Washington, D.C., agent Charles McGinnis. The sixteen-year veteran of the FBI had impressive credentials as a handwriting and fingerprint expert, which he delineated at great length. Hirsh rocked in his chair as if bored to tears. If the jury noticed Hirsh thought the credentials unimportant, perhaps they would, too. He certainly hoped so, because—aside from Bruce —McGinnis's testimony was the strongest link between David and TUCROB.

McGinnis, an obviously thorough man, had come well prepared

with a half dozen charts, graphs, and blowups of the various samples taken from the cars and hotel registration cards. Knauss walked him through the complex science of fingerprint identification as simply as he could, but the testimony went on for hours and was often confusing. Hirsh did his best to confuse it further on cross-examination, but when he sat down, he couldn't see how the jurors could not believe the prints belonged to David. He planned to call his own expert to rebut the claim, but McGinnis had him convinced.

Not so convincing was Bobby Gene Jones, the career criminal Knauss called for two reasons: to show that Brown had a great deal of money after his release for which to pay for an escape and to show that Bruce Fennimore did, indeed, have cause to fear for his life. Jones would testify that Brown had asked Jones to "hit" Fennimore, along with two other men Brown believed had stolen money from him.

Knauss attempted to head off the inevitable character attack by bringing out Jones's record first himself, although he did not do so in as much detail as he knew Minker would when he got his hands on the witness. Still, it took some time to get through the dozens of charges Jones had received over the years. And then Knauss had to bring out the fact that Jones had perjured himself at other trials in which he'd testified for the government.

Having put that unpleasantness behind him, Knauss moved on to Jones's meetings with Brown in the Nevada County Jail shortly after Brown's arrest in Denver. The prosecutor hit a nasty bump right off the bat when Jones testified that he did, indeed, know Doug Brown and proceeded to identify David Grandstaff when asked to point out the man he'd met.

Minker looked up quickly, unsure if this good fortune could really be happening. There was no question Jones had met Brown in the jail. The records were clear. How could he identify Grandstaff?

David leaned over to Doug, whispering, "I wonder why the asshole did that?" There was no question in David's mind the gaffe was deliberate.

Hirsh seized the moment to become accommodating to the prosecution.

"You want them to stand up?" he asked.

A flustered Knauss said yes, and after listening to Jones ramble about how he "didn't see too good," finally got him to make the correct identification.

Jones's direct testimony about his plans to spring Doug Brown and kill Bruce Fennimore was not entirely satisfactory. The Perkins Pancake House meetings in which he said Clyde handed over money were confusing and Jones added elements he hadn't described in earlier interviews. Describing Brown's discussion of various "hits" he wanted, Jones took some pleasure in revealing his business acumen.

"He agreed so quickly to the prices," he told Knauss, "that I kinda tried to double-dip him. . . . Other people would have to be paid a substantial amount of money—a higher amount of money to kill Fennimore than it would be to kill the other two."

It wasn't the kind of attitude anyone likes in their witnesses, but at least the testimony had not ended in the disaster in which it started. Until Minker got ahold of him.

After an exhaustive rundown of Jones's criminal history—in which Jones cheerfully admitted he was "one of the most active criminals in America"—Minker established that Jones could have been responsible for dismembering people in a St. Louis union hall bombing and shooting someone else in a bank burglary. It was all done over Knauss's objections and Minker never offered evidence of the crimes, for which Jones had not been charged, but the specter remained.

Minker then turned to Jones's relationship with the FBI, which began in 1978 and was still in effect. Jones would not say how much money he made through illegal activities between 1979 and 1981, but allowed that it was hundreds of thousands of dollars. All the while he was working for the FBI. During the year Jones dealt with Doug Brown, the agency paid him "eleven thousand dollars and change," not including the $5,000 the agency gave him to open a jewelry store, likely stocked in part with stolen jewels.

Minker: "And these stores. Did the FBI know you had these stores?"

Jones: "Yeah, they did."

Minker: "They were open for business to the public."

Jones: "Open for business."

Minker: "And you were there, on occasion."

Jones: "When I wasn't stealing stuff, I was."

Minker: "Right. And did (Agent Steven) Steinhauser ever come in and see you there?"

Jones: "No. He stayed away from my place."

Minker drove on relentlessly.

Minker: "In fact, to anyone who could see what you were doing, you were spending much more money on your living activities than you could show you were legitimately earning?"

Jones: "Yes. I was liquidating assets and spending it. I had a lot of jewelry and diamonds. I had real estate."

Minker: "But it's true, sir, that you couldn't account for all the money you had. From legal methods anyway."

Jones: "No, I couldn't as a matter of fact."

Minker: "And you were spending far more money than you were earning from your legal activities, including any jewelry you were selling."

Jones: "Yes."

Minker: "Considerably more."

Jones: "Yes."

Minker: "Did the FBI ever talk to you about that?"

Jones: "Yes, they did as a matter of fact."

Minker: "Did they ask you if you were out committing crimes?"

Jones: "And I said no."

Minker: "And what did (Agent Steven) Steinhauser do? Wink at you and say 'Don't commit any crimes'?"

●

After confusing Jones's already muddled testimony about the Brown escape attempt and the $35,000 paid to him by Clyde, Minker turned to the crucial Jones accusation—that Brown had wanted Bruce dead. Minker wanted to make his points crystal clear. That Jones had been in steady contact with the FBI during the time he planned an escape with Brown and had told them about the escape—but never about any murder plans. And that the only time a murder-for-hire plot surfaced was in 1984 when Jones found himself at Sandstone Penitentiary in witness protection with Bruce Fennimore. And finally, that Jones had been re-arrested at that time and was facing a twelve-year state sentence in Colorado and the Colorado authorities were not making any deals. He might have hoped the feds would help.

Minker: "And isn't it true, sir, that you never, ever, ever, told Steven Steinhauser while he's your control agent through '81 and '82 that you spoke to anybody about doing a contract killing? That you spoke to Doug Brown about doing a contract killing?"

Jones: "That's right."

Minker: "In fact, the first time it comes up is in 1984."

Jones: " '84? Probably."

Minker: "When you were with Bruce Fennimore."

Jones: "Right."

When Minker turned, exhausted, to resume his seat, he caught an approving glance from Hirsh. It might have been wishful thinking, but he thought even Brown nodded slightly before turning away. Well, at least Minker thought he might be able to sleep well one night during this doomed effort.

DESPERSIS

Hirsh had not planned on rebutting the government's fingerprint evidence. It was too compelling. It would be a waste of time and money, trying to find an expert who would disagree. But in the end, he decided it couldn't hurt to try. He was not obligated to report negative results. He decided upon Joseph Despersis, a twenty-five-year veteran of the Phoenix Police Department who had spent the last sixteen in fingerprinting before retiring into private practice several years earlier.

Hirsh met with Despersis for only one hour, but during that time Despersis said he disputed the FBI's contention that the prints and handwriting found on the San Diego car and the registration cards could be positively identified as David Grandstaff's. Hirsh was no fingerprint expert, but he was pretty sure the FBI was right. Still, he hadn't indicated what he wanted Despersis to say, and the man had sixteen years' experience with the Phoenix Police Department working with prints. As it was about to turn out, Despersis would prove valuable in quite another way.

Hirsh was not a believer in inundating juries—even superintelligent ones—with a plethora of technical facts it had taken experts years to master. If it didn't put them to sleep, it had the opposite, dangerous effect of making them believe they could learn it all by reading library books and come to independent—mostly erroneous—conclusions on their own. Hirsh thought McGinnis (and Knauss for that matter) in their zest to convince people of their expertise had made a mistake. He did not intend to handle Despersis that way.

Despersis shuffled into the courtroom unobtrusively, an elderly, white-haired gentleman with the air of a concerned grandfather. As Hirsh rose, he glanced at Knauss, who looked completely unconcerned. Knauss flipped through several letters with official letterheads on them, as if he were reminding himself of the true issue here. Hirsh knew what those issues were. He'd seen Knauss that morning in whispered conference with several of Arizona's Department of Public Safety (DPS) agents. Hirsh thought it was a mistake. He hoped it was, anyway.

Despersis took the stand without fanfare, arranged his glasses, and watched Hirsh without expression. It was the stance of a witness who had taken the stand more than 500 times and knew the drill. Hirsh was also appreciative of the Dick and Jane explanation Despersis offered for his drastically different opinion from the formidable Agent McGinnis's.

Yes, McGinnis had found six definite points of comparison on the fingerprints. Of course, the standard by law used to be twelve—just to be safe—but that had changed over the years. It was too bad.

But even with the six, some of them were "common" points. Yes, it was true that every individual's fingerprints were unique. But some "points" were common. In other words, the fingerprint as a whole was unique, but there were point traits that could be shared by more than one individual. Despersis believed that some of McGinnis's "definite" points were actually "common" points and that—unless he had many more points—the fingerprint could not absolutely be identified. It was, Despersis demured, only his opinion.

The Despersis opinion was a hell of a lot easier to understand and Hirsh was pleased. But he knew Knauss was not going to spend much time defending the testimony of his indisputably expert witness. He was going to attack.

Knauss: "You gave me a business card just like that one yesterday, did you not?"

Despersis: "Yes. I did."

Knauss: "Now, your business card, exhibit 105, says you're a certified latent examiner, does it not?"

Despersis: "Yes. It does."

Knauss: "In fact, your certification was revoked in October of 1986, wasn't it?"

Despersis: "Yes. It was."

Knauss was not finished with the explosions. He went after Despersis on the short period he'd spent evaluating weeks of FBI work. He pointed out that Despersis had brought no charts or graphs, just two, 3-by-5 cards. He proved that Despersis had had professional complaints filed against him in two separate Phoenix criminal cases, based on his testimony for the defense. Knauss indicated that Despersis still had a need to support himself. The implication was clear, but Knauss made it clearer.

Knauss: "How do you get paid?"

Despersis: "We arrive at a fee and I—"

Knauss: "How much are you getting paid for this case?"

Despersis: "Well, it all depends how long I'm on the stand. It looks like I'm going to be able to retire on what I make on this."

The courtroom erupted in laughter. David dropped his head so the jury could not see his smile. The old coot was not as helpless as he looked.

"How much are you getting paid in this case?" Knauss asked evenly, refusing to acknowledge the outburst.

"I'm getting paid mileage and I'm getting paid twenty-five dollars an hour for testifying in court and I'm getting paid ten dollars an hour for standby." Despersis's tone was mild.

Knauss repeated the figures meaningfully for the jury. Hirsh got to his feet on re-direct, sincerely annoyed. Knauss's tactic was understandable, but completely without merit. It was true that professional expert witnesses existed and perhaps Despersis was one. But Knauss knew Despersis had not been contacted until the last minute. There had been no possibility of coaching. Besides, Knauss well knew the background of the complaints against the elderly ex-policeman.

Hirsh: "There was never any complaint when you worked for the police department and when you were rendering opinions for the prosecutors?"

Despersis: "No. None whatsoever."

Hirsh: "And in fact, sir, the first complaint against you was when you were—"

"I'm going to object to the form of the question," Knauss cut in. "It's re-direct. It's a leading question."

Judge Bilby sustained the objection. Hirsh backtracked. He established that professional complaints were brought by Bill Watley, head of the DPS's fingerprint division, after Despersis had vehemently disagreed with two of his officers giving testimony in separate criminal cases in Phoenix. Despersis had been testifying for the defense.

Hirsh: "And was (Officer Steve) Anderson the man whose opinion you disagreed with?"

Knauss: "I'm going to object. When I was going back over those letters, I couldn't ask the basis because it was calling for hearsay. And now . . ." Knauss seemed stumped. ". . . And now this is calling for heresay again," he concluded.

Hirsh: "He *did* ask the basis, if Your Honor please. And I think I'm entitled to give an explanation."

Bilby had become increasingly impatient with Hirsh, often chastising him openly. "Well, *you* aren't entitled to an explanation," the judge spit.

"No, but the witness is entitled," Hirsh replied evenly.

"Well, but the question is leading," Bilby said, making a prosecutor's objection that was not on the table.

Hirsh sensed a dangerous turn of events. Whatever gains he had made could be destroyed if the jury thought the judge was against him.

"Well," he said contritely, "if the objection is a leading question, I'll rephrase the question."

"Well, if it is, I'm sustaining it," Bilby said sourly, knowing there was no such objection before the bench.

Hirsh: "Do you know a fellow by the name of Tabarino?"

Despersis: "Yes. Uh-huh."

Hirsh: "And is he in the courtroom today?"

Despersis: "Yes. He's sitting right there."

Hirsh: "And did you see him in consultation with Mr. Knauss this morning?"

Despersis: "Yes. I did."

Hirsh: "Who does Mr. Tabarino work for?"

Despersis: "He works for the DPS."

But he didn't always. Tabarino and Anderson both worked under Despersis at the Phoenix Police Department until his retirement. Despersis had been chairman of the Arizona Identification Association in 1984, a post inherited by Tabarino, who was instrumental in bringing the professional complaints against Despersis.

Hirsh: "Was Tabarino one of the complainants against you in '85 and '86?"

Despersis: "Oh, yes. He was the major, uh . . . one who formed the charges and forwarded them to the international. He was, I think . . . did most of the work on it."

Knauss: "Objection!"

On the basis of the complaints, Despersis had been required to retake his certification test—a test graded by the DPS.

Hirsh brought out that there were three parts to the test, and Despersis had received nearly perfect scores on the first two. The only reason he had failed was because he didn't have time to finish the third section.

Despersis: "Now, I don't question that I have slowed down since I retired, but I just didn't budget my time correctly and I didn't finish the number required to pass. They were all correct that I did, but I just didn't finish."

The jury looked at the retired policeman with understanding.

Hirsh felt decent about vindicating the old man, who nodded imperceptibly as he stepped off the stand.

46

CHRISTMAS

It was nearing Christmas, and the end of the trial. For the past twenty years, David had never felt one way or the other about the holiday season. He had spent too much time deliberately deadening the memories of going house to house for turkey, presents, and hugs to care about it much. But this Christmas in 1988 was a bit different. Hirsh and Minker were about to call "the convicts" to the stand. Some of them David had known since childhood and, he realized, it would be the last time any of them saw one another in street clothes.

He was not a fan of introspection, but he had given some thought to past images lately. Clanging bars and screams. The blue sheen of metal as it was cleaned and re-cleaned in an obsessive ritual to keep from killing or being killed. The terror on Pauline Welle's face or a dozen others, excluding Bud Grainger's, whose performance on the stand had been too much to take. The others' fear he had never fully understood, though he believed it was heartfelt. He just didn't comprehend the emotion.

The tables at Las Vegas he was drawn to, though he knew they were cheap. Virginia's angelic smile, coupled with her agonized tears. Nancy, laughing as she pretended to make her horse keep up with his. George's baby face, looking askance at a stringy pigeon. Mike See in rapture watching his horse lose at the track. Kenny and little Mark and Little Kenny, clamoring around his pant legs. His mother. Dead now. Lori. Beautiful Lori, stretched out on the sofa naked in the house on Palomino Parkway, a perfectly contented smile on her face. Two illegitimate sons he would never know. Did he have regrets? He didn't know. It didn't matter now.

Hirsh, David felt, had done a stand-up job. And the defense had had their moments. But there was just too much there. The gun, the fingerprints, the cars, Bert Williams. True, they'd never tied the money directly to them. But they had gotten in the fact that nearly $200,000 had been taken during the arrest in Denver. And they had a witness, no matter how distasteful, who pointed the finger right at them.

Although David frequently rebuked Doug's assertions that they were dead meat, he actually believed it himself. There was a rumor going around—circulated by the marshals—that Bilby had already decided on a sentence of 340 years for each of them. He would die there.

Knauss, David thought, might be his last chance at real entertainment. David would never read a book again. He had read too much already. That left television, which was only a phantom of images—like a negative of a photograph. He felt much that way himself these days. But a man like Knauss could never know that feeling. A man like Knauss, who thought himself so worldly, had not the slightest idea of what he was doing when he prosecuted check forgers and burglars. He had no comprehension of what he doomed them to.

David actually did not mind Knauss for this. He was, simply, a moron. David had more sympathy for him than he did the agents who flanked him. They took pleasure in their understanding of the cruel power they exercised. They slept well, knowing that John Cline had been unfairly convicted in the Kellogg robbery of 1968. Knauss didn't even believe such things happened. He was the man on the white horse, riding into righteous combat. David knew the agents themselves thought Knauss to be an idiot. They would lie to him as quickly as they would a defense attorney to gain their ends. In a way, David felt sorry for Knauss. He was so inconsequential, and he didn't even know it.

So it would be entertaining. Knauss, with his silly ideas of how to shame people, would go up against the "hard cons," as Knauss called them. David thought he must have heard the term in a Cagney movie.

That was the extent of the prosecutor's knowledge of who these men really were. Knauss had probably never seen anything more violent than a husband telling his wife she'd had too much to drink at a dinner party, but he thought he could crack these men. What he would never realize is that they knew him to the bone. They would crack him, and he would never know it. They knew the value of disguising intelligence before men who thought they were brilliant. The cons had to do it every day of their lives.

Clyde Brown was grave, denying everything Bobby Jones had said. Knauss did not puncture him. In his mind, Clyde was laughing.

One by one, the convicts took the stand. Knauss kept asking them about the "code"—a term no prison dweller uses but one which Knauss thought referred to the rule against snitching.

"You wouldn't ever consider testifying for the prosecution, would you?" Knauss asked accusatively, over and over, as if this were revealing. "That would go against the code."

Only Garvin White could not contain his amusement. "The code?" he asked bemusedly. Then got control of himself. "Well, I think that's mainly a myth."

"Well, you wouldn't testify for the prosecution, would you?" Knauss asked sturdily.

White had trouble again. "No. I don't think so." His voice was quavering with laughter.

Sean Duval, who had provided the defense with Fennimore's map of TUCROB, had some fun.

Knauss: "When was the first time you told anyone about your conversation with Mr. Fennimore?"

Duval: "What conversation are you referring to?"

Knauss: "The one you're describing . . . the one you testified to on direct examination involving the drafting of this diagram."

Duval: "Uh . . . I'm not sure anyone besides myself and Mr. Fennimore . . . possibly George Weir knows of this diagram that I drew up. I didn't publish it or show it about."

Knauss could barely contain his exasperation. "I'm talking about the conversation you had when the diagram was made. You testified that Mr. Fennimore said neither Mr. Grandstaff nor Mr. Brown participated in the bank robbery with him. Is that correct?"

Duval: "That is correct."

Knauss: "And when is the first time you told anybody that?"

Duval: "That they didn't participate?"

Knauss: "Yes! That Mr. Fennimore had told you Grandstaff and Brown did not participate with him."

Duval: "Well, it was common knowledge they didn't participate."

Bilby, barely able to contain his exasperation, intervened. "No. That wasn't the question. The question was, When was the first time you told somebody? That Mr. Fennimore had said that Grandstaff and Brown had not participated."

But Duval had known all along that wasn't the question. He was just having some fun.

Duval: "Well, to answer that question I'd have to first, uh . . . say that here was some compromising. . . ."

Bilby: "No! No! No! All you have to answer is when is the first time *you* said that to somebody . . . that . . . that Mr. Fennimore had told you that they had not participated in the bank robbery."

Duval: "I'm not sure I did. Uh, again, I probably spoke to somebody about it. . . ."

Knauss: "Well, you told Mr. Grandstaff, didn't you?"

Duval: "That what?"

●

Listening to his pals, Doug felt at ease for the first time during the trial. This was more to his liking. If the bastards could put on tight cuffs and hold him in solitary, they ought to get a little bit back for it. For himself, Doug would have thrown in a few profanities, but he didn't fault Duval for making discretion the better part of valor. It would prolong the activities. Knauss obviously thought Duval was just stupid.

Hirsh was making an objection. His hands waved; his hair stirred with every head movement as he walked around the courtroom.

"Would you talk to me and not talk to the audience?" Bilby shouted. "You always wander away. I'm the one that's important in this."

"I'm sorry, Your Honor," Hirsh said. "I was through and I trailed off."

"Now," Bilby said menacingly, "you do that with the jury and you do that with the witnesses because you're trying to effect something. And I haven't stopped you because I didn't want to embarrass you. But don't do it."

Hirsh: "I can tell you, Your Honor, it is nothing more than conditioning. . . ."

Bilby: "A lifetime habit that you've gotten away with."

Hirsh: "It's done unconsciously and I won't do it again. But it's done unconsciously, I can assure you."

Bilby harrumphed: "I won't have it."

●

David liked the way Hirsh got creamed in front of everybody. More specifically, he liked the fact that Hirsh was willing to take it—even invited it—to make his case. It forced David back into that introspection of what he might have done with his own brand of courage had he not become a career criminal. Dentistry still interested him, but recently he'd been thinking that he might have wanted to fly fighter jets. If he hadn't had that juvenile record when he applied for the Marine Corps, maybe that could have happened. He believed he would have been a fearless jet pilot.

●

Lori Brown entered the courtroom looking pale, but turning heads anyway. She was dressed demurely in a navy blue dress with a white Peter Pan collar. The little makeup she wore did not keep men from watching and women from envying—perhaps even hating. Lori kept her eyes away from the defendants' table and had one memorable contribution.

Minker: "Do you love your brother?"

Lori dropped her head, trying visibly to stop the shaking shoulders. Her tears rolled off her face onto the polished wood of the witness stand.

"Yes, I do," she said softly.

The jury lowered their eyes. Doug Brown, for the first time during the trial, looked anguished.

It was Minker's opinion that Dan Knauss did not question the last defense witness—Terry Lee Conner—at length because he was afraid of what Conner might say. It was clear somebody had briefed him thoroughly on the Tucson robbery. Conner had been out on one of his many prison escapes in 1981. He *could* have committed it, but everyone knew he had not. He admitted to it for another chance to escape. They had to transport him to Tucson.

Knauss could barely contain his outrage, but kept away from details nonetheless. If he got into it, it could go two ways. Either Conner would flub or he wouldn't. If he didn't, the jury might believe him. Instead, Knauss concentrated on Conner's penchant for admitting to crimes he hadn't committed so that he could be transported around the country.

Minker had been sorely uncomfortable with his direct examination of Conner, who had described in detail the TUCROB robbery. Hirsh had asked only three questions, never leaving the defense table, and then sat down.

Knauss: "Mr. Conner, when you were testifying on direct examination, you said that after you escaped and then went back to prison, you had told your story to some friends of Mr. Brown or they'd come to you. I ask you now, sir, everything you told the jury was a story, wasn't it?"

Conner: "Was a story?"

Knauss: "A story. Yeah."

Conner: "My life story, yeah."

Knauss: "No. I mean, not the truth. A story means it's not the truth."

Conner: "I'm sorry. I disagree with you."

Knauss brought McGinnis back to rebut Despersis's testimony. He brought newer and better charts and graphs, which he presented within feet of the jurors while pacing back and forth in an agitated condition.

"Look at this point," McGinnis said, putting the graph against the juror rail. "Look at it and you'll see what I mean!" The points from the original testimony had swelled from six to twenty-eight.

Juror James Rice tried to look at the blown-up print photographs, but it just looked like road maps to him. The future jury foreman, sitting behind Rice, leaned forward and whispered, "Why doesn't this asshole give us a break?"

After closing arguments, Hirsh and Minker limped from the courtroom toward their offices.

"Well, we gave them something to think about," Hirsh said. "That's as good as it gets."

"The good fight," Minker said. "How long do you figure?"

"Should take them at least a day. Maybe two," Hirsh said.

"I'm going home," Minker said. "Barbara's back from Egypt."

Neither one of the men went home. They went to their offices, ties askew, hair undone, and combed through many unanswered pink phone messages. WHILE YOU WERE OUT, they said on the top. Hirsh rocked in his chair, not looking at the beautiful black and red Navaho rug in his office. The sheaf of phone messages got warm in his closed hand.

●

David and Doug were shackled hand to foot, then led to a holding area for the verdict. One of the marshals—David would remember his name only as Joe—said "Good luck." The guy was black and had been good to them in their last appearances in court. The marshal had allowed them to walk in unshackled, and had demanded that they be given showers before court appearances, at the risk of unpopularity.

"Thanks, man," David said dully. "But I think it's too late for luck."

●

In the jury room, the smokers lit up and the nonsmokers fiddled around with the various accoutrements provided by the federal court system. Pitchers of water, glasses, and ashtrays were picked up and then put down as if messing with the items could magically make the jurors' decisions. Eventually, they got around to the easy part—picking a foreman. Unsure of what happened next, Foreman James Tate cleared his throat and suggested a trial run, a blind ballot —just to see where the chips had fallen.

Everyone agreed that would be a good idea and the jurors scribbled their verdicts on scraps of paper, folding them carefully, piling them in the center of the table. Tate gathered them up in his arms like a poker player collecting his winning chips. He opened each scrap, reading, and when he was done, he looked around the room.

●

Hirsh was trying to decide whether to eat or go home and nap when he got the call from Bilby's clerk, Virginia. He let his head drop to his desk with a painful thud. It had only been an hour and a half. He had not expected a guilty verdict this soon.

Minker joined him on the pavement outside the office so they could make the death march together.

"I expected two days, at least," Hirsh muttered.

"I really thought we gave them more to think about than this," Minker said miserably. His entire practice on hold for more than a month for an hour's worth of guilty.

The attorneys went to their clients' holding cell first. Doug was expressionless. Hirsh grabbed his own tie and held it aloft—as if hanging himself. David looked away, nodding.

"It's all right, man," he said. "You did the best you could. It was uphill anyway."

●

David did not bother to look at the jurors as they filed in. They were obsolete now, part of the past. He was concentrating his mind on the rest of his life in prison. He hoped it wouldn't be Marion, but it probably would. His escape record spoke for itself and he was certain the federal government would want retribution for the years of problems he'd caused.

He didn't remember rising as the verdict slip was passed from the jury foreman to the judge. He didn't remember the judge passing it to his clerk. David was looking somewhere behind the judge's head—far away into another universe. . . .

". . . find the defendant, David Grandstaff, not guilty. . . ."

David felt like he was having an out-of-body experience. He felt he was looking down from the ceiling, seeing everything in slow motion from above. The bitch had made a mistake. The stupid woman was going to have to reread the goddamn thing. This was a cruelty he didn't expect. It was just incomprehensible that he should be subjected to such a joke.

But the clerk hadn't stopped reading. It was not guilty again, but this time Doug's name was in front. It was not a mistake. David remembered nothing more until he was back in his cell, getting ready to serve the rest of his measly sentence on the Phoenix robbery. He would be out in three years. It was so astonishing, he didn't sleep for a week.

●

When Minker heard Grandstaff's verdict, his knees buckled. They nearly collapsed on him. A not guilty for Grandstaff meant a not guilty for Brown. It was unreal.

Hirsh shared David's sentiment that the clerk had made a mistake. When he saw that she hadn't, he looked at the jury in wonder. Juries that acquit normally like to view their handiwork with pleasure. They watch the defendants and smile at the attorneys. This jury was looking away, as if they were guilty accomplices.

Bilby's shock at his first, silent reading of the verdict had not worn off when the formalities were concluded. He didn't bother to thank the good citizens for their patience and participation—the normal routine after a trial.

"Thank you, ladies and gentlemen," he said briskly, and fled the bench, robes flying.

●

As it turned out, the jurors had reached a unanimous not-guilty verdict on the first ballot. They took a few more, but they always came up the same. Somewhat giddily, they decided to send out for evidence, just to make it look like they were thinking on it. They never looked at the evidence on the table except in passing.

While they whittled away time, it came out that they hated Bruce Fennimore, couldn't stand the FBI agents and how they'd comported themselves, and had smelled, vaguely, the scent of a setup. They weren't that crazy about the bankers, either. Leaving the courthouse, the juror who had been a bank teller for seventeen years beamed for the cameras and announced, "I knew those boys were innocent all along."

"Were they guilty or innocent?" a reporter asked James Rice years after the trial. He shifted uncomfortably at the kitchen table where the interview was taking place. His wife, Barbara, looked at him expectantly. He dodged the question.

But forty-five minutes later, after he was a little more comfortable, he said, "I never thought David Grandstaff, Doug Brown, and Bruce Fennimore divided that money equally." He shook his head as if considering the wisdom of this. "Anyway, I hope they're enjoying it."

INTERLUDE

In the fall of 1990, Bob Hirsh was asked to speak at the exclusive Canyon Ranch resort in Tucson. Being controversial, Hirsh was often asked to speak there and he wasn't about to disappoint the guests this time. He asked David Grandstaff and a writer to come along, too.

Sleekly hidden among the lush desert hills bordering the Catalina Mountains, the ranch is what Tucsonans—perhaps uncharitably—call a "fat farm for celebrities." Although the architects made a stab at adhering to elegant, simple desert architecture, the "ranch" does look more like something from Beverly Hills. The lavish, palm tree–lined driveway paved with expensive tiles many would put in their homes. The monolithic flower beds requiring more water a week than a Mexican family sixty kilometers south might use in a month. These touches, presumably, were a must to satisfy the wealthy patrons who come to the ranch to melt away waistlines at $400 a day or so. There is regulated exercise, no drinking, no salt, and extremely small portions of unseasoned food. The waistlines mostly come back after the guests return home to their Black Forest cakes.

Nightly seminars are held in an attempt to stave off the boredom

of the customers who willingly spend their money so that trainers can
force the rigid discipline they themselves are unable to exert at home.
The seminars mostly revolve around vitamins, food and muscle
groups, and diet. Many of the patrons, who would rather be at Spago
in L.A., tire of it quickly. To spice things up, guests like Hirsh are
sometimes brought in, although on this night, it was unknown he'd be
bringing an infamous bank robber with him.

When the doctors, investors, real estate moguls, and Hollywood
types discovered who they'd been trapped in a room with, seats were
shifted to avoid even accidental eye contact with David Grandstaff.
They focused on the well-dressed, confident attorney with the silver
hair—a man who clearly was in their ballpark.

David was quiet during the complimentary prespeech dinner in the
well-appointed dining room. He'd dressed immaculately in gray linen
slacks, a crisp white shirt, a burgundy alligator belt, and thin, gray
Italian shoes. He ordered a chicken breast that came with a sauce no
one else at the table wanted to sample, but he ate it dutifully while the
writer muttered murderously about the lack of salt. Hirsh laughed at
her.

When David walked into the seminar room, he took a chair near a
corner, watching silently as the men and women in their outrageous-
ly expensive warm-up suits filed in. He knew what he was in for.

Bob Hirsh began his talk easily, boiling complex legal questions
down to a level a layman could understand. He held court. He entertained. He cajoled in an attempt to get these folks to at least look at
his former client. It was not working, so he kept talking.

Eventually, the question came. It was: Shouldn't we have longer
prison sentences as a deterrent to crime? If anyone had been toying
with the idea of looking at David, they weren't now. The ceiling had
suddenly become extremely interesting and the man who asked the
question—a doctor from Cincinnati—looked flushed, as if it had tak-
en all his manhood to work up to the moment.

Hirsh deferred the question to David.

David considered the question. A few in the group flicked their
eyes toward him while others fidgeted. David appeared genuinely
nonplussed by the discomfort he was causing and answered the question simply by saying that prison sentences were not a crime deter-

rent in the large majority of cases. The vast majority of criminals do not consider consequences when they commit their crimes.

Despite themselves, the group was intrigued by the answer, which, after all, was from the horse's mouth. When Hirsh made no move to elaborate, a doctor from Michigan blurted out, "Why not? Do they want to go to prison?" David took the same thoughtful pose, considered his answer, and locked the doctor's gaze. The man had no chance to turn his head and he didn't.

Despite what the doctor might have heard, David told him, prisons were hellish places probably worse than many wars. Some were "softer" than others, but there was no such thing as a country club prison. No one wanted to go there. Criminals, David said, were an odd combination of upbringing, education, economics, and—it was true—genetics. A large portion of prison populations in the country were mentally ill. Some did not hold much intelligence and simply could not understand the nature of their acts. Yes, there were simply vicious men who needed to be in prison. But others had never had an opportunity to participate in the first place. They resented it, and turned vicious.

The answer sparked a barrage of questions, most of them aimed at trying to understand criminals so that sufficient protection could be put in place to keep them away. But eventually, the question on everyone's mind was put by the doctor.

"Do bank robbers commit other crimes?" he asked. "I mean, do they like rape or molest children?"

Although his expression did not change, David threw the writer a look she knew was bemused hopelessness, as if to say: "I told you this was ridiculous. I told you they are so far from understanding we cannot make them understand."

"Criminals specialize just like everyone else," the writer broke in. "Bank robbers only rob banks. Rapists commit rape. Even in prison, they rarely intermingle. And there are different levels of each category. . . ."

But the group was no longer interested in the writer—or the lawyer. Most had now shifted their chairs so that they could face David. All of them were looking at him, some leaning forward so as not to miss his answers. The women had relaxed. They wanted to hear the answer from David Grandstaff.

"As my friend says," David said, "bank robbers are specialists. I would no more want to hurt you than myself. Rapists," he shrugged, "are sick people I would never be in the same room with. I believe that is a group that must be locked up. Because I have never met one that can be rehabilitated."

As David spoke, they were convinced. He was not dangerous—at least not to them. He was just a bank robber and banks were pretty unsympathetic anyway.

"What a relief," the doctor said, smiling at his wife.

As the group broke up after two hours, several of the men lingered behind to shake David's hand and wish him well. David seemed embarrassed, but pleased.

"Good luck to you," said a buyer for a famous New York art museum. "I can see you're a man of good upbringing."

David gave an imperceptible smile.

"Just one more thing," said the doctor. "If you had had to use your guns, would you have?"

David looked at him for a moment.

"I see," the doctor said without any trace of judgment. "I'll keep that in mind if I ever find myself in a bank with you."

He wished David good luck before he left.

On the drive back, David said, "I think that went well." He seemed content.

EPILOGUE

•

David Grandstaff was paroled in 1989 after serving eight years for interstate transportation of stolen goods from the Phoenix jewelry store robbery. He lives in Des Moines, working for his cousin Ken Agee, who often has contracts to paint bank vaults. In December 1991, he ate next to FBI agent Dave Oxler at a fund-raiser held by one of the banks he'd painted. He enjoyed the evening.

Doug Brown was paroled within months of David and lives in the Los Angeles area with Linda and his brother, Dale. He trades in diamonds and real estate. He has sent Christmas cards to Agent Oxler, but has not received a reply. Doug granted the author interviews but later decided he did not wish to be associated with this project except to maintain his innocence of TUCROB.

Bruce Fennimore was paroled after serving eight years for his part in TUCROB. He lives in Des Moines, working for Riverside Auto Parts. He has had no contact with David Grandstaff, but was later arrested and released for allegedly stabbing one of the witnesses for the defense in the TUCROB case. He was bailed out by an officer from the Des Moines Police Department. He refused repeated requests to be interviewed.

Virginia Becks, formerly Virginia Fry, lives in Nebraska with her husband of fifteen years. She is happy, but her voice still quavers when she discusses David. She still wishes life had turned out differently for him.

George Weir resides in a federal penitentiary, where he was sent after a gun was found in his car during a routine traffic stop. George believes he has been repeatedly denied parole because of his involvement in the TUCROB trial, and allegations Bruce Fennimore made on an off the record to the FBI.

Mike See lives in Des Moines. He works as a house painter and still enjoys the racetrack. In 1985, he was acquitted of a bank robbery in which shots were exchanged with the police.

Terry Lee Conner resides in the federal penitentiary in Marion, as far as anyone knows. After spending years in lockdown, he was transferred to Leavenworth, but escape implements discovered in his cell caused him to be transferred again. There are no more crimes he can confess to and, unless he escapes again, he expects to die in prison.

Clyde Brown lives in Des Moines and plays a good game of golf.

Lori Brown recently moved back to Des Moines, after an unsuccessful love affair with a wealthy restaurateur. She works as a representative for Estée Lauder cosmetics.

Kenny and Terri Kauzlarich live in Des Moines. Their sons, Mark and Kenny junior, are doing well in school.

John Oliver lives in Springfield, Missouri. He works as a hairdresser and is still best friends with his ex-wife, Sharon Grandstaff.

Sharon Grandstaff lives in Des Moines where she does the best she can to manage a restaurant and still make sure her brother David has food in the refrigerator, since he is reluctant to shop for himself.

Mike Gabriel lives in Des Moines, working as a pipe fitter. After serving his time for the Phoenix robbery, Mike had lost all of his businesses. David wishes him well, but does not speak to him because he believes Mike spoke to the FBI off the record to have the Arizona state charges dropped. Gabriel declined direct cooperation in this project.

Ken Agee lives outside Des Moines on fifteen acres with his wife, Cheryl, several racehorses, a pool, and a good business. He makes a point of employing men recently out of prison who might turn to crime without income. He still rolls his eyes when he thinks about what David could have become.

Benny Grandstaff, David's father, lives in Des Moines and recently made peace with his son. Although conversation is stiff, it is ongoing.

Ava Grandstaff died while David was in Leavenworth. He declined to attend the funeral because he was told he would have to be shackled. He says her death was the only time he was tempted to cry since Benny hit him with the belt when he was twelve.

Kelly Grandstaff lives outside Des Moines with his wife, Pam, on a farm with several horses, including a new foal. He works as a house painter.

Nancy Lynch, David's lifelong friend and Virginia's nemesis, died in January 1992 of cancer. Despite his fear of illness, David visited her regularly in the hospital and served as pallbearer at her funeral.

Dave Oxler is still an FBI agent in Des Moines and—like all the FBI agents in this story—declined to be interviewed.

Larry Bagley retired from the FBI and is now a security specialist for Hughes Aircraft in Tucson.

Dan Knauss is still head of the District Attorney's Office in Tucson. He toyed with an interview but declined because he was still angry about the verdict.

Bob Hirsh lives in Tucson, Arizona, where he continues to give everyone in the state reasons to write letters to their editors.

Jeffrey Minker lives in Tucson, where he continues to be a highly successful attorney, philosopher, and connoisseur of travel and food.

Roxanne Conlin was embarrassed during an unsuccessful bid for the Iowa governor's office when it was disclosed she took advantage of income tax loopholes.

●

In the course of this book, I interviewed more than 100 people and moved across a half dozen states and several prisons.

I was fortunate to have the cooperation of the two attorneys on the case, who provided me with literally thousands of pages of FBI and police reports and interviews obtained through subpoena during the trial process. I also received the full recordings of the trial testimony, as well as the often reluctant statements from members of The Boys' clan, who felt they might be opening themselves for indictment but liked David enough to cooperate.

Finally, I must say that in fifteen years as a reporter, I have rarely met a subject as open as David Grandstaff. He gave me access to records of his personal life, including canceled checks, property deeds, photographs, letters, report cards, probation reports, twenty-year-old trial transcripts and a host of other paperwork accumulated over the years. It had to have been a very difficult thing to open a life like his up and I appreciate it. I also remember that, on our first meeting, he told me that he didn't care what conclusions I came to about his character.

"If you think I am a bastard, then write it that way," he said. "I only ask that what you write be true—and if there are other bastards out there that they be shown that way, too. No matter who they are."

INDEX

ABOUT THE AUTHOR

•

Debra Weyermann has been a newspaper reporter for fifteen years, mostly covering the criminal justice system. She has won awards for investigative reporting, series writing, and feature writing, including the American Bar Association's Certificate of Merit and the Arizona Press Association's Don Bolles Memorial Award. She lives in Tucson, Arizona.